T0414425

THE MANORS AND
HISTORIC HOMES OF
THE HUDSON VALLEY

THE MANORS AND HISTORIC HOMES OF THE HUDSON VALLEY

HAROLD DONALDSON EBERLEIN

With a New Introduction by Edward Renehan

EXCELSIOR
EDITIONS

Originally published in 1924 by J. B. Lippincott Company

Published by State University of New York Press, Albany

New introduction and other material © 2022 State University of New York

For information, contact State University of New York Press, Albany, NY
www.sunypress.edu

Excelsior Editions is an imprint of State University of New York Press

Library of Congress Cataloging-in-Publication Data

Names: Eberlein, Harold Donaldson, author. | Renehan, Edward, 1956–
  writer of introduction.
Title: The manors and historic homes of the Hudson Valley / Harold
  Donaldson Eberlein, Edward Renehan.
Description: Albany : State University of New York Press, [2022] |
  Series: New York classics | Originally published: J. B. Lippincott
  Company, 1924. | Includes bibliographical references and index.
Identifiers: LCCN 2022013233 | ISBN 9781438491035 (hardcover) |
  ISBN 9781438491042 (ebook) | ISBN 9781438491028 (paperback)
Subjects: LCSH: Hudson River Valley (N.Y. and N.J.)--History. | Manors--
  Hudson River Valley (N.Y. and N.J.) | Dwellings--Hudson River Valley (N.Y.
  and N.J.) | Historic buildings--Hudson River Valley (N.Y. and N.J.) | United
  States--Social life and customs--To 1775.
Classification: LCC F127.H8 E2 2022 | DDC 974.7/3--dc23/eng/20220503
LC record available at https://lccn.loc.gov/2022013233

CONTENTS

FOREWORD

"WOOL gathering" is a common failing amongst most people with reference to historical matters. Even comparatively recent history grows vague and hazy to them in its outlines amazingly soon, and they are apt to lose the thread of connexion between places and events. The sequence of events, too, becomes confused. Hence many a person falls unwittingly into the most absurd anachronisms. Those blessed with an active invention, and a decent degree of interest or pride in the past, ofttimes positively *know* a vast deal. "about things that are not so."

Houses and public edifices supply one of the best correctives for this nebulous mental condition. They are visible symbols and reminders of past life. They are specific tangible evidences. They are pegs on which to hang the links of memory, links that bind together the series of events and connect episodes with definite spots. They are finger-posts to guide us, markers to fix with clear-cut definition the sites of former happenings in which we have an interest. Above all, they afford a concrete setting for bygone men and deeds, and help us to visualise momentous actions and diverting incidents alike, with all the attendant circumstances.

Through force of association they make history a *real* and living thing to us. And whether we keenly pursue history or merely play about its fringes, whether we seek only to gratify a whim for romance or strive to learn somewhat from the experience of the past that may be of profit to us in the present, most chiefly do we need the sense of reality if our enquiries are to satisfy us and produce any lasting result.

If you are taken into a timber-ceiled room in a low-eaved house on the banks of the Hudson, and told that in that room, on such and such a day, the Society of the Cincinnati had its birth, you will ever after remember the place and the incident. One helps the other by association, and the occasion with its setting will be indelibly graven in the memory. If you go into the garden of another venerable house, farther up the river, and learn that "Yankee Doodle" was written by a young officer attached to General Abercrombie's staff, as he sate by the well, you will promptly acquire another mnemonic peg on which to hang a deal of romance and history. Again, if you enter a small study in a certain serene mansion in Cambridge, and discover that when a young subaltern popped in, without first knocking, to find General Washington down on his knees in fervent prayer, and that the great man, enraged at the intrusion, flung his scabbard at the youngster's head, swore roundly at him as he beat an hasty retreat, and then went on with his prayers, the whole occurrence will be so vivid that you will not soon forget the least detail. And, mark you, in each instance the house has been the mordant to make the story bite into the memory.

The Valley of the Hudson has that about it which makes one feel instinctively that it must have a story worth the telling, even though they may be wholly unaware of what has taken place since the first white men sailed up the river more than three hundred years ago. And it *has* an history well worth while. That history is inseparably bound up with the old houses that stand upon both banks of the river, and without them it would lose its dramatic force and become a dull, dead abstraction. They afford just so many points of vital contact with the past and help us to grasp the life of bygone days, the social, economic and political background from which the present has emerged. They aid us mightily, whether we make the river's chronicle a source of curious and romantic gratification, or whether we take a more serious view and regard it as a rich treasure house whence we may derive a clearer understanding of modern values. And surely the complex life of one of the greatest States of the country is worth making some effort to understand.

Even the names we encounter are fraught with meaning and have no end of history interwoven with them. To take only a single instance, how many realise why the name of Dutchess County is spelled with a "t"? The story is this. In 1683, the Assembly of the Province of New York set off and named the counties. Spelling was a variable quantity in those days and a "t" more or less made little matter, but the "t" has been kept, all the same, as a kind of heirloom. Dutchess County was really "The Dutchess's County," and was so named for Maria Beatrice d'Este, daughter of the Duke of Modena and second wife of James, Duke of York and Albany, and Lord of the Province of New York. If anyone wishes to crowd more history into the name they have only to glance through the annals of the Court of Louis XIV, to detect the scheming of "le Grand Monarque" to get James married to an Italian princess.

The houses and estates of the Hudson Valley reflect a system, social and economic, which, however much one may approve or disapprove it on general principles and judged by modem standards, profoundly affected the subsequent development of the State. Whatever flaws the doctrinaire democrat may pick in it, it unquestionably made for strength and stability in the early days of colonisation.

The systems of Patroonships and Manors, with their methods of land tenure and judicial administration, will be discussed in their appropriate place. We may, however, glance here at a picture of the social life of the region when the old *régime* had reached the flower of its growth, just before the War for Independence. In speaking of the upper part of the east bank, the writer says:

"Almost every sightly eminence was capped with a fine residence of one of the grandchildren of the first Lord and Lady of Livingston Manor. At all these mansions, cordial hospitality, abundant cheer, and what was then esteemed splendour, were to be found; and from the extreme limits of Van Rensselaer's Manor on the North to the Van Cortlandts' on the South, the eastern bank of the Hudson river from Albany to New York, and for a distance of from fifteen to thirty miles back from the river, was dotted by handsome residences of as care-free, fine-looking and happy a class as probably the society of any country has ever known. They had intermarried so freely that they seemed one great cousinry, all having a serene confidence in the invulnerability of their social position, which left them free to be jovial, hospitable, good-humoured, and withal public-spirited to an unusual degree. The men had their business offices and their business hours to confer with their stewards and tenants.... Into their capable and willing hands official positions naturally fell and were faithfully filled, but all these things were done in an atmosphere of large leisureliness, consequent upon the slow means of communication between distant parts."

And so life passed in an ample, dignified, idyllic way amidst surroundings that could scarcely be surpassed, the world over, in the mingled sweetness and majesty of their natural beauty.

A manner of life and a social order so firmly rooted could hardly be swept suddenly aside in its entirety by the political upheaval of the Revolution, and a good deal of the former method of existence lingered on into the early years of the nineteenth century. In 1819 it was said of Judge John Kane that he "could go from Albany to New York on horseback, or in winter by sleigh, and not spend a night nor take a meal outside of an house of a near relative." The hospitality was as spontaneous as it was universal.

No story of the Manors and historic homes of the Hudson Valley would be fully intelligible without some reference to the life that went on in the two urban centres, New York and Albany, with which most of the river gentry had close ties, whither they often went, and in all the affairs of which—social, commercial and political—they were accustomed to play an active rôle. Not a few of the grandees, who dwelt upon the banks of the upper Hudson, had their town houses as well as the broad estates upon which they passed a great portion of their time. For the sake of completeness, therefore, as well as for its own intrinsic interest, some account of town life and town houses is included in this volume.

Most of the houses built along the east and west banks of the river by the early lords of the soil, their tenants, and the small free-men with holdings of modest size were substantial but unpreten-tious. Nevertheless, they possessed charm of a very pronounced type and they were rich in the homelike domestic quality that is too often lost when a more formal and academic mode of expres-sion is consciously adopted. Although they were unassuming in their appearance outside, within they were furnished with every-thing that could contribute to either comfort or elegance.

As might be expected, these dwellings derived their inspiration from the lesser domestic architecture of the Netherlands. Many of them are almost exact replicas of their prototypes; others bear witness to the process of adaptation that went on, as local exi-gencies arose, until ultimately a characteristic Hudson River type was evolved. These homes were dear to the descendants of the original builders. They cherished them and added to them, when additions became necessary, rather than abandon them for domiciles of a more sumptuous and fashionable character. It was not until the eighteenth century was well advanced that Classic forms began to make their appearance to any appreciable extent in the architecture of either shore.

The desire to hold to the old houses, and yet appear fashionable, was responsible for much ruthless and absolutely indefensible disfigurement during the Victorian era. Old glazing in the windows gave place to big, vulgar, characterless panes. Silly gables burst forth above, where gables did not belong and could do no real good. Sillier barge-boards, fretted with jig-saw contortions and begotten of a besotted imagination, added their tawdry horrors to abominations that were already bad enough before. Even some of the later Georgian houses lost their purity of line and were transmogrified into marvels of atrocious ugliness. Nevertheless, not a few of the ancient structures escaped the hand of the nineteenth century spoiler and have remained intact for the delight of a generation at least more appreciative of antiquity if not more intelligent. These are they that have been chosen for illustration.

On looking at a map it will be seen that numerous streams on both sides debouch into the Hudson between New York and Albany. Some of them are navigable a short distance above their mouths for small craft of light draught; others are little more than brooks. The river was the natural, and for a long time the only, artery of traffic and communication. When the early colonists wished to penetrate into the heart of the country, they turned aside into these lesser waterways and followed them as far as they could go by sloop or canoe and, after that, took to their feet along the banks. It is, therefore, at the mouths and along the courses of these streams that we must look for the first settlements.

Furthermore, these tributaries of the Hudson offered another inducement to which the pioneers were not blind—they supplied abundant water power for mills, and mills were important nuclei of colonisation. The mill was a centre of distribution to which all were obliged to go to get the wherewithal for their daily bread. Oftentimes, until a church was established in the neighbourhood, they had no place else to go when they stirred from home, and after a church was established it was a common saying that thenceforth the people had *two* places to go—"to mill and to meetin'." Not seldom did the miller do a thriving business as fur trader and general storekeeper, so that the mill was the centre of local commerce.

Although roads of a very indifferent character had here and there been opened between neighbouring settlements—usually by means of widening Indian trails—it was not until the early years of the eighteenth century that any systematic attempt at road making for the benefit of the whole Province was essayed. Then, in 1703, the Provincial Assembly passed a "Publick Highways" act:

> "Publick and Common General Highway to extend from King's Bridge in the County of Westchester, through the same County of Westchester, Dutchess County, and the County of Albany, of the breadth of four rods, English measurement, at the least, to be, continue and remain forever the Publick Common General Road and Highway from King's Bridge to the ferry at Crawlier over against the City of Albany."

Even long after the whole length of the road had been pushed through and all the links completed, the river remained the chief highway; "traders followed it and settlers kept near its waters. The river bank was the most desirable land." The sloop or sail boat was the principal means of transit and the Hudson's bosom was dotted with sails. The "aquatic Dutch" appreciated its value and profitted by it. As time passed regular boat communication between New York and Albany, and between intermediate points, was established at regular intervals. An advertisement in the New York *Gazette*, in April, 1734, announces:

> "These are to give notice that Evert Bogardus now plys in a boat on the Hudson River, between New York and Esopus [Kingston]. If any Gentlemen or merchants have any goods to send to Ryn-Beck or Esopus, he will carry such goods as cheap as is usually paid for carrying to Esopus. He will be at New York once a week, if wind and weather permits, and comes to Coenties Slip."

Not only was the Hudson the great highway of the Province in the days of its beginnings; it was later the chief line of strategy during the War for Independence. This phase of its history we must not overlook. It was the British aim to control the river throughout its whole length and thus completely cut off New England from the Middle Colonies and the South. It was Washington's aim to control it and thus keep open an interior means of communication, whatever might befall along the seaboard. For this reason the Hudson's shores are most intimately associated with the struggle between the Colonies and the Mother Country. Hence do they derive no little share of interest, for many of the most momentous as well as most dramatic events in the history of the war occurred in or near the houses described in this volume.

In the performance of any task, however congenial it may be, it becomes necessary to set limits. The limits within which lie the houses treated in this book are the shores of the Hudson from New York to Albany. On the West Shore are not included those houses within the boundaries of New Jersey, for New Jersey's historic houses form a subject by themselves. Neither are the houses in Long Island and Staten Island included, for there are so many of them to which great historic interest attaches that it would be impossible to put them into one volume with the Hudson Valley houses and do justice to them. It seems better, therefore, to reserve them for separate discussion. Hence the scope of this volume is confined to the east side of the Hudson, from New York to Greenbush, now called Rensselaer, and the west side, from Albany to the New Jersey border.

The author wishes to acknowledge with thanks his deep indebtedness to Miss Anne S. Van Cortlandt, Miss Haldane, H. Strong, Mrs. William Verplanck, Miss Crary, Dr. Chorley, of St. Philips-in-the-Highlands, Dr. John Deyo, of Newburgh, the late Dr. George W. Nash, Mr. Wall, of the New York Historical Society, Mr. Shelton's book on the *Jumel Mansion* and Dr. Edward Hagaman Hall's *Philipse Manor Hall* for valuable and important data, the Pennsylvania Historical Society, the Library Company of Philadelphia, the New York Public Library, and, last of all but by no means least, his friend and colleague, Roger Wearne Ramsdell, for his invaluable aid while these pages were in preparation.

EASTER, 1924

HAROLD DONALDSON EBERLEIN

INTRODUCTION
EDWARD RENEHAN

Harold Donaldson Eberlein's *The Manors and Historic Homes of the Hudson Valley* has been considered an essential and elegant resource ever since its first publication by J.B. Lippincott in 1924. Profusely illustrated with drawings, classic prints, and photographs (many of the latter taken by the author himself), the book not only discusses the architecture and beauty of more than 35 historically relevant estates and homesteads, but also contextualizes their varied histories amid key social and political disruptions, these ranging from the rise of the Dutch through to the American Revolution and the heyday of the patroonships overseen by such families as the Livingstons and Van Rensselaers and Van Cortlandts.

Eberlein himself was an interesting man. By the time he died in July of 1964 at the age of 89, he'd authored or coauthored some 50 books. The majority of these focused on historic houses and architecture, but Eberlein also wrote biographies such as *The Rabelaisian Princess* (1931), focusing on Elisabeth Charlotte, Duchess of Orleans, and contemporary of Louis IV. An 1896 graduate of the University of Pennsylvania, Eberlein at various times worked on the editorial staffs of *The Philadelphia Evening Telegraph* and *The Philadelphia Public Ledger*. In his later years, he served on the Department of the Interior's Board of Advisors to the National Park Department's Historic American Buildings Survey. He also held memberships in the Historical Society of Pennsylvania, the Philadelphia Society for the Preservation of Landmarks, the Maryland Historical Society, and the Columbia Historical Society (Washington, DC).[1]

---

1 See Eberlein's obituary: "Howard D. Eberlein, A Historian and Author of 50 Books, Dies," *New York Times*, 28 July 1964, Obituaries Section, p. 29.

Writing in 2001, Bradley C. Brooks said of Eberlein:

His success as an author was the result of several factors. He was extraordinarily industrious, particularly during the first two decades of his career. He was a sharp-eyed observer, with a gift for developing multiple works from a given source or group of sources. . . . To his good fortune, Eberlein's output found a market among readers who needed historical information for many reasons, most of them linked to the influence of the colonial revival that flourished during the first half of the twentieth century. Some probably needed practical information on historic architectural or decorative styles. As the twentieth century moved into its second decade, Eberlein helped to codify and disseminate new standards of taste that required greater knowledge of those styles.[2]

Eberlein dedicated *The Manors and Historic Homes of the Hudson Valley* to his friend Anne Stevenson Van Cortlandt (1847–1940), whom he cited as the primary instigator of his undertaking. At the time of her death just short of her 93rd birthday, she was the very last lineal descendant of Stephanus Van Cortlandt (1643–1700), the founding patroon of Van Cortlandt Manor. When she passed, she did so in the old manor house at Croton-On-Hudson, near the confluence of the Croton and Hudson Rivers, where she'd been born nine decades before.[3]

It is perhaps because of Anne Van Cortlandt's specific interest in the periods during which her family had been most prominent—the Dutch era, the pre-Revolutionary/Colonial era, and the Revolutionary and immediate post-Revolutionary period—that Eberlein chose to focus on structures from those times. Thus, he largely ignored historic homes of a more recent vintage, such as John Jacob Astor's *Rokeby* on the Hudson at Barrytown, built in 1811, or the Livingston family's home of later generations after that of *Clermont* near Tivoli—the home

---

2 Bradley C. Brooks, "The Would-Be Philadelphian: Harold Donaldson Eberlein, Author and Antiquarian," *The Pennsylvania Magazine of History and Biography*, Vol. 125, No. 4 (Oct., 2001), 373.

3 See Anne Stevenson Van Cortlandt's obituary: "Anne Van Cortlandt Dies in Croton at 92: Last Direct Lineal Descendant of Founder of Family Here," *New York Times*, 6 June 1940, Obituaries Section, p. 36.

called *Edgewater*, at Barrytown, built 1824. Nor did he discuss *Lyndhurst*, on the banks of the river at Tarrytown, designed and built by Alexander Jackson Davis in 1838 for William Paulding Jr. In 1924, the year of the publication of Eberlein's book, this mansion was still in the hands of the family of Wall Street financier Jay Gould, who'd purchased the place in 1880.

Any modern work purporting to survey the historic homes of the Hudson Valley would necessarily have to include these establishments, as well as numerous others. Not the least of these are the elaborate Frederick Vanderbilt mansion at Hyde Park, built in the 1890s, and the 1905 Palazzo of Standard Oil partner and Treasurer Oliver Hazard Payne, which stares down the Vanderbilt edifice from its perch on the opposite Hudson River shore at the hamlet of West Park, in the town of Esopus.[4]

No small part of what makes Eberlein's book important is the attention he pays to the history of the Hudson Valley as evidenced in its historic homes. In fact, Eberlein saw the old manors and historic homes of the region as vital signposts to that history—a history "inseparably bound up with the old houses that stand upon both banks of the river, and [a history which] without them ... would lose its dramatic force and become a dull, dead abstraction." For Eberlein, the homes and buildings he discussed represented "points of vital contact with the past ... the social, economic and political background from which the present has emerged."[5]

All of these important buildings are, as Eberlein tells us, "visible symbols and reminders of past life ... specific tangible evidences ... [and] pegs on which to hang the links of memory." For Eberlein, as for us, these elderly and elegant structures make history come alive "through force of association."[6] Even the

---

4 *Rokeby* today remains in private hands. *Edgewater* is today owned by Classic American Homes Preservation Trust. *Lyndhurst* is owned by the National Trust for Historic Preservation. The Frederick Vanderbilt Mansion is now a National Historic Site administered by the National Park Service. The Payne mansion is today owned by Marist College and operated as the Raymond A. Rich Institute for Leadership Development.
5 Harold Donaldson Eberlein, *The Manors and Historic Homes of the Hudson Valley*, p. vi.
6 Ibid., p. v.

names associated with the homes and manors reek of history: Van Rensselaer, Verplanck, Van Cortlandt, and Livingston being the standouts among them.

Unlike when *The Manors and Historic Homes of the Hudson Valley* was published in 1924, many of the homes mentioned in the book are today open to the public. For example, *Clermont*—the original manor house of the patroon Livingston family (built 1740, burned by the British in 1777, and subsequently rebuilt)—was still in the hands of several Livingston heirs (those not living at the aforementioned *Edgewater*) at the time Eberlein did his work, but is today a State of New York Historic Site. As has already been mentioned, Van Cortlandt Manor in Croton was as well still occupied by Eberlein's friend Anna. Today, however, the Van Cortlandt Manor is owned and administered by the nonprofit Historic Hudson Valley. And the Mount Gulian manor house of the Verplanck family, in Beacon on the eastern side of the river, is now—after being destroyed by a fire set by an arsonist in 1931 and restored by a Verplanck descendant in the late 1960s and early 1970s—a museum run by a nonprofit.

The story of the most striking resurrection and restoration since Eberlein's time relates to Alexander Hamilton's mansion, The Grange, built in upper Manhattan in 1802. At the time Eberlein wrote, this once grand edifice was a shadow of its former self. The mansion was privately held by disinterested owners, empty, and had long before been moved two blocks south of its original location. Much of its beautiful exterior ornamentation had been removed, and the house cringed in the shadow of a six-story apartment building. Eberlein evidently did not have the heart to relay the grim contemporary truth of The Grange to his readers. Instead, he stressed its importance historically and described the house as it once had been. Fortuitously, however, in that same year of 1924, the place was purchased by The American Scenic and Preservation Society, which restored it and opened it as a museum in 1933. Today owned by the National Park Service, The Grange sits at St. Nicholas Park, facing West 141st Street, next to the City College campus of the City University of New York, and thus still sits within the bounds of Hamilton's original estate, having been moved there in 2008.

Other dwellings and buildings have also opened up. Thus, today's reader of Eberlein's book has a decided advantage over Eberlein's original audience in that a good deal more of the sites Eberlein discusses are ones that the reader may actually visit.

All this being said, Eberlein's book remains as enduringly timeless as the manors and homes he discussed and described so passionately. Here we have the elegant, engaging, and enlightening prose of a man who researched exhaustively and thought deeply about his subject matter—a man who embraced his work as something of a sacred trust and mission to breathe life into key architectural relics of the American past. And for this, we, of another generation, owe him a great debt.

I.

TOWN HOUSES AND TOWN LIFE IN NEW YORK

SEVENTEENTH CENTURY

"THE counting house there is kept in a stone building, thatched with reed; the other houses are of the bark of trees. Each has his own house. The Director and Koopman live together; there are thirty ordinary houses on the east side of the river which runs nearly north and south. The Honourable Pieter Minuit is Director there at present; Jan Lempe Schout; Sebastiaen Jansz Crol and Jan Huyck, Comforters of the Sick, who, whilst awaiting a clergyman, read to the Commonalty there on Sundays, from texts of Scripture with the Comment. Francois Molemaecker is busy building a horse-mill, over which shall be constructed a spacious room sufficient to accommodate a large congregation, and then a tower is to be erected where the bells brought from Porto Rico will he hung. . . . . . .

"Men work there as in Holland; one trades upwards, southwards and northwards; another builds houses, the third farms. Each farmer has his farm and the cows on the land purchased by the Company; but the Milk remains to the profit of the Boer; he sells it to those of the people who receive their wages for work every week. The houses of the Hollanders now stand without the fort, but when that is completed, they will all repair within, so as to garrison it and be secure from sudden attack."

So reads a contemporary description of New York City soon after its first emergence from the status of a mere trading post to the condition of a settlement where the people had planted themselves with a mind "to remain there." This was in 1626.

To have reached even the modest measure of permanent establishment implied by the foregoing description, however, any venture in coloniation must needs have had some antecedent history. That antecedent history in the case of the plantation amongst the Manhattans was this. Early in May, 1623, dropped anchor at Manhattan the ship "New Netherland," Cornelis Mey skipper, and director of the emigrants. On board were thirty families, "most of whom were Walloons," we are told, and thus, at the very outset, were planted the seeds of that polyglot cosmopolitanism that has reached such astounding proportions in the New York City of our own day. Most of the settlers were carried up the river to Fort Orange, while only eight of the "New Netherland's" passengers were left at Manhattan, so that Albany, it seems, can lay claim to prior settlement or, at least, more substantial settlement at an earlier date than the city at the mouth of the "Great River."

Apparently the eight immigrants left at Manhattan were all men, "who lived for a time in the traders' makeshift shelters," the only habitations hitherto erected by the Dutch at that spot. Just how much building they essayed at first it is impossible to say, but they seem to have made themselves reasonably comfortable and content. Baudartius, in 1624, quotes a recent letter from New Netherlands which says:

> "Here is especially free coming and going without fear of the naked natives of the country. . . . . . . Had we cows, hogs and other cattle for food (which we daily expect by the first ships) we would not wish to return to Holland, for whatever we desire in the paradise of Holland is here to be found. If you will come hither with your family you will not regret it."

The "cows, hogs and other cattle for food" reached New Amsterdam in 1625. In that year Pieter Evertsen Hulst, one of the Directors of the West India Company, at his own charges fitted out three ships, two of them laden with seed, farming implements, swine, sheep, and more than a hundred head of cattle. From Wassenaer we learn that "each animal had its own stall. . . . . fixed as comfortable as any stall here [in Holland]. Each animal had its respective servant who attended to it and knew its wants, so as to preserve its health, together with all suitable forage, such as oats, hay and straw." This was a bit of characteristic Dutch care and foresight and explains why only two of the animals died on the voyage.

The third ship bore to Manhattan "six complete families with some freemen, so that forty-five newcomers or inhabitants are taken out to remain there." Upon the advent of this company "to remain there" were begun some of the buildings that figure in the previously-quoted description, and thus, in good earnest, were laid the foundations for the future city of New York.

On May 4th, 1626, came the ship, "Hot Meewtje" (The Little Sea-Mew) bringing the new Director, Pieter Minuit, the first Director to bear a formal title—Director-General of New Netherland. According to pre-determined plan, the Director-General and several of the Company's officials moved into the houses inside the walls of the fort, when these dwellings were completed, but the rest of the settlers "remained as yet without the Fort, in no fear, as the Natives live peaceably with them." The "thirty ordinary houses on the east side of the river," alluded to in the description, as a matter of fact, were not built along the east bank of the North River, but much nearer the shore of the East River, which was then the chief water front, and about this nucleus most of the other houses arose for a number of years subsequently.

In forming our mental picture of the infant settlement's appearance, we must not take too seriously nor too literally the contemporary chronicler's statement that the houses were "of the bark of trees." In all probability they were framed of hewn logs. Since no saw-mills had yet been set up, the logs were sheathed, after the fashion of shingling, with pieces of thick bark from the chestnut or other suitable trees, while the roofs were thatched with reeds.

Another possible, but not nearly so likely, explanation of the chronicler's meagre description might be drawn from Van Tienhoven's words. Cornelius Van Tienhoven, Secretary of the Province, put forth in 1650 a pamphlet containing "information Relative to Taking Up Land in New Netherland." Therein he writes:

> "Those in New Netherlands and especially in New England, who have no means to build farmhouses at first according to their wishes, dig a square pit in the ground, cellar fashion, six or seven feet deep, as long and as broad as they think proper, case the earth inside with wood all round the wall and line the wood with the bark of trees or something else to prevent the caving in of the earth; floor this cellar with plank and wainscot it overhead for a ceiling, raise a roof of spars clear up and cover the spars with bark

or green sods, so that they can live dry and warm in their houses with their entire families for two, three and four years, it being understood that partitions are run through these cellars which are adapted to the size of the family."

This explanation may be taken for what it is worth, remembering, however, that Van Tienhoven's veracity was open to more than serious question upon numerous occasions. Whether the original "thirty ordinary houses" and their immediate successors were of this fashion or of the more likely type first noted does not much matter, for in any case they were regarded merely as temporary expedients and were very soon abandoned in favour of more permanent, more substantial and more comfortable abodes.

Two causes materially affected the physical growth of the town and the aspect of the houses at a very early date—first, the Director-General's purchase of the whole island of Manhattan from the Indians; and, second, the arrival of a sawmill. Some time during the summer of 1626 Minuit effected the land transfer and the record of this momentous transaction is preserved in a letter, despatched to the States General by their delegate representing them in the Assembly of the XIX at Amsterdam, which runs:

"High and Mighty Lords,

"Here arrived yesterday the ship Arms of Amsterdam which on the 23d September sailed from New Netherland out of the Mauritius River. They report that our people there are of good cheer and live peaceably. Their wives have also borne children there. They have bought the island Manhattes from the savages for the value of sixty guilders. It is 11,000 morgens in extent. They had all their grain sown by the middle of May and harvested by the middle of August. They send small samples of summer grain, such as wheat, rye, barley, oats, buckwheat, canary seed, beans, and flax.

"The cargo of the aforesaid ship is:

7246 beaver skins,	36 wildcat skins,
178 half otter skins,	33 minks,
675 otter skins,	34 rat skins,
48 mink skins,	Much oak timber and nut-wood.
"Herewith	

"High and Mighty Lords, be commended to the grace of Almighty God.

"At Amsterdam, the 5th of November, A 1626.

"Your High Mightinesses' Obedient

"P. SCHAGHEN."

Thus was bought for about twenty-four dollars the whole island of Manhattan.

Soon after 1626 arrived the machinery for a saw-mill of the sort driven in Holland by wind-power. Mill and mechanism were forthwith set up on Governour's Island—Nut Island it was then called—whither logs could easily be floated from the neighbouring shores and where, also, there was an abundant supply of highly desirable standing timber. The sense of definite establishment imparted by Dutch acquisition of the land from the natives, and the possibility of now getting sawn timber proved a double inducement and justification for a better type of housebuilding.

The "five stone houses" in Winckel Street—a short thoroughfare that once ran closely parallel to the lower end of Whitehall—belonging to the West India Company, plainly shewed the increasing confidence of tenure and facility in building materials; and they were a conspicuous feature of the town's first decade of growth. They were two, or perhaps three, storeys high and were given over to the industries carried on under the eyes of the Company's officers. Therein were the workshops of the carpenter, the blacksmith, the cooper, and the armourer, along with the shops of the tailor, the shoemaker and the hatter. There was likewise an appurtenance in the shape of a boat house at the rear, built in Van Twiller's time, according to the Company's records of the year 1639, to shelter the animals sent as a present to the Director-General by Sir John Harvey, Governour of Virginia. As the records state that these five stone houses were "in need of considerable repair" in 1638, and as they appear in the earliest view of New Amsterdam—Hartger's View, which seems attributable to some time between 1628 and 1630—they were undoubtedly amongst the earliest structures of any importance in the city.

The "spacious room sufficient to accommodate a large congregation," "constructed" in 1626 over the horse-mill for grinding tan-bark—the site is now occupied by numbers 32 and 34 South William Street—did not long answer for the needs of the growing town, for in 1633, on the site now covered by 39 Pearl Street, was built a wooden church with a modest parsonage just to the east of it. It was within this parsonage, in all likelihood, in the autumn of 1642, that the historic wedding of Doctor Hans Kiersted and Dominie Bogardus's eldest stepdaughter, Sara Roelofse, took place, upon which occasion Director-General Kieft displayed some of his Machiavellian cunning.

Captain De Vries relates how one day Director-General Kieft was felicitating himself "that he now had a fine inn, built of stone, in order to accommodate the English who daily passed with their vessels from New England to Virginia, from whom he suffered great annoyance and who might now lodge in the tavern." To this De Vries rejoined that

> "it happened well for the travellers but there was great want of a church, and that it was a scandal to us when the English passed there and saw only a mean barn in which we preached; that the first thing which the English built, after their dwellings, was a fine church, and we ought to do so, too, as the West India Company was deemed a principal means of upholding the Reformed religion against the tyranny of Spain, and had excellent materials therefor, namely, fine oak-wood, good mountain stone, and lime burnt of oyster shells, much better than our lime in Holland. He then inquired who would superintend the work. I answered, the lovers of the Reformed Religion who were truly so. He then said I must be one of them, as I proposed it, and must give a hundred guilders."

To this proposal De Vries consented, and added that the Governour, too, must give on his own account, and more largely still on behalf of the Company. As a matter of fact, the Director promised 1000 guilders contribution from the Company, and then, at the wedding feast in the house of Dominie Bogardus, with whom at that time he was on good terms, deeming it a good occasion for his purpose, he "set to work after the fourth or fifth drink; and he himself setting a liberal example, let the wedding guests sign whatever they were disposed to give towards the church. Each then, with a light head, subscribed away at a handsome rate, one competing with the other, and although some heartily repented it when their senses came back, they were obliged, nevertheless, to pay; nothing could avail against it."

This church with an high-pitched, twin-gabled roof, a dominating feature in the old pictures of New Amsterdam, was placed within the fort. It was seventy-two feet long, fifty-four feet wide, and the walls sixteen feet high to the spring of the roof. Although the people paid for their church, Kieft, nevertheless, with characteristic assumption, placed upon it this insinuating inscription:

**"A°. D°. MDCXLII. W. Kieft Dr. Gr. Heeft
de Gemeente dese Tempel doen Bouwen."**

which, being translated, is

**"Anno Domini, 1642, William Kieft, Director General,
hath the Commonalty caused to build this temple."**

The City Tavern, upon the erection of which the Governour was congratulating himself, begun about 1640 under the auspices of the Company, completed in 1641, and occupied early in 1642, stood quite apart from the other houses and occupied a conspicuous position near the shore of the East River. From such documentary evidence as has been preserved, the City Tavern seems to have had a frontage of about forty-two feet and a depth of about thirty-three feet. It was a building of two full storeys with a basement underneath, and spacious lofts overhead in the steep-pitched roof with its gables crow-stepped according to the Dutch fashion of the period.

While this inn served chiefly for the lodging and entertainment of travellers and other strangers, and likewise as a rendezvous for convivial gatherings of the townspeople, it was furthermore used from time to time as a place of detention for suspected persons and political prisoners until they could be conveniently dealt with by the Company. In 1654 the Company turned the City Tavern over to the use of the municipal authorities and thenceforth, ceasing to be an hostelry, it was known as the State House or Town Hall. With the change in its fortunes, a portion of the building was also set apart for the town gaol, thus perpetuating the tradition previously instituted.

Of quite different character was another early structure anent which we have certain explicit information. In 1642, one Adam

Roelantsen, built himself an house on the north side of Stone street. Roelantsen had come out from the Netherlands as one of the earlier colonists and was certainly settled in New Amsterdam by 1633. Nominally the schoolmaster, he seems to have left little impress upon the community in his professional capacity, and we hear far more of him in very different connexions. Besides teaching the young, it appears to have been incumbent upon the holder of the office to assist the parson by acting as "consoler of the sick," precentor, and clerk, and by turning the pulpit hour glass. As an additional activity it appears, from court records, that he took in washing, or at least conducted a laundry. His tongue and his temper were always getting him into hot water with all his neighbours so that the career of this tattling, prying, peeking, gossiping clerk-pedagogue-laundryman was tempestuous so long as we find any trace of him.

At all events, in 1642, he built him the new house aforesaid in Stone Street, and this was the manner of it:

> "It was a clapboarded structure, covered with a reed roof, and eighteen by thirty feet in size. Like most of the buildings in the thickly settled districts, it stood with its gable end to the street. At the front door was the usual 'portal' with its wooden seats. Outside of the frame a chimney of squared timber was carried up. Within, the fireplace was provided with the luxury of a mantelpiece, and we may presume that the living room was ornamented with the 'fifty-one leaves of wainscot,' for which Adam Roelantsen had contracted a few years before. The house contained the usual 'bedstead' or permanent frame built in, for state occasions, being somewhat of the nature of a bunk."

Adam did not long enjoy the occupancy of this house, for within a few years after its completion he made a voyage back to the Netherlands. While he was gone his wife died, leaving two young children altogether unprovided for, so that the Council decreed that they should be placed under the care of his four nearest neighbours—Philip Geraerdy, who kept the White Horse Tavern, Doctor Hans Kiersted, Jan Stevense, who had succeeded to the post of schoolmaster, and Oloff Van Cortlandt—who, as curators and guardians, were to look after the children "till the arrival of the father or some news of him." When he came back, shiftless, busy-body Adam sold the house and then promptly got into more trouble by insulting and brawling with a neighbour's wife, whereupon the Council adjudged that he should be publicly flogged and banished the Colony.

So much for the houses of private individuals in seventeenth-century New Amsterdam. Now let us look for a moment at the abode of the highest official. The Governour's house, built in 1654, by William Kieft, was one hundred feet long, fifty feet deep, and twenty-four feet high. It was a comfortably built mansion and, for the time, one of the most imposing items in the architecture of the city.

Many of the streets, even till well after the seventeenth century had entered its second half, bore little resemblance to the metropolitan character they were to assume in the years to come. Broad Street was formerly nothing more than an open ditch through a marshy piece of ground. It was first built up and planked along its sides in the year 1657. The paving laid down in front of the Van Cortlandt house was amongst the first, if not the very first, effort made in that direction of improvement in the infant city.

Notwithstanding the primitive and unfinished condition of things, New Amsterdam must have been a pleasant place to live in during these days of beginning. A contemporary description emphasises the rural—one may almost say the paradisiac—quality of the place. "The town," says the writer, "is well-shaded and like a garden most pleasant to walk in. There are frogs as well as birds in the trees and these animals make such a clamour as to make it difficult to make oneself heard in conversation."

Even from the beginning, New Amsterdam had assumed a cosmopolitan and polyglot character, and people of foreign tongues were soon numbered amongst her citizens as well as amongst the visitors whom the occasions of trade brought within her gates. Walloons and French Huguenots had come with the very early colonists and later, after the revocation of the Edict of Nantes, a large contingent of Huguenot refugees had sought asylum in the New World where they might enjoy liberty of conscience—the kind of liberty they desired being not contrary to the ideas of the Dutch as were the tenets, or at least the behaviour, of the Quakers.

Not a few of this later migration sate down at New Rochelle, but they had strong affiliations with New York. Their connexion with the city was especially close during the period before their own place of worship was built at New Rochelle, and even after it was erected their frequent intercourse with New York continued. The Huguenots, although they amounted to about only four per cent, of the population, contributed an extremely valuable element to the composite race of New Yorkers for they were conspicuously "earnest and upright and never engaged in race hostilities." At the time of their first settlement at New Rochelle they were accustomed to tramp down to the city on Saturday nights, carrying their arms. "On Sunday morning they washed, ate and rested at the Collect Pond, sang the 60th Psalm, and then spent the day in the services of their church in Marketfield Street." After the day's services were over, they visited their friends and then walked home at night.

Although the general tenour of seventeenth-century town life was even and uneventful, and there was little excitement to distract the wonted simplicity of existence, nevertheless, the people were not wholly without organised diversion and amusement. They were, at least, not quite so restricted as the people in scattered settlements up the river whose outside relaxations were confined to two things—going "to mill and to meetin'." For one thing, in which the city dwellers had the advantage of their country neighbours, the first English Governour, Colonel Richard Nicolls, by one of his early acts—in May, 1665, to be exact—established a race-course on Long Island.

British rule must have come as a relief, in many ways, to the paternal strictness and all-embracing supervision of Governour Stuyvesant. Stuyvesant was conscientious in the discharge of what he conceived to be his duties, but he was somewhat narrow in his outlook on life and painfully intolerant of anything not comprehended in the Dutch scheme of civil and religious policy. His intolerance is well exemplified in his treatment of the Quaker Hodgson. The Quakers of that day were not always the placid folk their successors generally shewed themselves, and they could be—and often were—extremely contentious and irritating. But even their greatest proficiency in the gentle art of being annoying seemed scarcely to merit the harsh measures Stuyvesant meted out to Hodgson. He fined and imprisoned him, had him chained "to a wheelbarrow and whipped by a negro, hung up by the hands, and again whipped."

However intolerant and severe some of the higher officials might be upon certain occasions, nevertheless, the people at large believed in and practised a comfortable, easy-going mode of life. Taken all in all, the New York Dutch were wholesome-minded, human folk as different as they could possibly be from the austere, gloomy religionists and dyspeptic theologues of conscience-ridden New England. To give only one instance of their liberal outlook upon life, and their desire both to be comfortable themselves and to make the strangers within their gates comfortable, too, they encouraged the building of taverns. At the same time, like the thrifty folk they were, they had an eye to profit, and one reason why taverns were encouraged was that a substantial tax might be collected from them.

The taverns were carefully regulated by law, and the statute not only prescribed the prices for the tankard of beer or the mutchkin of rum, but also the cost of beds with sheets and beds without sheets. While the New Amsterdam Dutch are said to have promulgated the first excise law in the New World, by putting a tax on wine and beer, they also looked after the behaviour of the people and imposed a penalty on excessive drinking. When a drunken man was discovered, if the authorities could not find out who was the seller of the liquor that had caused the inebriety, they levied a fine upon every drinking house in the entire street.

The liquor traffic was not the only business to be closely supervised by the constituted powers. The milling and bolting of flour was an important New York industry almost from the very planting of the Colony. In 1694 it is said that 600 of the 938 buildings in the city were connected with or dependent upon the trade in flour, and that two-thirds of the inhabitants, in one way or another, were engaged in the business. For many years the city enjoyed a flour monopoly—the exclusive right to bolt flour and pack it for export. The Bolting Act, safeguarding the monopoly, was finally repealed in 1694, to the great disgust of New York City, but to the joy and satisfaction of the rest of the Province.

Trade between the Indians and the citizens of early New York was jealously overlooked by the City Fathers and the officers of the West India Company. Both sets of officials seem to have been tenderly solicitous for the health of the red men, as we may judge from the ordinance of 1653 which forbade selling white bread or cake to the natives. In their wisdom, doubtless, the Dutch authorities felt it inadvisable that the Indians should be pampered with delicacies to which they and their stomachs were unaccustomed, to the detriment of their digestion. This law, apparently, was not a dead letter, for the records shew that in 1655 Jochim, the baker, was tried for selling the redskins sugar cakes.

The mere mention of digestion calls to mind the unpleasant subject of medicine. The practice of the medical science was but indifferently followed in New Amsterdam for many years after the founding of the city—perhaps to the great benefit of the inhabitants. Doctor La Montagne, an Huguenot refugee of an ancient and noble French family, was a man of more than usual attainments, according to all accounts. He was a graduate of the University of Leyden and settled in New Amsterdam in 1636. He was, we are told, "the only doctor in Manhattan in whom the settlers had any confidence." We may gather somewhat of the state of affairs and understand the lack of confidence in the average medical practitioner when we read that, in 1652, it was enacted, "on the petition of the Chirurgeons of New Amsterdam," that "none but they be allowed to shave, the Director-General and Council understanding that shaving doth not appertain exclusively to Chirurgery, but is an appendix thereto: that no man can be prevented operating on himself, nor to do another this friendly act, provided it be through courtesy and not for gain, which is hereby forbidden." It was furthermore ordered that "Ship Barbers shall not be allowed to dress any wounds nor administer any potions on shore without the previous knowledge and especial consent of the Petitioners, or at least of Doctor Johannes La Montagne." This latter provision seems to indicate an attempt to prevent quackery, but then it worked in various other ways as well. Besides, so far as most of these barber-surgeons were concerned, it was very much like the pot calling the kettle black. Nor is there wanting the suggestion of attempting to maintain a trades-union monopoly. In 1663 there was sent out from Holland a supply of drugs for a clergyman "versed in the art of Physick and willing to serve in the capacity of Physician." His presence, as a medical man, may or may not have been a gain to the community; but considering much of what had gone before, it could scarcely by comparison have been a detriment. By 1680 we find the old Five Houses of the West India Company converted into an hospital, so from this we may infer that systematic attempts were being made to raise the status of the medical profession and provide more adequately for the needs of the people.

But this book is not primarily an history of New York City, and we must not spend too much time on the subject of city life or we shall be betrayed into committing an whole volume before getting to the real subject proposed. The aim here is to give only a bare idea of the town life to which the people up the river resorted, either when business interests called them or when they felt the need of as near an approach to a metropolitan atmosphere as they could command without crossing the water.

EIGHTEENTH CENTURY AND AFTER

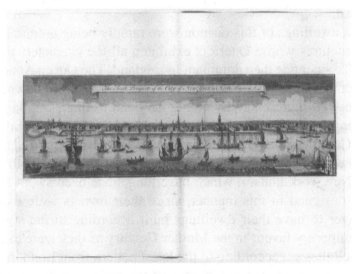

**SOUTH PROSPECT OF THE CITY
OF NEW YORK, 1746.**

Between the manners and conditions of the seventeenth century and those of the eighteenth we can trace no sharp line of distinction. The transition was gradual and imperceptible, as it was bound to be. The utmost we can do, in order to form an adequate mental picture, is to note some of the salient contrasts afforded by features and incidents belonging distinctly to the eighteenth century when compared with what had gone before.

To begin with, very early in the eighteenth century, the aspect of domestic architecture began to undergo a clearly perceptible change. There were still remaining many of the typical houses of the Dutch period—built of yellowish-tinted brick of Holland pattern, with peaked roofs and gable ends to the street. The gables tapered upwards by a succession of "crow steps" on each side—so constructed, it is said, to enable the chimney-sweeps to reach the chimneys from the gables—and were often surmounted by fanciful weathervanes of wrought iron. The heads of anchoring irons coming through the gable ends of the houses were fashioned into numerals, indicating the year of erection, or into the initials of the owner and his wife, and these stood out in strong relief against the ground of the wall and supplied a feature of marked decorative interest.

But dwellings of this fashion were rapidly being outnumbered by structures whose exteriors exhibited all the characteristics of the Classic mode then dominant in England. The Queen Anne and the Early and Middle Georgian fashions are so well known, and are so well represented by numerous good examples throughout the length and breadth of the States formed from the original thirteen Colonies, that it is unnecessary to enter here into a detailed discussion of their distinguishing features. The eighteenth century New York houses, which have long since been swept away, were designed in this manner, since their owners were usually as eager to have their dwellings built according to the style in contemporary favour in the Mother Country as they were to have their clothes cut according to the latest pattern from London.

The city of the second quarter of the eighteenth century presented a low-roofed aspect; the houses of the newer fashion had dormer-windowed attics and were, at most not over three storeys in height, but more commonly of two storeys. One of the finest houses in the city at this time was the home of Stephen De Lancey, on the west side of Broadway. It was quite representative of the best English domestic traditions of the period and was designed in the early Georgian manner. It was described as "plain, but strong and neat," and on top of the roof had an "outlook with a balcony." This means to say that its composition was marked by the restraint and elegance commonly exhibited by the Classic manner, that its elevations were symmetrically disposed, and that it had a flat deck on top of the hipped roof, surrounded by a balustrade. The materials ordinarily used in the construction of city houses were brick and stone; in many cases the walls were wholly of brick, while in other cases a combination of brick and stone was employed, the stone being used for bases, quoins, string courses and other items of architectural amenity. The woodwork was very generally painted white.

FRAUNCE'S TAVERN, BROAD STREET

Detroit Publishing Company, Library of Congress, Prints and Photographs Division

It is possible to get some idea of the appearance of the better dwellings of the period if we look at what is now Fraunce's Tavern, at the corner of Broad and Pearl Streets—a building about which "cluster more interesting historical associations than attach to any other pile of brick and mortar" now standing in New York City. The site belonged originally to Stephanus Van Cortlandt but was conveyed by him, in 1700, to his son-in-law, the Huguenot Stephen De Lancey. The house was built in 1719 and, in time, descended to Oliver De Lancey. About 1757 it became the home of Colonel Joseph Robinson, and later on it was used as the store and warehouse of De Lancey, Robinson & Company, merchants engaged in the East India trade.

This erstwhile dwelling "did not begin its career as a public house until 1762." In that year it was sold at auction and bought in by Samuel Francis or Fraunce, usually considered a West Indian on account of his swarthy skin. He opened the house "as a tavern, called the Queen's Head, under the sign of Queen Charlotte." It immediately became one of the most popular gathering places in the town and was used for all manner of civic meetings as well as for convivial assemblages. Here, in the Long Room, on the 8th of April, 1768, the New York Chamber of Commerce was organised, consisting of twenty-four merchants and importers, with John Cruger for its first president. Here, in 1774, the Sons of Liberty and the Vigilance Committee held a meeting of protest against the landing of the tea from the ship *London*, at the East India wharf nearby, and all of those present thereupon determined to march to the dock and throw the cargo into the river. Thus New York, as well as Boston, had its Tea Party. Here, also, was organised the Committee of Correspondence, the body that had so much to do with bringing about soon afterwards the formation of the Continental Congress. Here, too, on the 25th of November, 1783, Governour George Clinton gave a dinner to celebrate Evacuation Day when the British forces finally quitted the city where they had been so long established. Amongst those present at this dinner were General Washington, the Chevalier de la Luzerne, and other distinguished officers. Last of all, the event for which the Tavern is most famous took place on the 4th of December, 1783, when, at a dinner holden in this favourite inn, General Washington bade farewell to a great gathering of the officers who had been with him through the campaigns of the Revolutionary War. The complete history of the building, and a catalogue of all the notable events that have taken place there, may be found fully chronicled in other volumes.

GOVERNMENT HOUSE (1790–1815)

New York Public Library Digital Collections

The second quarter of the eighteenth century was a time marked by the inauguration of various civic improvements and the institution of sundry facilities of intercourse with other places, all of which changes were gladly welcomed. In 1733 the irregular bit of ground at the foot of Broadway, that had hitherto been only an unkempt "common," was laid out and set aside as a bowling green—the Bowling Green with which we are familiar, since this initial effort at civic beautification and the creation of a park system has retained its identity to the present day. Just one year before this was established a monthly stage service to Boston, while a weekly post to Philadelphia maintained regular relations between New York and what was then the metropolis of the Colonies.

In our survey of eighteenth century New York we must not forget the public buildings that were erected from time to time. Of these one of the most notable was the old City Hall.

It was erected at the head of Broad Street in 1699, an oblong, two-storeyed structure, somewhat like the letter H, with peaked roof, dormer windows, and a cupola. Therein were the common council room, a court room, a room for the jury, the fire-engine room, the debtors' prison, and a dungeon for criminals. In 1740, accommodations being provided elsewhere for some of the previous functions of the building, it became the official residence of the Mayor, John Cruger. Later, it was altered and added to and, under the name of Federal Hall, became the seat of the Federal Government when New York City was the national capital. It was under the portico of this structure that the oath of office was administered to General Washington at his inauguration as first President of the United States. In after years this time-honoured building was demolished to give place to the Sub-Treasury Building.

**CITY HALL, WALL STREET,
BEFORE THE REVOLUTION**

New York Public Library Digital Collections

FEDERAL HALL, WALL STREET

New York Public Library Digital Collections

The Governour's House in the fort, at the Battery, was another important public building and continued to be the Governour's place of residence up to the 29th of December, 1773, when it was burned, during Governour Tryon's occupancy.

When we turn to look at the social life of the eighteenth century city we find that it took the form of evening clubs for men, and concerts and assemblies for the ladies, with the occasional dissipation for all of theatrical performances, when chance sent a troupe of actors thither for a short stay. Although the theatre was patronised, when the actors made their infrequent appearance, this form of amusement was severely frowned upon by a large element of the community.

Of the ladies, in his history of New York before the Revolution Smith says: "They are comely and dress well, and scarce any of them have distorted shapes. Tinctured with Dutch education, they manage their families with becoming parsimony, good providence, and singular neatness." But he unkindly adds, "There is nothing they so generally neglect as reading, and indeed all arts for the improvement of the mind."

"Indeed, education generally seems not to have been of an high grade. The schools were not good, for the instructors were incompetent. Speech was corrupt, and, in public and private, there were abundant evidences of a low standard of taste in thought and language."

Smith tells us further that the pre-Revolutionary New Yorkers were "not so gay a people as their neighbours at Boston and several of the Southern Colonies," nor was there any great inequality of wealth, for the most part, "as is common in Boston." As an evidence of "low standards in taste," the severe critic of early New York might, perhaps, have pointed to the exhibitions of bull-baiting, held now and then, or to the beguilingly hysterical diversion of "flying horses" that itinerant shewmen sometimes provided. These non-intellectual amusements doubtless got their patronage at the time of fairs when, it is interesting to note, ready justice was administered for incident emergencies by the courts of "pypowder," held as they were of old in England and presided over by a proper person delegated for that purpose by the Government.

Slavery flourished, "quite one-sixth of the population being blacks." Most of the negroes, however efficient or inefficient as servants they might be individually, were peaceable and well-behaved, although there were times when their number and temper gave occasion for distrust and alarm. This feeling we see reflected in an act of the Assembly, passed just after the middle of the century, by which it was declared unlawful "for above three slaves to meet together at any time," or "at any other place than when it shall happen they meet in some servile employment for their masters' or mistresse's profit, and by their masters' or mistresse's consent," under penalty of being whipped.

It is interesting to note that duelling now and then occurred, but without in the least disturbing public equanimity beyond an occasional flutter of excitement amongst the friends or relatives of the parties immediately concerned. The *Daily Advertiser*, of the 25th of September, 1787, informs us that "at eleven o'clock at night a duel was fought on the grounds near Bayard's Mount in which the noted Chevalier de Long-champs was unfortunately killed. It is said that his antagonist was a Frenchman (Captain Verdier, late an officer in Count Pulaski's Legion) who had served in the late American Army; he had thought himself much injured by some assertions made by the Chevalier and meeting him in

William Street on Tuesday (25th) afternoon, an affray took place which in the evening terminated in the melancholy catastrophe above mentioned. The gentleman who killed him has since sailed for the West Indies."

The French residents of New York, whether ex-soldiers or refugees, were not all so contentious as the above-named gentleman "who has since sailed for the West Indies." We learn of one exiled French aristocrat, M. Auguste Louis de Singeron, who determined to make the best of the new order of his changed fortunes and, possessing both skill and excellent judgement in culinary matters, set up in business as a caterer, an employment in which he was rewarded with substantial success. He seems to have had a vivid recollection of his escape from the mob at the Tuileries during the French Revolution, and this memory he perpetuated in the marchpane façades of the Tuileries for which he found no little demand. Molasses taffy, wrought in decorative patterns, and gilt gingerbread effigies of Louis XVI and Marie Antoinette helped to augment his income.

It is highly amusing to compare the municipal appropriations of 1801, for certain city expenses, with the appropriations for the like items today. In that year the sum of $25,000.00 was set aside in the budget for the maintenance of the watch, in other words, for the expenses of the police department. For the paving and repair of streets, the munificent sum of $5,000.00 seemed sufficient, while $15,000.00 was deemed adequate for the purchase of new lighting equipment and keeping the lamps in order and lighted on nights when there was no "light moon." At that time the city occupied only the lower end of Manhattan Island and the Battery was the favourite promenade.

During the early Republican period wealth materially increased and there was a corresponding spread of luxury and elegance. The domestic architecture of the period, and the interior appointments of the houses, also reflected the changes that had taken place. Fascinating as this subject is, we must not allow ourselves to be diverted longer from the principal purpose of this volume. For those to whom these matters afford a lively interest, no better book can be recommended for its vivid portrayal of the life and manners of the day than Griswold's *Republican Court*.

PARLOUR IN CITY HOUSE, BEFORE 1815

**TWO INSURANCE OFFICES
AND ABANK,** *circa* **1800**

**THE INMAN HOUSE (FORMERLY AT
25th STREET AND 7th AVENUE)**

II.

THE PATROONSHIPS

To the Patroonships of New Netherlands attaches a certain historical glamour, very intriguing in its way, and conducive to the sense of old-world romance with which it pleases the imaginative to invest nearly everything connected with the Hudson Valley prior to the humdrum days of the nineteenth century. The unfortunate part of it all is that so many people are content to accept the glamour without troubling their heads about any exact historical facts, and consequently their conception of what happened is extremely hazy and inadequate. If they did but know it, their enjoyment of historic associations and the remaining visible memorials of notable personages and events would be immeasurably enriched by a modicum of accuracy in their retrospect, an accuracy that would endue the characters and doings of pioneer days with a lively and truthful reality. The Patroonships and Manors of the Hudson have furnished the intellectually lazy and the historically careless with an excuse for all manner of fanciful imaginings; their true story is tenfold more engaging than the fancies that have been spun about them.

At an early date in the history of New Netherland, the West India Company recognised the urgent need of taking active measures to encourage immigration and stimulate more permanent and substantial forms of settlement if the Province was ever to be other than a mere chain of trading posts for the collection of peltries, or if it was to produce any enduring return for the moneys already expended on their colonial venture. Hitherto the quasi-ephemeral character of the Dutch settlements on the Hudson had been chiefly due to a general predisposition to concentrate all activities upon the alluring trade in peltries rather than upon the tilling of the soil, a form of pioneer industry upon which all attempts at really permanent settlement must of necessity be based.

Bounden as it was, by the terms of its charter, to "advance the peopling of those fruitful and unsettled parts" that fell within the scope of its broad control, and to "do all that the service of those countries, and the profit and increase of trade shall require," the Company was deeply concerned to put affairs on a more satisfactory basis. It was plainly essential to attract thither men with the will and the means to push forward the development of a region of vast promise and untold resources. The result of their extended deliberations, carried on during 1627 and 1628, was that the Assembly of the XIX determined to prepare a plan giving special privileges, powers, and exemptions, to such members of the Company as would, at their own private expense and risk, send out expeditions and establish separate and distinct plantations in any part of New Netherland, Manhattan Island excepted, which the Company reserved to its own corporate control. Each detail was carefully weighed and, at last, on the 7th of June, 1629, the plan was finally approved and adopted by the Assembly of the XIX, and ratified and confirmed by their High Mightinesses, the States-General.

This plan or charter, as it might, perhaps, be more correct to style it, was entitled "Freedoms and Exemptions, Granted by the Assembly of the XIX of the Privileged West India Company, to all such as shall plant any Colonies in New Netherland." The word "colonie" in the Dutch sense, it should be observed, means a "plantation or settlement, and includes people, cattle, tools, stock of all kinds, as well as the lands on which all were to be placed," and has not the more extended sense we commonly attach to it in English, connoting a common, public undertaking directly controlled in all essential details by the duly constituted judicial and legislative authorities.

The first of the articles of the charter of 1629 immediately affecting the status, privileges and obligations of Patroons is the third, which sets forth that:

"all such persons shall be acknowledged Patroons of New Netherland, who shall, within the space of four years next after they have given notice to any of the chambers of the Company here [in Holland], or to the Commander or the Council there [New Amsterdam], undertake to plant a colonie there of fifty souls, upwards of fifteen years old; one-fourth part within one year, and within three years after the sending of the first, making together four years, the remainder, to the full number of fifty persons, to be shipped from hence, on pain, in case of wilful neglect, of being deprived of the privileges obtained; but it is to be observed that the Company reserve the island of Manhattes to themselves."

The fourth article provides for the privilege of changing sites, when there is good and sufficient cause. The sixth article specifies:

"The Patroons, by virtue of their power, shall and may be permitted, at such places as they shall settle their colonies, to extend their limits four miles [sixteen English miles] along the shore, that is, on one side of a navigable river, or two miles [eight English miles] on each side of a river, and so far into the country as the situation of the occupiers will permit; provided and conditioned that the Company keep to themselves the lands lying and remaining between the limits of the colonies, to dispose thereof, when, and at such time, as they shall think proper, in such manner that no person shall be allowed to come within seven or eight miles of them without their consent, unless the situation of the land thereabout were such, that the Commander and Council for good reasons, should order otherwise."

The seventh article guarantees that the *venia testandi*, or liberty to dispose of their heritage by testament, shall "be granted to all Patroons who shall desire the same."

"The privilege of becoming Patroons, with all their rights, powers, and exemptions, hereditary and otherwise, was confined solely to the members, that is the stockholders, of the West India Company. Other persons, could, with the permission of the Director and Council of New Netherland, take up as much land as they could improve, 'and enjoy the same in full property either for themselves or others, but without any of the advantages and privileges conferred upon the Patroons. These were styled Free Colonists.' "

Broad as were the powers and privileges conferred by this instrument, it failed to bring results commensurate with the hopes and expectations of the Company. Various disagreements arose between the Patroons and the Company on the score of fur trading, and it also became evident, from a careful study of economic conditions, that far more colonisation was urgently needed. It was, therefore, determined to throw open the country on broader and more generally inviting terms, without, however, working any prejudice to the rights of the Patroons who had already undertaken settlements, and without discontinuing the system of Patroonships. This determination brought about the issuance of a new Charter of Freedoms and Exemptions, generally known as the "New Instrument," on the 19th of July, 1640.

According to this revised and more liberal schedule, by which all the points in dispute between the Company and the Patroons had been adjusted, the privilege of becoming Patroons was open to "all good inhabitants of the Netherlands, and all others inclined to plant Colonies in New Netherlands." By this enlarged charter both the status of Patroons and the status of others undertaking plantations were more specifically set forth and defined.

Owing to sundry difficulties that arose, at the end of Governour Kieft's administration and during the earlier years of Stuyvesant's, between the Commonalty and the Company over restrictions of trade, delegates were sent by the Commonalty to Holland to lay their complaints before the States General. After the matters in question were explained and thoroughly discussed, a third Charter of Freedoms and Exemptions was enacted on the 24th of May, 1650. This modified somewhat the clauses of that of 1640 relating to trade, and the administration of justice in some minor points.

The latter charters were exceedingly liberal according to the views and standards of the seventeenth century, and it is by the standards of the time that we must judge them. It is important to observe, too, that the later charters made provision for a class of colonists who were not Patroons, in these words:—

> "For Masters of Colonists, shall be acknowledged, those who will remove to New Netherland with five souls above fifteen years; to all such, our Governour there shall grant in property one hundred morgens, two hundred English acres Rhineland measure, of land, contiguous one to the other, wherever they please to select."

By making this explicit provision for a body of lesser gentry there were definitely established and recognised in New Netherland the two upper classes then dwelling in the Republic of the United Provinces. The accepted social distinctions obtaining in Holland were transplanted, as a matter of course undeserving of any special comment, and were perpetuated on this side of the water. This social system contemplated nobles and commoners. The latter were of two sorts, first those who were of gentle birth and entitled to bear arms and, second, the boers or common people. Both the nobles and the gently born commoners brought out the third class, the boers, who were the men and women whom they settled upon their "colonies" and farms.

It was both natural and wise that the accepted order in the parent country should be transferred overseas to the venture in the New World. In this connexion it is well to bear in mind Edward De Lancey's very lucid summary of the whole situation. In his treatise on the Manors of Westchester County he writes:

> "It was this combined and harmonious system of mingled municipalism and aristocracy which gave the United Netherlands their great power and made them such a strong, conservative, and successful nation. It was a system they had tried, and under which they had lived, for more than two centuries, which all classes approved, and with which they were fully satisfied and thoroughly familiar. Hence it was, that when the West India Company undertook to colonise New Netherland, they naturally adopted for that new possession the same system which they knew had always worked well in the old, which they had always been accustomed to, and which was in entire consonance with the views, habits, manners, and customs, of the people of the Batavian republic."

> "It was not this system in New Netherland, but the ways and means of putting it into operation and carrying it out, which produced the delays, disputes, and changes, that began soon after the enactment of the Charter of Freedoms and Exemptions of 1629" and only ended with the adoption of the revised and amended charters to date."

It is a great errour to imagine that the mediæval institution of feudalism was transplanted to the colonies in America. This was not at all the case. The accepted social system and judicial organisation of the Netherlands were, quite reasonably, transferred to the colonies. It is hard to understand how anything else could have been done, or why the West India Company should have felt called upon to devise an wholly new order out of whole cloth. But no new feudal fiefs of the old model were ever created as they had already ceased to be created in Holland. The old feudal fiefs carried with them certain obligations incumbent upon the holders that no one ever dreamed of perpetuating in the new land. What was transplanted, and what misguided persons, athirst for the glamour of romance, are pleased to construe as feudalism, was the method of landholding along with the Dutch local system of judicial administration that went with it.

III.

THE MANORS

Quite as much nonsense has been written about feudalism and the Manors of the Province of New York as about feudalism and the Patroonships. The erection of Manors in the Royal Province of New York did not imply the establishment or continuance of feudalism in any respect.

The statute "Quia Emptores," of the year 1290, put an end to the creation of new feudal manors, so that even in England, after that date, the development of feudalism was restrained.

Manors of subsequent creation were *freehold* manors. The Manor of East Greenwich in Kent, a Crown possession, was the model upon which all the manors in the Province of New York were formed. "When William and Mary directed their Government to call General Assemblies, with the advice and consent of the Council, and when the first Assembly held in New York, under those sovereigns, met in April, 1691, that Assembly, in the Second Act it passed, declaring the rights and privileges of their Majesties' subjects in their Province of New York, enacted 'That all the Lands within the Province, shall be esteemed and accounted Land of Freehold and Inheritance, in free and Common Soccage, according to the tenour of *East Greenwich* in their Majesties' realm of England.' "

The favoured County of Kent, in which lay the Manor of East Greenwich, had never been wholly reduced to the new military tenures brought in by the Norman Conqueror. Most of the landholders there, in consequence, owed no claim for suit or services, or other obligations, than those of fealty and allegiance. "Hence it was that when the tenure of the British grants in America came to be settled, it was described as 'of our Manor of East Greenwich in the County of Kent,' that Manor being held only 'in free and Common Soccage'. The object of this was to give to the new possessions in America the most favourable tenure then known to English law." This desire to deal generously with the colonists is a point too frequently overlooked in our day.

The fixed "service" or "rent", on which New York was held in soccage by the Duke of York, was the yearly payment of "forty beaver skins when they shall be demanded or in ninety days after." When the Duke became King, in 1685, this nominal rent ceased and he held the Province from that date as Sovereign of England. Under him and his successors, therefore, from that year until the peace of 1783, by virtue of this fact, New York continued to be a Royal Province, under Royal Governours, commissioned by its British monarchs under their signs manual.

As such representatives of their Sovereigns, all grants of Manors and other great and small tracts of land, were made by the Governours of New York as long as New York continued to be a Royal Province. The tenure of all land was the same as that in the Patents from Charles II, to the Duke of York, "in free and common soccage as of our manor of East Greenwich in the County of Kent." The fixed services or rents varied, but were merely nominal in all cases. "In some of the minor incidents of the grants of manors, and of lands not manors, they also varied, but the *important* thing, the tenure itself, was the same in all."

The Manors of New York, by reason of their being erected subsequent to the Statute of Charles II. (12 Charles II., Anno 1660), which abolished military tenures and turned them into free and common soccage, "never possessed, nor were their lords ever invested with, the powers, privileges, rights, duties, and burdens of the old feudal manors of England." Owing to ignorance of this fact, or the concealment of it, as the case may be, "much misconception has been generated in the popular mind, by some writers, and also by some lawyers and men in public life. . . . . No grant of a feudal manor in England, at any time from their first introduction ever carried with it a title, and much less did any grant of a New York freehold manor ever do so. Both related to land only. The term 'Lord of a Manor' is a technical one, and means simply the owner—the possessor—of a manor, nothing more. Its use as a title is simply a work of intense, or ignorant, republican provincialism. 'Lord' as a prefix to a manor owner's name was never used in England, nor in the Province of New York."

Under the manor system there were two kinds of land tenure for that part of the land not reserved to himself by the Lord of the Manor—*freehold and copy-hold.* The freeholders were those to whom the Lord of the Manor sold land outright, and this land they held in fee simple and were entitled to dispose of it by sale or otherwise, as they saw fit. They remained, however, a part of the manor in its aspect as a political unit.

The part of the manor retained by the Lord was called his demesne or domain. The cultivable portion of the demesne was tilled by a class of tenants called in ancient times "villeins." These villeins originally could not leave the land and their service to the Lord of the Manor was obligatory. They were permitted, however, to cultivate specified portions of the land for their own use and profit. Although their occupation of the soil was at first at the pleasure of the Lord of the Manor, it eventually became a qualified right, recognised at first by custom and finally by law. In course of time the services and obligations due the Lord of the Manor by this class of tenants were almost wholly commuted to a money payment or rental. This form of land tenure was known as *copy-hold.*

When the manor system was established in the Province of New York the obligations of the copy-hold tenants consisted almost altogether of such money payments as have just been mentioned. Their actual status did not differ very materially from that of tenants nowadays who pay stipulated annual rents to the landlords of the farms they cultivate, those rents being partly in kind and partly in money, or wholly in money, according to the terms of agreement between landlord and tenant. When a copy-holder conveyed his land to another, he surrendered it to the Lord of the Manor and paid him the customary fine or transfer tax, whereupon the Lord granted the holding to the person nominated by the outgoing tenant. This custom was rigidly adhered to on the Manor of Philips-borough and also on some of the others.

The Court Leet, consisting of the freeholders presided over by the Lord of the Manor or his steward, was the centre of local jurisdiction and was under the control of the Royal Government of the Province. The Court Baron, on the other hand, was a purely local court held by the Lord of the Manor and made up of the manor freeholders; its functions were the redressing of grievances, the judgement of misdemeanours, and the settlement of disputes, in any of which particulars the tenants of the manor might be concerned. The copy-holders were not members of the court baron, but approached the court as petitioners.

The foregoing explanation of the manor system has been undertaken in the interest of historical accuracy and for the clearing away of a false sentimental glamour that those unacquainted with the facts have delighted to attach to the manner of land holding and civil administration that obtained in certain portions of the Province of New York in the seventeenth and eighteenth centuries. A knowledge of the true facts in the case does not destroy the romance at all, but rather enhances it by giving it the firm foundation of veritable circumstance.

Some of the Hudson manors succeeded the patroonships of the Dutch period, like the Manor of Rensselaerwyck or the Manor of Philipsborough, which latter really comprised most of the earlier Patroonship of Colen Donck. Some of them, like Pelham Manor or Fox Hall Manor, were in effect confirmations of land grants made before the erection of manors under the English *régime*. Still others were created virtually *de novo*.

In nine of the manors the tenure was that of the Manor of East Greenwich, in the County of Kent, and the grantees were privileged to hold Court Leet and Court Baron. These manors, in the chronological order of their erection, were as follows:— the Manor of Fordham, granted to John Archer, the 13th. of November, 1671; the Manor of Fox Hall, near Kingston, granted to Thomas Chambers, the 16th. of October, 1672; the Manor of Rensselaerwyck, granted to Kiliaen van Rennselaer, the 4th. of November, 1685; Livingston Manor, granted to Robert Livingston, the 22nd. of July, 1686; Pelham Manor, granted to Thomas Pell, the 25th. of October, 1687; the Manor of Philipsborough, granted to Frederick Philipse, the 12th. of June, 1693; the Manor of Morrisania, granted to Lewis Morris, the 8th. of May, 1697; the Manor of Cortlandt, granted to Stephanus van Cortlandt the 17th. of June, 1697; and the Manor of Scarsdale, granted to Caleb Heathcote, the 21st. of March, 1701.

Besides these, there were seven other manors within the Province of New York, references to which occur in the early records, and it is not at all unlikely that there were others of which all substantial traces have disappeared. The exact status of these manors it is extremely difficult to determine because of the loss or inaccessibility of the original records. The manors in this group of which we have some knowledge were the Manor of Gardiner's Island, at the eastern end of Long Island, granted to the Earl of Stirling, the 10th. of March, 1639; the Manor of Plumme Island, consisting of Plum Island and Gull Island, granted to Samuel Willes, the 2nd. of April, 1675; the Manor of Cassiltown (Castleton) on Staten Island, granted to John Palmer, the 20th. of March, 1687; the Manor of Saint George, in Suffolk County on Long Island, granted to William Smith, the 5th. of October, 1693; and the Manor of Bentley, often called Billopp Manor, on Staten Island, granted to Christopher Billopp, the 6th. of May, 1687. On Cadwallader Colden's Map of Manors and Grants there appears a manor, designated Fischer's Manor, to the north of Newburgh, while various documents about 1697 make mention of Queen's Manor, on Long Island, held by the Lloyd family.

In the United States, it is quite true, the social and economic conditions have altogether outgrown the manorial system, while in England it "has become almost obsolete, except so far as the customs developed and rights acquired under that system have become ingrafted in our common law." Nevertheless, we are bound in justice to recognise the fact that the manor system was a useful and beneficent institution when it was in full operation and that it contributed more than most people are aware to the social and political stability and progress of the English-speaking race. Not to cherish and hold in reverent esteem the memory of the manor system, "because the feudal idea which it recalls is inconsistent with modern American ideas," is exceedingly narrow-minded and savours of the spirit that would demolish what remains of the Coliseum because gladiatorial combats are repugnant to the standards of the present age—or, at least, are assumed and said to be.

In one of its important aspects, the manor system afforded a simple, direct, effective and easily-worked method of local administration. The local government, carried on through the agency of the manor courts, was just and economical in its operation, and the people were satisfied and happy. In other words, the system *worked*, and without needless complexities. Furthermore, it was a safeguard for the tenants. It established a reasonable measure of local self-government and it defended many popular rights against encroachment. We hear a great deal about the rights and privileges enjoyed by the Lords of the Manors—too much, per- haps—and we forget that with those rights and privileges were inseparably connected great and often onerous responsibilities. We hear far too little about the privileges of the tenants, and yet, if we impartially examine all the facts and data, candour compels us to admit that "in return for the privileges which the Lord of the manor enjoyed he had to render a very substantial return to his tenants in the privileges which he guaranteed to them and was bound to protect." Not the least valuable of these rights guaran- teed by the Lords of Manors were those of the courts.

The manor system was not a one-sided scheme of economic existence devised for the sole pleasure and profit of the great land-owners. It was a system based upon the mutual interest of the great and lowly, the common profit of landlord and tenant, and for the advantages each derived he had to render a substantial *quid pro quo*. It lasted and prospered as long as it did because it was firmly established on this ground of mutual interest and each side recognised the value of the benefits derived. It had its defects, to be sure, but what scheme of ownership and tenancy, what plan of local administration, what relationship of capital and labour has not its drawbacks! The millennium has not yet arrived, and, so far as can be judged from present indications, its arrival in the near future does not seem likely. The manor system was swept away as a consequence of the Revolutionary War, but it may be honestly questioned whether the usages and relationships by which it was supplanted have appreciably increased the profit or happiness of those who now occupy the lands once embraced within the old manorial jurisdictions.

IV.
THE PATROONSHIP AND MANOR OF RENSSELAERWYCK

PATROONSHIP 1630–1685

MANOR 1685–1783

On the 7th. of June, 1629—as already stated in the discussion of the Patroonships as an institution—the "Charter of Freedoms and Exemptions," after mature deliberation, was adopted by the Assembly of the XIX and ratified by their High Mightinesses, the States General of the Netherlands. The way was now open, by the creation of the proper legal and administrative faculties, for the stable colonisation of the Province of New Netherland. All that was needed was the willingness of eligible persons, with the means and the desire, to undertake the responsibility of planting "colonies" in the new land under the conditions laid down.

The Jonkheer Kiliaen Van Rensselaer, a nobleman of the Province of Guelderland, was one of the original "Lords Directors" of the Dutch West India Company and likewise a member of the Amsterdam Chamber in the Assembly of the XIX. Moved by the spirit of enterprise and adventure, Kiliaen Van Rensselaer signified to his colleagues his intention of becoming a Patroon under the newly-created instrument. Accordingly he sent his agents to New Netherland to choose out for him land suitable for the planting of a "colonie" and upon the strength of their report, in the months of April, May, July and August, 1630, he procured to be purchased for him from the Indian proprietors several large tracts on both the east and west banks of the Hudson so that by mid-August, when these purchases were confirmed by formal patents, bearing the signatures of Director Pieter Minuit and the members of the Council at Manhattan, a great portion of the present counties of Albany and Rensselaer was in the hands of the Patroon and Fort Orange, with the land immediately around its walls, was all that remained in the neighbourhood under the sole jurisdiction of the West India Company.

By subsequent purchases, made during the next few years, the boundaries of the Patroonship were enlarged until a princely domain had been created, on both sides of the Hudson River, extending approximately twenty-four miles north and south by forty-eight miles east and west, and including most of what is now Columbia County, as well as the counties previously mentioned. The patents for these purchases, issued by the resident Director and Council in New Netherland, were afterwards approved and confirmed by the West India Company and when New Netherland passed under English control, in 1664, these great holdings were likewise endorsed by the English Governour and Council. Thus arose the Patroonship of Rensselaerwyck, destined to play so important a part in the history of New York.

Although other Patroonships were created at about the same time, or within a brief space afterward, within the bounds of the territory over which the Dutch West India Company then claimed jurisdiction, the "Colonie" of Rensselaerwyck was the only venture of the sort that continuously prospered and had a permanent existence, and it was the only one that left an appreciable mark on New York's colonial life.

The stable foundation and substantial success of the Patroonship of Rensselaerwyck as a venture in colonisation and concentrated local government were altogether due to just one person, and that one person was Kiliaen Van Rensselaer, the first Patroon. He never had the gratification of seeing his vast overseas domain, and yet he laboured so assiduously, so wisely and so well, that no one of the early pioneers who was actually on the ground, combatting face to face the dangers and hardships of subduing the wilderness to tractability, is more to be reckoned a founder and maker of the country. They toiled with their hands, and sweated, and in their bodies endured the physical discomforts incident to early settlement; they also had the satisfaction of seeing the tangible results of their effort and sacrifice. Van Rensselaer sate in his counting house in Amsterdam, planned with painful anxiety, devised ways and means to meet the endless needs of a venture that entailed an enormous outlay and brought in little return, directed with meticulous care every detail of his distant under-taking, and shewed his faith by unflinching devotion to the fur-therance of a scheme that he must well have known could never be of profit to himself personally and could bear fruit only for succeeding generations; and Van Rensselaer's only meed of sat-isfaction was derived from the reports of his agents which, often enough, were insufficient, perplexing and far from encouraging. Yet Van Rensselaer toiled on unremittingly. Although an absentee landlord, he deserved none of the odium usually attaching to that class, and for what he did he richly merits the honour and grati-tude of posterity.

Modern critics frequently exhibit a rancorous bias against any-thing they think savours of feudalism, and they are inclined to cavil at a project to transplant what they are pleased to interpret as feudal principles to a new soil. Nevertheless, candour should impel them to admit that at the time, and under the conditions then obtaining, it was a sane and feasible scheme, not perfect, perhaps, in its provisions, but as nearly so as circumstances would permit. Both common sense and experience shewed the extreme difficulty of inducing the small tenant of slender means to venture the expenses, hazards and discomforts of emigration; to invite the organisation of blocks of settlement in Patroonships was an alter-native that commended itself to hard-headed Dutch shrewdness. And to attract the establishment of Patroonships, under propri-etaries with large holdings and charged with choosing the per-sonnel of the colonists, the formulation of a detailed scheme of management, and the responsibility of advancing the requisite capital, it was obviously necessary to offer substantial induce-ments to the "adventurers in chief" in return for the risks and the executive burden they were assuming. It is true that the privi-leges with which the Patroon was invested were great, but so also were the responsibilities to counterbalance them. The holding of a Patroonship was not "all beer and skittles" for the Patroon by any manner of means. The game, if it was well played, was worth the candle, in the end; but the playing entailed vision, faith and patience to an untold degree, qualities just as essential, after all, to the happy outcome of any colonial venture, as brawn, hardihood and physical endurance.

After the lands purchased by Kiliaen Van Rensselaer were "transported" or patented to him, no time was lost in sending out colonists, building houses for them, and equipping them with the necessary live stock and implements so that they could make a good start in carrying on fanning operations. Many of the early settlers sent out were chosen from amongst Van Rensselaer's own tenantry in Holland or from amongst people more or less personally known to the Patroon through his church associations. Through this careful choice of colonists and close supervision of the personnel many difficulties and contentions were avoided that would otherwise have been inevitable.

From an examination of the Bouwier manuscripts, amongst which are preserved many documents relating to the intimate affairs of the colony in its early days, we may gather enough incidents to convey a fairly lively impression of what was going on in the everyday routine of building the settlement. For example, we learn that on the 7th. of July, 1631, "appeared before the meeting [of the Amsterdam Chamber of the West India Company] Mr. Kiliaen Van Rensselaer, who requested that he be permitted to send over by the ship *d'Eendracht* some colonists and eight or ten calves."

An ensuing entry reads:

"In regard to which it was decided first to hear the skipper, who declares that he will do all he can, whereupon his honour's request is granted, on condition that the skipper in case he should be inconvenienced thereby, may throw them overboard or allow them to be eaten, without thereby obliging the Company to give any compensation."

Although the record does not specifically say so, it is to be presumed that the discretionary powers entrusted to the skipper of throwing overboard or eating part of the Patroon's shipment, should he "be inconvenienced thereby," referred to the calves, not the colonists, although one cannot help wondering whether, in the course of a long voyage, it might not at times have been a satisfaction to the said skipper if the option of disposal had been all-inclusive.

The minute directions for the management and governance of the colony sent by Van Rensselaer to his agents are full of homely details that serve to bring the daily life of the settlers very close to us. In case the agents "think it advisable to erect a brandy distillery or brewery, they shall ask the director [of the Company] for the large brewing kettle and brandy kettle which is at the Manhattes and sell the brandy and beer either at Fort Orange or at the Manhattes or elsewhere." With well-balanced judgement and a sane, sympathetic comprehension of the divers needs of humanity, while taking thought for the *spirituous* comfort—as indicated by the memorandum just quoted—the Patroon concerned himself with the no less necessary *spiritual* comfort of his people, for he enjoins Commissary Planck "before all things to promote piety and take care that means be found to send a minister," and instructs Pieter Cornelissen that he shall, meanwhile, "cause the people to assemble every Sunday, to train them in the commandments, the psalms, the reading of the Holy Scriptures and Christian authors, in modesty, love and decency." This happy combination of brewing and preaching, the inculcation of piety and the distilling of brandy, plainly indicated the Patroon's catholic outlook and his fitness to be at the head of a colonisation venture in which human nature was bound to play so large a part. It is altogether a more pleasing picture to contemplate than the contemporary New England combination of potells of rum and preachments of damnation.

Van Rensselaer's directions concerning the religious welfare of the settlers on his estate were no mere idle chatter indulged in for the sake of propriety and what other people might say. To Arendt Van Corlaer he writes:

> "In the box is a wooden model of a small church; please use diligence in erecting it at the least cost, if the [building of the] farmhouses does not prevent it. I have at Craloo a farm house of that shape, which is 60 feet wide. This church would be but 48 feet wide, so that it ought not to cost so very much. However, the upper structure is somewhat heavier and a storey higher. It is my definite intention that this church be put opposite Castle Island, north of the small grove and south of the farm of Gerrit de reux, deceased, not far from the small grove on a small hill, near or on the bank of the river. Cornells Theunissen would perhaps rather have it on the west side of the river, but I am firmly resolved to have it on the east side, at the aforesaid spot. Near the church ought to be built also a dwelling for the minister and one for the sexton."

In another letter to Van Corlaer, he writes:

"I again commend to you the building of the church; . . . . It ought not to be a very complicated matter, the shape being mostly like that of an eight-cornered mill; it cannot cost a great deal either as it is small, its greatest width on the outside measuring but 48 feet."

From the two foregoing references, it is evident that the projected church was to be an octagonal building with an approximately conical roof.

When Dominie Megapolensis arrived in the colony, in 1642, his first business, of course, was the cure of souls but, at the same time, he was expected to take a very active advisory interest in the temporalities of the settlement. The Patroon's letter to him, that he was to peruse and ponder on the outward voyage, contains a summary of terms for farmers which throws valuable light on the substantial methods of colonisation. It stipulates that:

"each farmer must take with him at least two servants and one boy who understands farming, and himself equip them; the patroon, on his part, provides their board till they arrive in New Netherland at the Island of *manhatans* and on their arrival in the colony causes them to be provided upon condition of repayment with grain for eating and sowing and with a suitable site on which to establish their farm, where the patroon will once and for all have a good house with [hay] barrack and barn built for them, which according to the custom of that country are usually placed near the river, the waters of which flow by clear and fresh and full of fish; the patroon causes them also to be provided once with a waggon and plough and what else is needed for farming, the same to be kept in repair and replaced by the farmer; he will further assign them 30 or 40 morgens of land toward the interior, consisting of beautiful woods filled with excellent game, such as deer, turkeys and all sorts of nourishing fowls; he also turns over to them on each farm, from the surplus of animals in the colony, four horses and four cows, of which they are to have half the increase, the other half to be paid to the patroon in money or in kind."

The really paternal interest of the Patroon in the welfare of his colony was abundantly manifest all through his correspondence. It is not difficult to appreciate his feelings, for instance, when he says that "those in the colony (even if I were not their lord) need me here [in Amsterdam] more than I need them there, for who will supply their necessities if I do not? Who will furnish them the money if I do not?" We see his solicitude for law-abiding and seemly behaviour when he orders that "if any farm hands or even farmers or anyone else should misbehave themselves, especially those who through quarrelling or fighting, through laziness or drinking, neglect the profit of their patroon, they must be corrected and punished according to the laws of this province of Holland, without regard to person." It was not unreasonable that the Patroon should expect loyalty to his interests from the colonists for, as he justly observes, "they have no expenses in the world and gain whatever they gain through my investment."

Although the sending out of "one brandy still, weighing 115 pounds," with condensing coil, is duly recorded, Van Rensselaer expected the people of Rensselaerwyck to exercise self-control— as witness the foregoing injunctions about the punishment of drunken brawling—and use their liberty wisely; in his wisdom he knew that free will and the opportunity to conquer temptation were more conducive to strength of character and good conduct than silly inhibitions and interference with the indefeasible rights of personal liberty.

Amongst the thousand and one matters that demanded attention were formal amenities, and the outward symbols appropriate to official dignity were not forgotten. In a list of items shipped out at a very early date there is noted "a silver-plated rapier with baldric and a black hat with plume, to be presented to Rutger hendrixsz van Soest in his capacity as officer and Schout of Rensselaerwyck," also "four black hats with silver bands, to be presented in my name to the following persons, whom I have designated as schepens and councillor of Rensselaerwyck," after which they are mentioned in due order, along with various hints about preserving a spirit of wholesome amity.

Kiliaen Van Rensselaer died in 1647 and was succeeded in the Patroonship by his son Johannes who was not yet of age and, by his father's will, was left under the guardianship of his grandfather and his cousin, Wouter van Twiller. The guardians appointed Herr Brandt Arent Van Schlechtenhorst, the scion of an ancient Holland family, as Director of the Colony of Rensselaerwyck. Van Schlechtenhorst was a vigorous, diligent and capable director, of undeviating loyalty to his charge and determined to uphold all the claims of the Patroonship against infringement from any quarter. It was during his incumbency of the office that the famous controversy with Governour Petrus Stuyvesant occurred over conflicting claims of jurisdiction. The Governour fearing, it seems, the ascendancy of the Patroonship over the interests of the West India Company, sent a written order that no buildings should be erected by the Patroon within six hundred paces of the fort at Albany.

"Van Schlechtenhorst paid no attention to the mandate. A sheriff was then sent up the Hudson to prevent the erection of a fort for the Patroon on Beeren Island. The quartermaster of Rensselaerwyck, in his turn, entered a formal complaint for the 'meddlesome interference,' saying the fort was only to exclude the 'canker of freedom from the colonie of Rensselaerwyck,' and it was completed, cannon planted, and the Patroon's flag hoisted. The next document informs us that Gouvert Loockermans, of the sloop *Good Hope*, was ordered to strike its colours while passing Beeren Island, and not obeying, a shot was fired from the fortress through the sloop's mainsail."

"Matters were approaching a crisis. Stuyvesant's willing hands were full in straightening all sorts of crooked affairs for a short time after he reached the little Dutch dorp which is now New York. But as soon as other duties permitted he went to Rensselaerwyck with a military escort. Arriving at the fort he summoned Van Schlechtenhorst into his presence to answer for contempt of authority. He came at once and charged Stuyvesant with proceeding contrary to all ancient order and usage, as if *he*, the Governour, were lord of the Patroon's colony! Stuyvesant retorted with offended dignity, and Van Schlechtenhorst retorted in turn."

"Stuyvesant said the buildings were objectionable, and endangered the fort [in Albany], and Van Schlechtenhorst declared hotly that the soil on which they stood belonged to the Patroon, and that the Governour's argument was a mere pretext, adding several forcible expressions in Dutch which it would be difficult to translate into good English. No definite results were obtained, and the parting was in high temper on both sides. As soon as Stuyvesant sailed for New York, Van Schlechtenhorst continued his improvements, precisely as before."

The next act in this diverting colonial drama—to us, looking at it from a distance of nearly two centuries, it seems a comedy;

to the actors it was anything but a comedy—reveals Stuyvesant, greatly annoyed and perplexed, seeking the advice and endorsement of the Amsterdam Chamber. The upshot of it all was that Van Schlechtenhorst was captured, taken to New York and imprisoned for four months in the fort on the Battery, whence he ultimately made his escape, secreting himself on a sloop bound for Albany. As soon as he was back at his post in Rensselaerwyck, Van Schlechtenhorst had all the people of the colony, whatever their status, renew their oath of allegiance to the Patroon and his representatives, and asserted his control more firmly than ever over the populous little settlement about the fort at Albany.

Then came the irate and choleric Stuyvesant with a military force and sent orders to the manor house bidding the Director to strike his flag. Van Schlechtenhorst flatly refused, whereupon the soldiers entered the grounds, fired a volley from their muskets, and hauled down the flag themselves. Stuyvesant next proceeded to establish a court of justice in the village independent of the Patroon's court. The notice proclaiming the constitution of this court was torn down in a twinkling and, in its place, appeared a proclamation asserting the authority of the Patroon.

When the whole matter finally came before the States General in Holland, the members of that august body inclined to favour the claims of the Patroon. The controversy dragged on for years until New Netherland came under English dominion and became the Province of New York, when the points at issue were amicably adjusted and Albany was eventually (1686) incorporated as a city independent of the Patroonship of Rensselaerwyck which, however, retained all its prestige of jurisdiction in every other respect.

Jan Baptist Van Rensselaer, an half brother of the second Patroon Johannes, succeeded Van Schlechtenhorst in the Directorship before the settlement of the contest over jurisdiction—a contest to which, naturally, he fell heir—and Jan Baptist was in turn succeeded by his next brother, Jeremias, who managed the affairs of the colony with "acceptance and discretion," he, too, having to apply all his tact in the still unsettled dispute.

Kiliaen, the son of Jeremias Van Rensselaer and Maria Van Cortlandt, was the third Patroon and took to wife his cousin, who bore the same name as his mother, Maria Van Cortlandt, the daughter of Stephanus Van Cortlandt, first Lord of the Manor of Cortlandt. The Van Rensselaers were now closely bound by marriage ties with the Schuylers and Livingstons as well as the Van Cortlandts and these family alliances counted for much in the influence they exerted upon the growth of the Province. That influence, it should be added, was a most beneficial factor in the development of the country. Kiliaen, the third Patroon, sate in the Provincial Assembly from 1691 to 1703, and was the first Lord of the Manor of Rensselaerwyck when the Patroonship was erected into a Manor in the new order of things under English rule. Kiliaen's two sons, Jeremias and Stephen, were successively Lords of the Manor, Jeremias, the elder, dying without issue. Stephen died in 1747, leaving a son, Stephen, five years of age who, about the time of reaching his majority, built the second manor house which, when its demolition was impending a few years ago, was carefully removed to Williamstown, Massachusetts, to be preserved as a valued historical and architectural monument.

This second manor house in Albany, which was completed in 1765, took the place of a much older structure that had served not only as the home of the Patroons, and more or less as the seat of the local manorial government, but had also been used as a fortress in the earlier days of the colony. To this new manor house the family removed, the old structure nearby being relegated to other uses. The new manor house, a stately and commodious structure, designed with the utmost urbanity and elegance characteristic of the period of its erection, was far more in keeping with the station of its owners than was its predecessor, and far more suited to the lavish and constant hospitality dispensed. It was an imposing dwelling in the Georgian manner with a great central block flanked by wings of one storey. Across the central portion of the main front was a portico of four columns, reached by a broad flight of steps. The exterior was graced with all the amenities of orders, balustrades and balconies, besides a wealth of exquisitely wrought ancillary details. The interior was nobly planned with rooms of spacious and well-considered dimensions, while the details of the panelling and carved woodwork were even more distinguished than those of the exterior. As may be imagined, all the appointments were consistent with the fixed setting they were intended to complete and combined all the comforts of a polite manner of life with the utmost elegance of which an elegant age was capable. So long as this house was occupied by the Van Rensselaer family the guests welcomed within its doors were the most notable personages who came to Albany and the functions held there brought the presence of many whose names are familiar in the historic annals of the country. Although it is a thousand pities that an house of this character should be lost to the community in which it played so important and conspicuous a part, posterity may be thankful that it is carefully preserved as an inspiration for future generations.

The earlier history of the Patroonship and Manor, as well as much of the personal history of the family, centred about the old manor house which was built about 1660. There were several thousand tenants upon the manor and "their gatherings were similar to those of the old Scottish dans. When a Lord of the Manor died these people swarmed about the manor house to do honour at the funeral. They regarded the head of the family with reverence, a feeling shared by the whole country." On rent days and on the days when the manor courts were held, there were also notable gatherings of the tenantry. The manor always had its own representative in the Provincial Assembly and was regarded as an extremely important factor in the administrative system of the Province. The Lord of the Manor, as head of this great estate, was always a conspicuous personage wherever he went, and when it was announced in New York that he was "coming to the city by land, the day he was expected crowds would turn out to see him drive through Broadway with his coach and four."

The manor house was "well peopled with negro slaves," and, with a sufficient domestic retinue for all emergencies, the numerous family connexion and innumerable friends were always sure of a cordial and hearty welcome whenever they descended upon the master of what was in effect a veritable principality.

Stephen Van Rensselaer, the last Lord of the Manor, bridged the chasm between the old order and the new. He belonged in a manner to both systems. He was the scion of an "aristocracy that had a legalised and legitimate growth, yet the country did not contain a more conscientious republican than he was. His mother was Catherine, daughter of Philip Livingston, the signer of the Declaration of Independence. He was born . . . the subject of a king, with immense inherited estates as well as chartered baronial rights, the proprietary of a landed interest remarkable for any country," yet he "favoured from his earliest youth the changing sentiment in America . . . nor during his entire life did he ever lament the loss of his power and consequence. When he came into possession of his vast domains, shortly after peace was restored, he is said to have leased as many as nine hundred farms of one hundred and fifty acres each, on long terms."

He married a daughter of General Philip Schuyler and was thus brought into close relationship with both Schuyler and Alexander Hamilton. He served his State and country faithfully in many official capacities, and was ever a public benefactor and philanthropist. "No individual in the State, at the time, carried with him a more potent personal influence." It has been well said of him that "he was a Christian, a philanthropist, and a patriot, as well as a gentleman. He assumed nothing, he offended no one."

V.

THE PATROONSHIP OF COLEN DONCK

1646–1666

A DRIAEN VAN DER DONCK, first and only Patroon of Colen Donck, while one of the most outstanding figures in the early history of New Netherland was, at the same time, one of the most unfortunate. His case is peculiarly pathetic. He was pursued by a series of untoward events and he seems to have been foredoomed to disappointment, now through obstinacy, now through petty jealousy or spite on the part of those sundry officials into conflict with whom an unkind fate thrust him, thwarting his best efforts to be useful to the infant land, although his integrity and sterling abilities commanded the respect of his neighbours and led them to repose their confidence in his discretion for the conduct of affairs nearly touching their closest interests.

He appears on the scene, plays his rôle, and then vanishes, leaving behind him no such enduring traces of his career as did the patroons of Rensselaerwyck or the Lords of the greater Manors. His only lasting memorials are his writings, oft quoted but little read, and the name of the town of Yonkers, corrupted in the course of years from the possessive of "Youncker" or "Jonkheer," meaning "the son of a gentleman," a title by which he was commonly known as early as 1645. A very substantial personality in his own day and generation, to posterity he seems little more than a shadow flitting across a dim and far-off stage.

Adriaen van der Donck, a Dutchman of gentle birth, was a native of Breda, a graduate of the University of Leyden, and a doctor of both the civil and canon law. He was the first lawyer in the Province of New Netherland, and his name occurs as signatory on many of the important documents of early date. In the autumn of 1641 he was sent out as Schout-Fiscaal of the Patroonship of Rensselaerwyck. The Schout-Fiscaal was a public functionary whose office combined the duties of a sheriff and an attorney-general. In a domain so extensive and so active in the processes of its growth as was the Colony of Rensselaerwyck, the post carried with it no little responsibility.

Prior to sailing from Amsterdam van der Donck, "probably as part of the terms" agreed upon between them, received from Kiliaen Van Rensselaer, the first Patroon, a lease of the westerly portion of the first island on the west side of the Hudson below Albany, an island known successively as Welysborough, Castle Island, and Van Rensselaer's Island, and here, upon landing, he built himself an house.

Owing to sharp differences of opinion and difficulties with the Patroon's Commissary, Arendt Van Corlaer, in 1643, van der Donck was minded to sever his connexion with Rensselaerwyck and arrange for the planting of a "Colonie" at Catskill of which he himself might be the Patroon. Van Corlaer considered van der Donck "covetous and monopolising," and said so; van der Donck is said to have "heaped abuse and slander upon the Commissary." The fact of the matter seems to have been that they were both men of decided character and vigorously expressed convictions and between such, unless there be singular unanimity of outlook, friction is apt to arise. Besides, Van Corlaer had been first on the spot and, for that reason, may have assumed a certain superiority that was bound to be irritating to his fellow officer. Van der Donck's action in seeking to found a Patroonship of his own in the immediate neighbourhood, it appears, would have been an infraction of several articles in the charter of Freedoms and Exemptions and Kiliaen van Rensselaer insisted that the Schout-Fiscaal, as his "sworn officer," should desist from the undertaking. This put an end to the project of the Catskill Colony, the belligerents patched up their quarrel, and van der Donck stayed on at Rensselaerwyck in his former capacity.

In January, 1646, van der Donck's house burned down when he was on the point of selling the remainder of his lease and new dissensions broke out between him and the Commissary over the responsibility of rebuilding the dwelling. The upshot of it all was that van der Donck dwelt in an hut beside Fort Orange till spring and then, wearied and disgusted with the vexations to which he was subjected, went down the river to New Amsterdam.

Here he was *persona grata* to Director Kieft, thanks to the great services he had done the hot-headed Governour a short time previously "in advancing the requisite funds and settling the terms of peace with the Indians" at the close of the war Kieft had wantonly provoked several years before.

Meantime Kiliaen van Rensselaer had died at Amsterdam and with his death van der Donck's official connexion with the Patroonship of Rensselaerwyck ceased. Still minded to become a Patroon, van der Donck chose what is now the lower part of the County of Westchester and the northern part of New York City "between the rivers Hudson and Harlem, on the west and south, and the Bronx on the east." This domain, to which was given the name "Colen Donck" (Donck's Colony), was granted by Director Kieft and his Council in 1646.

The new Patroon had scarcely entered into possession of his estate, and begun to set his establishment in order, when the troubles between Kieft's successor, Peter Stuyvesant, and the people became acute and van der Donck was chosen one of the committee of three whom the Commonalty of New Netherland were sending back to Holland to lay the popular grievances before the supreme authorities. Here he was detained and underwent many annoyances for a long period. He did not return to New Amsterdam till 1653.

In 1655 van der Donck died, having willed his Patroonship, as he was privileged to do, to his wife, Mary Doughty. With her children she subsequently removed to Patuxent, in Maryland, where she married Hugh O'Neale. In October, 1666, conformably to the precedent established by Governour Nicolls when the Province passed under English control, a confirmation of the grant of "Colen Donck" was issued, naming Hugh O'Neale and Mary his wife as joint proprietaries. Later in the same month they transferred their interests to Elias Doughty, Mary's brother, and he proceeded forthwith to dispose of the lands by sale to sundry purchasers. Thus, after only twenty years duration, the Patroonship of Colen Donck came to an end, part of it going to form what was afterwards Fordham Manor, part being absorbed in the tract that was later erected into the Manor of Philipsborough, while the rest was parcelled off in smaller holdings. The one reminder of the broad Patroonship granted to "one of the most noted and intelligent of the leading men of New Netherland" survives in the name of the town that grew up on the land that once belonged to the "Youncker" or Jonkheer Adriaen van der Donck.

VI.

THE MANOR OF FORDHAM

ERECTED THE 13TH. OF NOVEMBER, 1671

IT HAS already been pointed out that the Patroonship of Colen Donck, after the death of the Patroon, Adriaen Van der Donck, was parcelled out and sold off by his heirs. Part of this land was incorporated within the Manor of Fordham and the greater portion was later absorbed into the Manor of Philipsborough.

John Archer bought the southern portion of the erstwhile Patroonship and also a certain tract of land lying to the south of it. Thereon he began "a township in a convenient place for the relief of strangers, it being the road for passengers to go to and fro from the main, as well as for mutual intercourse with the neighbouring Colony." "For all encouragement unto him, the said John Archer, in prosecution of the said design, as also for divers other good causes and considerations," Governour Francis Lovelace did grant and issue a patent constituting the Manor of Fordham, of which John Archer was the first Lord.

The Manor of Fordham was patented to John Archer "in as large and ample manner, and from and with such full and absolute immunities and privileges as is before expressed, as if he held the same immediately from his Majesty the King of England, and his successors, as of his Manor of East Greenwich in the County of Kent, in free and common soccage, only yielding, rendering and paying yearly and every year unto his Royal Highness, the Duke of York," a peck of good peas, when it shall be demanded.

The Manor House of Fordham Manor has not survived to our day and there is nothing of moment to record concerning it.

VII.

FOX HALL MANOR

KINGSTON-ON-HUDSON

ERECTED THE 16TH. OF OCTOBER, 1672

THOMAS CHAMBERS, who became the first Lord of Fox Hall Manor, by grace of Royal Charter and letters patent, in 1672, made his first appearance in the records of New Netherland on the 6th. of May, 1642. At that time he is described as an English carpenter contracting to build an house in New Amsterdam for Jan Janse Schepmoes. The contract after stating that the dimensions of the house were to be twenty by thirty feet, continues:

"It shall be enclosed all around and overhead with clapboards tight against the rain, inside even as the mason's house, one partition, one bedstead and pantry, two doors, one double and one single transome window. The carpenter shall deliver 500 clapboards for the house; Schepmoes shall furnish the nails and the food for the carpenter during construction, which commences this day, and for eight weeks, when the house, accidents excepted, must be ready, and when the whole shall be duly completed, Schepmoes shall pay to Thomas Chambers in addition to board, the sum of one hundred and sixteen guilders computed as twenty stivers the guilder, for the which the carpenter and Schepmoes submit to all courts, provided the carpenter shall hew the timber to the best of his ability."

The one hundred and sixteen guilders named in the contract would have been about forty-six dollars and forty cents. The disparity between building costs and the price of labour then and now would dismay the modern artisan. For many years Chambers was commonly known as "De Clabbordt" or "The Clapboard," seemingly in allusion to his occupation and his building the clapboarded house for Schepmoes. Goosen Gerritse calls Chambers by this name in the record of an horse purchase.

The next mention of Chambers occurs in the records of the Patroonship of Rensselaerwyck where he appears as a tenant farmer. The lease agreement reads:

"IN THE NAME OF THE LORD, AMEN: This day, 7th. September, anno 1646, the presiding officers of the Colonie Rensselaerwyck on one side, and Thomas Chambers on the other, have agreed and consented about a certain parcel of land lying right opposite the Bouwerie called the Flatt [deVlachte], on the east bank of the river, between the two kills, which land he, Thomas aforesaid, shall occupy as a bouwerie for the term of five successive years, commencing the 15th of November, 1647, on the following conditions. . . ."

Subsequent allusions to Chambers in the records of the Colony of Rensselaerwyck seem to indicate that he continued to ply the trade of carpenter, and that he was an active factor in helping to develope the prosperity of the settlement. That Chambers pursued the trade of carpentry and joinery was no indication of the walk of life from which he had come before his migration to New Netherland. He seems to have claimed the right to bear arms, as we shall see by-and-by. In an infant colony, from force of circumstances nearly everyone, regardless of rank, was obliged to perform manual labour or to practise some branch of artisanry. It is the same to-day when cadet members of distinguished families undertake ranching or farming in newly settled territory. Whatever the degree of his birth, certain it is, at all events, that Chambers was a man of parts and of the type that furnishes good pioneer timber.

Seeing the advantages to be derived from the ownership of extensive lands, and fired by the ambition of independent action, he determined to withdraw from the Colony of Rensselaerwyck and purchase lands from the Indians, in which he might at length exercise the rights of proprietary overlordship with all the benefits and privileges thereto appertaining. Accordingly, as early as 1652, he and several others settled along the Esopus, near the present site of Kingston, and began to acquire lands from the Indians by purchase. These holdings they increased from time to time and, in spite of repeated troubles between the Indians and some of the settlers, their settlement grew in numbers and their land purchases multiplied.

The story of Kingston's early days is told elsewhere in this volume, so that we may here go on with the specific narrative of Thomas Chambers and the erection of Fox Hall Manor, which was independent of the town, had its own separate civil and judicial administration, and antedated the division of the Province into its original Counties. Until the setting off of Fox Hall Manor, in 1672, however, the growing estate of Thomas Chambers was incorporated in the settlement of Esopus. If his discreet advice had been more consistently heeded by his fellow colonists from the first, there is little doubt that the course of Kingston's infancy would have run far more smoothly than it did, and that many of the discomfitting frictions with the Indians might have been averted or, at least, appreciably mitigated.

Although the other early settlers at the Esopus were sometimes headstrong and unwilling to hearken to Chambers's counsels, he nevertheless held a conspicuous position of influence in the colony in 1668, when the newly arrived Governour, Sir Francis Lovelace, was making a tour of inspection through the Province in company with Colonel Nicolls, who was about to go back to England. It was natural that their Excellencies should visit Chambers as they passed through Kingston on their way along the west bank of the Hudson. While they were the guests of William Beckman, during the two days they remained in the neighbourhood looking into military matters and the general ordering of affairs, they "spent an evening of great hilarity" with Thomas Chambers, at his house and seem to have been much impressed with their reception.

By this time the rich lands along the Esopus had become the Egypt of the Province. The products there raised were feeding not only the people of the Hudson Valley, but Esopus maize and wheat were exported in considerable quantities to the West Indies. During the year 1672 twenty-five thousand schepels of corn had been raised on the Esopus lowlands. Surely now was the time when Thomas Chambers, one of the chief citizens and land owners of the neighbourhood and the backbone of the community from the date of its establishment twenty years before, might hope for substantial recognition from the Provincial Government.

This recognition came and Chambers's ambitions were realised when his lands at the Esopus were erected into a manor, on the 16th. of October, 1672, and he became Lord of the Manor of Fox Hall.

It is evident, from the wording of the patent, that there was at that time a substantial house "commonly called Ffox Hall," and that it was fortified against Indian attack, doubtless having loopholes in the walls like those at Fort Crailo or the Van Cortlandt Manor House at Croton-on-Hudson. Unfortunately, this manor house in which Thomas Chambers lived has long since disappeared.

In 1686 Governour Thomas Dongan granted Chambers a new patent, confirming the former patent issued by Governour Lovelace, and more specifically defining the manorial rights of the grantee. At the same time, he added three hundred acres to the Manor, bestowed the right to hold Court Leet and Court Baron, and confirmed the right of advowson or patronage of any churches within the bounds of the Manor. The Manor of Fox Hall, though lying adjacent to the town of Kingston, and just to the north of it, was in no way a part of it but constituted an altogether separate and independent jurisdiction. When the original counties of the Province were established and their boundaries defined, it was decreed for "the County of Ulster to containe the Townes of Kingston, Hurley and Marble Towne, Fox Hall and the New Paltz and all the villages, neighbourhoods, and Christian Habitations on the West Side of Hudson's River from the Murderer's Creeke near the Highlands to the Sawyer's Creeke." This mention of the Manor as separate from the town of Kingston indicates the distinction that was always observed; owing to the proprietary rights of the grantee, the Manor occupied a peculiar relation to Ulster County. As it was not "within nor part of any town," "it was necessary that the taxes levied upon the Manor be laid with a separate warrant for collection, and addressed to the collector of the Manor."

Thomas Chambers had no children. In order to transmit the Manor, to preserve the entail, and to perpetuate the name of Chambers, he made a will with most intricate provisions sufficient, as *he* hoped, to meet all contingencies. His wife was the widow of Dominie Laurentius Van Gaasbeek. Chambers made her son Abraham Van Oaasbeek, his heir and stipulated that he should assume the name of Chambers. If Abraham died without issue, the estate should go to Jannetje, a sister of Abraham, on condition that she and her children "take the name of Chambers, as well as whoever should marry her." Should she leave no children or should they not assume the name of Chambers, the property passed to the next sister, Maria Salisbury, on similar conditions, and her son was to inherit the property and assume the Chambers name. It was entailed until the tenth son, or if no sons survived to pass down through the daughters, beginning with the eldest. The Manor property in all cases was to be kept intact.

A curious document in the Court Records of Ulster County shews that Thomas Chambers, Lord of the Manor of Fox Hall, not only claimed the right to bear arms but also, in the absence of a duly constituted College of Heralds for the Province of New York, was ready to undertake the duties of the Heralds and devise appropriate bearings for his stepchildren. This document reads:

"CAPT. THOMAS CHAMBERS DECLARES by the present that, out of free favour (vrye gunste) and affection he has presented to Jan Mattysen and Mattys Matty sen, sons of Margarite Chambers, they being her sons by another marriage, a portion of his coat of arms, viz.: one of the burning fireworks (branden vaurwerken) and the crest which shall be as a complete coat of arms to them.

In testimony of the truth I have subscribed to the present with my own hand in the presence of the Magistrates this November 28, 1679, at Kingston.

(Signed) THOMAS CHAMBERS
To which testifies,
(Signed) WM. MONTAGNE, Secretary."

Chambers's efforts to found an enduring Manor and to perpetuate his own name in the Lordship of that Manor were unavailing. The entail was broken not long after his death, the Manor of Fox Hall disintegrated, and the very burial place of the first Lord was neglected and quite forgotten until a few years ago when his body was removed, re-interred, and the spot marked that posterity might not forget the name of the man who really founded Kingston.

VIII.
FORT CRAILO, GREENBUSH
EASTERN MANOR OF RENSSELAERWYCK
1642

**FORT CRAILO, WEST FRONT,
GREENBUSH (RENSSELAER)**

Library of Congress, Prints and Photographs Division

FORT Crailo, at Greenbush—now called Rensselaer—opposite Albany, is one of the earliest homes, perhaps we should say the earliest, of the Van Rensselaer family in America. It is, without question, the oldest continuously inhabited dwelling in the state of New York, if not in the whole United States. Its history forms part and parcel of the story of the Patroonship and Manor of Rensselaerwyck, of which it was an integral part until the separation of the estate into the Eastern and Western Manors, but it has such a strongly individual history of its own that it must be considered separately.

In 1704, Hendrick Van Rensselaer received Fort Crailo and the Eastern Manor from his elder brother the Patroon, as his own share of the estate, when the whole of the Van Rensselaer estate in America was finally settled after paying off the other heirs who still remained in Holland. From Hendrick Van Rensselaer Fort Crailo descended to his son, Colonel Johannes Van Rensselaer, a man prominent in colonial times for his public services and patriotism. His was the longest life identified with the old house. He was born there, in 1708, and always lived there until his death, in 1783.

Of the house itself, we are told that "the small stone fort on the east side of the Hudson, at what is now Greenbush, was built by order of the first Patroon. . . . It served as a place of defence and refuge for his colonists when hard pressed by the hostile Mohicans." As a matter of fact, the colonists of Rensselaerwyck had little need of the protection of a fort for, thanks to the wisdom, fairness and tact of the Directors and officers of Rensselaerwyck, the colony's relations with the Indians were generally amicable, but when "the Indians attacked Wiltwyck [now Kingston] and massacred many of the inhabitants, on the 17th. of June, 1663, 'the farmers fled to the Patroon's new fort Crailo at Greenbush for protection.' "

The original part of the house is said to have been built in 1642, and all documentary and circumstantial evidence seems to agree in the assignment of this as the correct date of erection. On a stone in the cellar wall, inside the oldest portion of the building is the inscription "K.V.R. 1642 ANNO DOMINI." On a similar stone in the opposite wall is the inscription "DO. MEGAPOLENSIS." As the shipping lists bear evidence, Dominie Megapolensis, accompanied by his wife and children, left Amsterdam in one of the Patroon's ships for Beverwyck, as Albany was then called, in January, 1642. Van Corlaer, in one of his letters, alludes to the Patroon having sent out in 1642 a ship load of stone, bricks and tiles for building and roofing purposes. This ship, *De Houttyn,* brought Dominie Megapolensis and his family. "It has been suggested that the

Patroon, with his remarkable faculty for ordering the minutest details of the management of his 'Colonie,' may have sent over his cornerstones all graven and ready for use by the hand of his Reverence, the 'well-learned Doctor Johannes.' " The presence of these inscribed stones in the cellar of Fort Crailo, together with what we know of the coming of the dominie, the arrival of the building materials, and other incidents connected with the history of the settlement, all form links of corroborative evidence that the house was built in 1642. The house, or rather the fort, for it was both at the beginning, was named Crailo after the estate of Crailo, near Huizen, in Holland, which Kiliaen Van Rensselaer had purchased in 1628. The name means "Crows' wood." Whether Crailo was immediately upon its completion occupied by Dominie Megapolensis, or whether it was leased by the guardians of the young Patroon to "Arendt Van Corlaer for six successive years," as one document seems to indicate, we have no means of certainly determining. We do know, however, that without question the house was occupied by the Van Rensselaer family from 1704 onward.

In 1740, Colonel Johannes Van Rensselaer made very substantial additions to the house and brought it to its present form. These additions comprised the dining room, with the rooms over it, forming the whole north-western portion of the building, together with the broad central hallway, the cross hallway, to the rear of the dining room, and the whole of the L extension at the back. It will thus be seen that Colonel Johannes's additions of 1740 more than doubled the size of the house. The initials J.V.R., inscribed on a stone beside the north door, with another opposite bearing the date 1740, commemorate the period of the enlargement. Owing to this very great enlargement, the plan of the house is curious; nearly "all the rooms connect with each other, usually by means of closets, but as there are several levels on the same storey the doors in some cases open several feet above the floor of the lower room. There is no apparent reason for this difference of level unless it was purposely designed to increase the difficulty of capture," in case the house should be taken by an enemy. Tradition has it that Fort Crailo sustained several Indian sieges at different periods before the Revolutionary War.

The "beautiful Katrina," the daughter of Colonel Johannes Van Rensselaer, married General Philip Schuyler, whose daughter Betsy became the wife of Alexander Hamilton. There was thus an intimate intercourse kept up between Fort Crailo and The Pastures as well as between Fort Crailo and the old Manor House and, later its successor, in Albany. From Colonel Johannes Fort Crailo passed by will to his grandson John Jeremias, who made many alterations in the old house in the early part of 1800, "putting in new window frames in the library and dining room,". . . while "Italian marble mantels, costly and novel, took the place of the old-fashioned wooden ones. They were the wonder of the country round."

Notwithstanding the changes wrought, in the taste of the day by John Jeremias, the prevailing character of the interior is still strongly reminiscent of the date of the earlier enlargement when Colonel Johannes spared neither pains nor expense in the panelling and other robustly detailed woodwork then installed.

The exterior of the house exhibits excellent brickwork which is a credit to the taste and skill of the old masons who constructed the fort or erected the subsequent additions. There are still visible some of the old loopholes in the walls of the ground floor, eloquent reminders of less peaceable days. The original doors and shutters, and many of the old window frames and sashes have long since disappeared and been replaced by others of later date and indifferent character, but the texture of the walls, the details of the brickwork, the general features of the composition, the structure of the roof, and the entire contour convey an adequate idea of what the house must have been in the hey-day of its prosperity when it was surrounded by gardens and orchards, with broad lawns in front sloping down to the Hudson and enclosed by high hedges of lilacs.

In order to avoid confusion it should be explained that Greenbush and Claverack together formed what was called the Eastern Manor and belonged to the younger branch of the family, after Kiliaen the Patroon conveyed it to his younger brother Hendrick in June, 1704, while Rensselaerwyck, or the Western Manor, belonged to the head of the family in the elder branch. The purchase from the Indians on both sides of the river was concluded at the same time, in 1630, the lands on the east side of the Hudson comprehending about one fourth of the original Patroonship. The Claverack tract was acquired at a slightly later date from the Indians by two purchases, the first on the 27th. of May, 1649, by Brandt Van Schlechtenhorst, then Director of Rensselaerwyck, and the second on the 15th of June, 1670, by Jeremiah Van Rensselaer. The Van Rensselaer holdings in the Eastern Manor were generally spoken of as the Upper Manor, or the Greenbush Manor, of which Fort Crailo was the Manor House, and the Lower Manor at Claverack, of which the Manor House is still to be seen a short distance to the east of the town of Claverack. The lands of the Greenbush Manor comprised 1800 acres, while those of the Lower Manor consisted of some 60,000.

In the back garden of the Greenbush Manor House or Fort Crailo is an old well which is intimately associated with the writing of "Yankee Doodle." The story goes that during the French and Indian War, when General James Abercrombie with his staff made the Manor House his headquarters on his way to defeat at the hands of Montcalm, at Ticonderoga, on the 8th. of July, 1758, the British officers were the guests of Colonel Johannes and his wife, Angelica Livingston. On General Abercrombie's staff was a young surgeon who was greatly amused by the spectacle the raw American recruits presented as they straggled in from the countryside, arrayed in all manner of motley garb, thoroughly rustic and not at all military. Sitting on the kerb of the well in the back garden, he scribbled the doggerel verses which alone preserve his name and "were destined to be adopted and proudly sung by the boys of '76." His name is variously stated to have been Shuckbergh, Shackberg and Stackpole, of which the first is more generally accepted. There is said to be a secret passage connecting the cellar with this well, and in the floor of the passage a trapdoor, supposed to have been designed "as an oubliette, to engulf a stealthy and unsuspecting foe," but if there is such a trapdoor it was doubtless contrived for some other purpose, and if the passage really exists it was in all likelihood made to allow the occupants of the house to get water without danger in case of attack by Indians.

In June, 1775, the Continental Army, then on its way to Ticonderoga, had its cantonment in the gardens back of Fort Crailo. General Schuyler also made Fort Crailo his headquarters on one occasion during the Revolutionary struggle.

The hospitality of the master and mistress of Fort Crailo was proverbial and many were the guests entertained at their well furnished board. Nearly all the American and French officers of note who came into the neighbourhood dined or supped there, including the Marquis de la Fayette and General Washington. In later times Daniel Webster and Harrison Gray Otis were numbered amongst the distinguished visitors.

The Van Rensselaer family continued to occupy Fort Crailo until the death of Doctor Jeremiah Van Rensselaer, in 1871, since which time it has gradually fallen into a state of sorry dilapidation and decay from which, it is to be hoped, means may be found to rescue it and preserve it in a manner becoming its historic significance.

IX.

LOWER VAN RENSSELAER MANOR

CLAVERACK

EASTERN MANOR OF RENSSELAERWYCK, 1685

IN WHAT particular year the Lower Manor House of the Van Rensselaers, at Claverack, should be reckoned as becoming, technically speaking, a manor house, it would be hard to say. It was built in 1685 by Hendrick Van Rensselaer, and has sometimes been called the "Van Rensselaer Outpost" as it was at the lower end of the Van Rensselaer lands and conveniently placed for the transaction of manor business in that extreme portion of the estate which was much too far away for the average tenant to be expected to journey to Albany or Greenbush when rent days or court days came round.

MANOR HOUSE, LOWER VAN RENSSELAER MANOR, CLAVERACK

The house seems to have grown gradually into the manor status with the increasing performance of manorial functions within its walls. Its early history is inseparably bound up with the history of Fort Crailo, at Greenbush. When the Eastern Manor was finally set apart as a separate estate and manorial jurisdiction, the Claverack lands formed a part of it, and the house at Claverack became what might be called an alternative manor house for convenience in the transaction of manorial business. The Eastern Van Rensselaer Manor, in other words, was very much like a State having two capitals. Fort Crailo, the *real* Manor House, sharing its honours with Claverack.

The Lord of the Eastern Van Rensselaer Manor lived at Fort Crailo, while one or another of his sons lived at Claverack. On rent days, and at other times when it was customary for the Lord of the Manor to be readily accessible to his tenants, he went to the Lower Manor House. When he could not be there in person, one of his sons acted for him. Hence the Claverack house was identified with the collection of rents and other functions of manorial administration and is, therefore, entitled to be ranked as a manor house, certainly from the time when the Eastern Manor became a separate entity.

Unlike Fort Crailo or the later Van Rensselaer Manor Honse in Albany, the Lower Manor House at Claverack can lay no claim to urbanity or studied grace of architectural style. It is simply a Dutch farmhouse of Colonial type, staunchly built, commodious, and comfortable, but wholly devoid of any of those elegancies of plan or structure that gave an air of courtly dignity to many of the other manorial homes of the Hudson Valley.

Standing a short distance back from the road to Great Barrington, about a mile to the east of Claverack town, it is substantially built of brick, with walls two feet thick, and the whole is encased in a jacket of broad clapboards painted white. At the rear of the building, sundry additions have been made, but all of the original structure remains intact. The roof is unpierced by dormers and displays, towards the south or road front, a broad and steep slope extending to within a few feet of the ground so as to include the verandah beneath its spread. There is no flaring kick-up at the eaves, such as we find at the Van Cortlandt Manor House or other houses of nearly the same date, and the undeviating continuity of straight lines from ridgepole to verandah imparts a curiously beetling and determined aspect that is altogether individual and distinctive.

It will avoid mental confusion if we remember that Greenbush and Claverack together made up the Eastern Manor, which was held by the cadet branch of the family while Rensselaerwyck was the property of the head of the family, the "Patroon" of the Dutch *régime.*

During the Revolutionary War, the Claverack portion of the Eastern Manor played an important, though prosaic and often forgotten, rôle. In other words, it was the chief source of food supply for the Northern Army, at first under the command of General Schuyler and later under the leadership of his successors. From 1776 to 1783 a thankless but most necessary duty devolved upon Colonel Henry Van Rensselaer, namely, "to induce the tenants to remain upon the Manor, to plant and cultivate the land and then dispose of their produce to him upon the faith of future payment by a Revolutionary Government." His brother, General Robert Van Rensselaer, was then Representative of the Manor in the Assembly and lived alternately with his father, Colonel Johannes Van Rensselaer, at Fort Crailo in Greenbush, or else at Claverack. That they might maintain good order in the Manor during this unsettled period, the brothers acted in harmony and were wholly successful in their efforts. "No Tories as in Schoharie County, nor Cowboys as in Westchester" were permitted to cause disturbance. Those disposed to give trouble were promptly court-martialled and every attempt at disorder was put down with a firm hand.

If the exterior of the Lower Manor House at Claverack was unprepossessing and even crude in aspect, the interior was far otherwise. Though it may have lacked architectural distinction, its appointments were not only ample and comfortable, but elegant. Excellent furniture, fine silver, linen and pictures there were in abundance. Curiously enough, in the Claverack branch of the family there is a paucity of portraits, a lack, however, to be explained by their prejudice on this score. Some of them had made a visit to a certain manorial home where they discovered an ancestral portrait doing duty as a fireboard, and they had no mind to have their likenesses perverted to any such purpose when they were dead and gone. One can readily sympathise with their point of view.

X.

THE MANOR OF LIVINGSTON

ERECTED THE 22D. OF JULY, 1686

ROBERT LIVINGSTON, the first Lord of the Manor of Livingston, can very properly be regarded as a good example of the canny Scot blessed with an unerring intuitive instinct ever prompting him what to do and—what is quite as important—when to do it. Robert landed in the New World with his way to make, and he made it, doing exceedingly well unto himself long before the end of his life and, incidentally, doing well unto many others also. Robert landed at Charlestown, near Boston, in 1673, but soon determined that Massachusetts was not for him; and journeying to New York, in 1674, he proceeded up the Hudson to Albany where he correctly jaloused that opportunities were awaiting a man who knew how to make himself useful in the right way.

Robert Livingston was the son of the Reverend John Livingston and Janet Fleming, and a direct descendant, through a cadet branch, of the Lords Livingston of Callendar, so that he had back of him all the traditions of ability and breeding that stood him in good stead in the task of making a name and competency for himself in the new land whither he had migrated after the death of his father. Besides his mental equipment, he was fortunate in possessing an address and personality that commended him to those with whom he came in contact.

Arrived in Albany, Livingston's native abilities, superior education, and ready versatility soon won him favourable recognition, as a result of which he obtained "many public appointments, including the Secretaryship of Indian Affairs," a post that not only required great tact and discretion for the successful discharge of the duties attached to it, but also afforded ample scope for profitable trading ventures of which, doubtless, Livingston took every legitimate advantage. Thanks to the numerous opportunities within his grasp to improve his circumstances, it was not long before he had acquired comfortable means, and by careful management he readily increased the comfortable means to affluence. On the 9th of July, 1679, he married Alida Schuyler, the daughter of Philip Peterse Schuyler and Margareta Van Schlechtenhorst. "The latter was the only daughter of Brandt Van Schlechtenhorst, the celebrated Director of Rensselaerwyck," who matched wits and words and swords not unsuccessfully with Governour Peter Stuyvesant when the latter had tried to override the prescriptive rights of the Patroon. "Thus Robert Livingston became united with one of the largest and most powerful land-holding families of the Colony. The estates of the Schuyler family, like those of the Van Rensselaers, were measured by square miles rather than by acres."

"Robert soon saw that the power of the Colony lay with the great land owners, and on the 22d of July, 1686, he obtained from Governour Dongan a Manor grant of the lands lying for ten miles on the east bank of the Hudson River, about thirty miles south of Albany and extending to the New England boundary line, a total of about 160,000 acres." Thus the Manor of Livingston—if we leave out of account the Manor of Gardiner's Island and the Manor of Plumme Island, which are not treated in the present volume—was the fourth manor to be created in the Province of New York.

"On this estate in 1699 Livingston built his Manor House, the site of which was on the Hudson River near to what is now the railway station of Linlithgow. It remained standing for over a century, but about 1800 it was taken down by the great-great-grandson of the founder." There is thus, strictly speaking, no Livingston Manor House at the present day and only the important Livingston houses within the Manor boundaries can be considered. Although "credulous natives will still point out various old Livingston houses as 'Manor Houses,' and one may even see such designations on picture post-cards sold in the vicinity, this information is absolutely erroneous and without any authority whatsoever. The Livingston Manor House is not now, nor has been, in existence for over a hundred years." It is wholly incorrect, therefore, to speak of a Livingston Manor House to-day.

Since the erection of the Manor, in 1686, there had always been some annoying uncertainty about the original boundaries and also difficulty in identifying the Indian landmarks. Livingston, therefore, petitioned the Government for a new patent and, accordingly, on the 12th of October, 1715, Governour Hunter issued a confirmatory manor grant definitely settling the boundary questions and also conferring the privilege of having a manor representative in the General Assembly of the Province, an honour previously enjoyed only by the Manors of Rensselaerwyck and Cortlandt. Thenceforth, from 1716, until he retired from active life in 1725, Robert Livingston sate for the Manor in the Provincial Assembly, and for seven years of that time presided as Speaker.

Robert Livingston was solicitous that missionaries should be sent amongst the Indians and by his earnest representations on this score effected the despatch of two clergymen for this work by the Society for the Propagation of the Gospel in Foreign Parts. He was also keenly alive to the public needs of the Colony and strongly urged "preparedness" on the authorities in England, pointing out the necessity of repairing the forts at New York and Albany and storing therein an adequate amount of military supplies, timely precautions about which the Government at this time had become inexcusably lax.

On the 1st of October, 1728, three years after he had laid aside the burdens of public life, Robert, first Lord of the Manor of Livingston, died, "bequeathing the bulk of his estate, including the Manor House, to his son Philip," who had already undertaken the official duties relinquished by his father. A considerable tract of land in the southwestern portion of the manor was left to a young son, Robert. Robert Livingston, the elder, true to the character of benevolent canniness ascribed to him at the beginning of this chapter, did well unto himself in founding a great manorial estate which, apart from personal considerations touching him or his family, was also a factor of stability in the upbuilding of the Province; he likewise displayed the public spirit, vision, energy and initiative that comport with the rôle of a great pioneer and entitle him to high rank amongst the makers of the country.

Philip Livingston, the second Lord of the Manor, already embarked upon a distinguished career before coming to the headship of the family, was unlike his father in many respects. In her *History of the City of New York*, Mrs. Lamb tells us that he "was less subtile, less persevering, less of a financier and a much handsomer man." To the same source we are indebted for the information that "in his youthful days he was dashing and gay; he had a winning way with women, and went about breaking hearts promiscuously." Whatever promiscuous heart-breaking the dashing Philip did, however, must have been done by 1707, for, in September of that year, he married Sarah Van Brugh, the daughter of Peter Van Brugh, sometime Mayor of Albany, and Sarah Cuyler, his wife.

Just as the first Lord of the Manor had shewn much concern for the religious welfare of the Indians, so his son Philip was concerned for the tenants of his manor, and it is told of him that he was continually building churches throughout his domain, all of which he painted red. His interest in the spread of religious teaching amongst his tenantry did not by any means indicate that he had become a narrow religionist averse to the lighter amenities of life, for he is reported to have "supported three princely establishments, one in New York, one in Albany, and his Manor House," in all of which he maintained "a style of courtly magnificence." It is to be regretted that the Livingston Manor House, the scene of so much of this engaging mode of life, was demolished; for when an house disappears most of its historic associations vanish with it.

Philip died in February, 1748, in New York, and Sedgwick, in his *Life of William Livingston*, records of the second Lord of the Manor that "his obsequies (for so they may be called) were performed both at that place and at his residence in the Manor of Livingston. In the City the lower rooms of most of the houses on Broad Street, where he resided, were thrown open to receive the assemblage. A pipe of wine was spiced for the occasion and to each of the eight bearers, with a pair of gloves, mourning scarf and handkerchief, a monkey spoon was given. At the Manor the whole ceremony was repeated, another pipe of wine was spiced, and besides the same presents to the bearers, a pair of black gloves and handkerchief were given to each of the tenants."

Robert, the third Lord of the Manor, had taken his seat in the Provincial Assembly in 1737 as representative of the Manor, and this seat he continued to occupy for twenty-one years, at the end of which time he "retired in favour of his talented younger brother, William, then recognised as the leader of the Presbyterian or opposition party in the Province, of which the Livingstons had become the champions, and which at this period had become so identified with this family that it was generally known as the 'Livingston party'; while the Episcopalian, the party in power, took the name of 'the De Lancey party' from their leader, the Lieutenant-Governour— the Honourable James De Lancey."

As early as 1753 the aggressive and unjustifiable behaviour of the Massachusetts squatters and their attempted thievery of the manor lands had caused alarm and Robert Livingston's life was endangered. In fact, he escaped kidnapping at that time only through the friendly warning given by a neighbour, one of the Van Rensselaers of Claverack, who besought him to be on his guard "as he had been credibly informed that the New England people intended to carry him off either 'dead or alive.' " "Again three years later the threats of murder and arson were so serious that the New York Government sent a military force to guard the Manor and the iron mines." The boundary dispute was ultimately adjusted, but not before it had occasioned much anxiety and ill-feeling.

When the Revolutionary War came, Robert Livingston, the third Lord of the Manor, held no official post in the Government of the revolting Colonies, but his sympathies with the new order were attested by his action in placing his iron mines and his foundry at the disposal of the Committee of Safety, and his sons and many other members of his family played an active part both in the contest and in moulding the governmental policy of the infant country. One of Robert Livingston's sons, Peter, besides being a member of the Provincial Congress and of the Assembly, was Colonel of the Manor Regiment; Walter, likewise a member of the Provincial Congress and Speaker of the Assembly, was Deputy Commissary General of the Northern Department; John was aide-de-camp to Governour Clinton; and Henry, the youngest, was Lieutenant-Colonel and Commander of the Manor Regiment at the battle of Saratoga.

The third Lord of the Manor lived until 1790. In consequence of the Revolutionary War and the new principles of administration, the entail to the estate was broken and the manor lands were divided amongst Robert Livingston's children.

CLERMONT

Robert Livingston, the first Lord of the Manor, sent his third son, Robert, hack to Scotland to he educated. The following story, quoted from Mrs. Delafield's *Biography of Francis and Morgan Lewis*, explains how the southwestern portion of the manor came to he separated from the rest of the estate and bequeathed to this third son, as previously mentioned.

> "The first summer that young Robert passed with his father at the Manor, (after his return from Scotland,) his attention was attracted one afternoon by what seemed to him an unusual number of Indians skulking around and keeping within the shadow of the woods. That night, after he was in bed, he heard a noise in the chimney. He lay quite still and watched; presently a pair of legs descended upon the hearth. Robert sprang from his bed, seized the fellow before he could extricate himself, exclaiming at the same time, 'Villain, confess!' The man, utterly confounded, confessed that he was one of a gang who had fixed upon that night to rob and murder the whites. His father was so pleased with his intrepidity that he gave him the lower end of the Manor—a tract consisting of about thirteen thousand acres."

At his father's death, in 1728, Robert took possession of this estate and, about 1730, built thereon, upon a cliff over looking the Hudson, a commodious brick and stone house in the Georgian manner, which he called "Clermont." From this circumstance, Robert was afterwards known as "Robert of Clermont," to distinguish him from his nephew, Robert, who later became the third Lord of the Manor. When General Sir Henry Clinton made his expedition up the Hudson in October, 1777, and burned Kingston, his men fired many of the houses along both banks of the river. Clermont was one of the houses burned. The flames gutted the structure, but some of the walls were left standing and the house was rebuilt the following year virtually as it was before. When the Manor House was demolished in 1800, Clermont became the oldest Livingston house in the manor bounds. The exterior of Clermont has undergone many modern changes that obscure its Georgian character.

Robert of Clermont was a picturesque figure. He was a most courtly and genial person, and until his dying day he retained the costume of men of his rank worn at the period when he withdrew from an active part in public affairs. "His only child, the Judge, was to him the light of his eyes and the joy of his heart. The most perfect confidence existed between them. In both, religion was the ruling principle. They were both gentle in their temper and affectionate in their dispositions; both were inflexible where their duty was concerned." The master of Clermont was devoted and liberal to his grandchildren, and they adored him. If his grand-daughters were about to make a trip to town, he was wont to put a note in their hands, saying, "For your ribbons, my dears." He always said that he liked to see ladies well dressed, and thought brocade far more becoming than chintz. Whenever Mrs. Church, General Schyler's daughter, and a famous belle of her day, came to Clermont, she always insisted on seeing the old gentleman, even when he was confined to his room. "No one," said she, "flatters me so much to my taste as he does."

The rare devotion of Robert of Clermont to his son, the Judge, was not merely a matter of strong family affection. The Judge possessed such sterling qualities of character that he was esteemed and honoured by all who knew him, and beloved by those who knew him best. He has been described as an "eminent Christian, Statesman and Patriot," of whom his intimate friend, the Honourable William Smith, the historian and Chief Justice of Canada, was accustomed to say, "If I were to be placed on a desert island, with one book and one friend, that book should be the Bible and that friend Robert R. Livingston." He was Judge of the Admiralty Court and of the Supreme Court of the Province of New York, and in these capacities rendered most valuable public service.

In 1742 Judge Livingston married Margaret, the only surviving child and heiress of Colonel Henry Beekman, of Rhinebeck. Margaret Beekman brought with her not only one of the largest estates in the Province, but also an endowment of exceptional character, good common-sense, and rare executive capacity that marked her as one of the most notable women of her day.

When hostilities began, at the outbreak of the Revolutionary struggle, Judge Livingston left his town house in New York and removed his whole family to Clermont, no trifling undertaking at that period when the cabin of a sloop had to be engaged, berths furnished with bedding, crockery, knives, forks and the like provided, and enough food cooked to last for several days. It was little short of having to furnish a small house. Not long after this family migration, both Robert of Clermont and Judge Livingston died and Margaret Livingston was left with the entire management of the vast estate, her eldest son Robert being wholly engrossed with pressing public duties. To this task, however, she was fully equal.

After her house was burned by the British forces, nothing daunted she soon began rebuilding, for in a letter to Governour Clinton, in November, 1778, she tells him that she needs many hands, "such as masons, carpenters, brick burners, stone and lime breakers and burners," thus indicating that nearly all the materials for the house were taken from the place itself. But the management of the estate and the rebuilding of Clermont were not the only duties resting on the shoulders of Margaret Livingston. Besides these and the sundry calls of charitable and relief work that the women of the Revolutionary period assumed, she had the education of her children to superintend and the care of her large household, the last named an exacting obligation that would appal and overwhelm many a modern housekeeper.

In the kitchen, in the garden and on the farm, the work was done by negro slaves. At Clermont most of them were either inherited or bom on the place, just as they were in Virginia or Maryland. While the abundance of labour was a great advantage, there was also the need of constant supervision and instruction; those who know the black race know how soon and how readily they and the character of their work deteriorate directly they are left to themselves without the watchful oversight of a white master or mistress. And the white master or mistress must know, too, exactly how things should be done in order to require a proper performance of duties. Mrs. Livingston could not have been well served unless she herself had been thoroughly skilled in all the mysteries of pantry, kitchen, dairy and poultry yard.

Insistence on having work well done was not at all incompatible with kindness and consideration for the slaves, for they were always kindly treated at Clermont. In many ways the *régime* was like that on a southern plantation. On Christmas morning Mrs.

Livingston sate in her drawing room, a table near her, on which lay piles of Madras handkerchiefs, rows of pocket knives, bags of silver coin, and other gifts that would be appreciated. Then all the servants came in and wished her a "Merry Christmas" and received a present from her. How much the slaves felt themselves a part of the place, and how content they were to be there, may be gathered from the following anecdote. It is said that Mrs. Livingston once offered freedom to a slave woman of ungovernable temper on condition that she would leave Clermont and never come back. The reply to this offer was an indignant refusal:—"I was born on this place and have as good a right to live here as you have. I do not want to be free. "

The hospitality of Clermont was proverbial, and the hospitality of the table was not the least important factor that went to make up the welcome of all who crossed the threshold. There were always great preparations in the kitchen against winter. Then all hands were busy, "pickling beef and pork, curing hams, preparing sausages. The good housewife had always well filled shelves of mince-meat, cheese and preserves, apples were plenty, and the buckwheat cake regularly appeared at breakfast. As soon as the river was free from ice, the shad made their appearance, then calves and lambs were due, and wild ducks and geese flew northwards, so by spring there would be nothing to complain of in the way of fare." We cannot leave this subject without quoting Mrs. Stockton's enthusiastic reminiscence of Clermont muffins—they were "not pastry, nor like the Scottish short-bread, nor the beaten biscuit of the South; they were more like the croissant roll of the Paris *petit déjeuner*, but round and flat, cut out with the top of a wine glass, and nothing but silver and glass must touch them in the making. They were as light as a feather when finished."

Besides her other responsibilities, Mrs. Livingston had to devise means for the education of her younger children. Schools were closed during the war, and it was not easy to find the right man as tutor. "Finally, she was fortunate in procuring the services of Dominie Doll, a learned minister, capable also of teaching the German language. By another good chance she obtained an excellent music master, who taught the children to play upon the spinet. She was herself a French scholar, so no doubt she taught that herself to her children, when other aid was not to be had. Mrs. Livingston felt so sorry that Dominie Doll's only child should be away from him that, when the long cold winter set in, she sent for the girl to make one of the Clermont household!"

It was Mrs. Livingston's habit to leave her drawing-room at an early hour in the evening and spend some time in reading and correspondence before going to bed. She seems always to have kept well abreast of all that was going on, "and her opinion had weight with those in public affairs. Shortly before the delegates, who declared New York State independent, met at Kingston, a number of the most influential Republicans met at Clermont to consider, among other questions, who should be the first governour. A valid objection to every person was raised until Mrs. Livingston proposed George Clinton. Her suggestion was received with acclamation:—"He is the man! Why did not we think of him at once?"

ARRYL HOUSE

Little more than a stone's throw from Clermont, and like Clermont overlooking the river, stands Arryl House. Unfortunately it is now in ruins, the interior gutted by a fire that occurred a few years ago, the roof gone, and the walls gradually crumbling. Enough remains, however, to shew plainly what an admirable piece of domestic architecture it was, and even now it would be possible to restore it to its pristine grace.

**RUINS OF ARRYL HOUSE,
CLERMONT, NEW YORK**

Immediately after the Revolutionary War, in 1783, Chancellor Livingston built Arryl House for himself. Although the Clermont estate had been left to him at his father's death, in 1775, he desired his mother to continue as mistress of Clermont and, in accordance with his wishes, she remained there the rest of her life, dying in 1800.

Chancellor Livingston had conceived a warm admiration for French domestic architecture of the Neo-Classic type and Arryl House was built from a design by Bunel, inspired, it is said, by the Château of Beaumarchais. It was a most urbane and finished conception, and unquestionably one of the finest examples of domestic architecture on either side of the Hudson between New York and Albany. Indeed, it would be hard to find anything finer anywhere, even amongst the best of the modern work patterned in the same school of delicate elegance. The house was built in the form of a capital H. Between the two projecting wings of the river front was an elevated, stone-paved terrace, upon which were set orange, lemon and myrtle trees in tubs, after the contemporary French manner. The conservatory ran the whole depth of the house on the south side, and here on great occasions the dinner and supper tables were set, the tables being so constructed that large plants rose from their centres. Two skilled gardeners took charge of the conservatory, the greenhouse and the flower gardens; the rest of the servants were negro slaves.

When Chancellor Livingston returned to America after his diplomatic residence in France, he brought with him many fine pieces of furniture, and also tapestries and silver plate, all of which he had bought from returning *émigrés* who were impoverished and glad to sell their household treasures to the wealthy American who had exquisite taste and sincerely appreciated them. His young relatives used to tell how " 'Cousin Chancellor' would walk about among the young people, relating the history of each piece, which would prove as interesting as any story book." One of the most fascinating features of the house was the splendid library, "containing more than six thousand books, besides quantities of pamphlets—books not only in English and the learned languages, but in Spanish and French, both of which tongues the Chancellor read and spoke with ease."

Chancellor Livingston's eminent position and personal charm alike brought to his home a constant stream of visitors. Arryl House was nearly always full of guests, and these were amongst the most distinguished persons of America, as well as visiting foreigners of note. "Many a bearer of an ancient and honoured name of the old French *noblesse* was here sheltered for months, and even years, for the Chancellor used to say 'he loved all Frenchmen for the sake of those who fought for us.' " In 1824, when the Marquis de la Fayette made his triumphal tour through the United States, he visited Arryl House. Here a great reception was given in his honour, "when the lawn for half a mile was crowded with people, and the waters in front were white with vessels freighted with visitors from neighbouring counties; and all the cups, plates, ladies' gloves and slippers bore the image and name of la Fayette." There was also a *fête* to all the tenantry, as a part of the celebration, and likewise a review of the county militia. Marshal Grouchy, who was looking on from a window of Arryl House, lost his balance and fell out, breaking his arm. The excitements and festivities of this occasion closed with a great ball in the evening, opened by Mrs. Montgomery, the Chancellor's sister, and the Marquis.

Riding was always a favourite pastime and exercise with the Chancellor and he spent much of his time in the saddle. When he made calls, however, or went abroad on any formal occasion, he drove in a great gilded coach drawn by four horses. Alluding to this custom of the master of Arryl House, a descendant observes "from this we may surmise that, while politically the strictest of democrats, the style of living congenial to him continued to be that of the Lords of the Manor."

OAK HILL

OAK HILL, NEAR LINLITHGOW, NEW YORK

When Robert Livingston, the third Lord of the Manor, died in 1790, he bequeathed a part of the manor lands to his son, John, who built himself a house in the northern part of the estate in 1795. This house he called Oak Hill.

The story goes that before deciding upon the site where he would build his dwelling, John Livingston climbed to the top of one of the tallest oak trees on the place, and, taking a survey from this airy perch, he chose the spot that pleased him best. This portion of the tract was always covered with flourishing oak trees, and hence we have the name of the house. These oaks have been carefully preserved and remarkably fine specimens still abound. Until a few years ago two oaks of great height, with trunks about five feet in diameter stood in front of the house, and it was one of these, in all likelihood, that John Livingston climbed to make his observations.

The situation of the house is unique and cannot be surpassed by any other on the family lands. "Placed upon a height rising direct from the Hudson, just where the river bends towards the southwest, the view is unimpeded over the water for quite ten miles, while in front one gains a view of the Catskills very different from that seen from any other part of the Manor."

The house is a spacious rectangular brick building designed in the late Georgian manner, bnt the real beauty of its lines has been somewhat obscured by nineteenth century irrelevanoies in the shape of a verandah and a mansard roof. The ample rooms within and the beauty of the interior details, however, still convey the true character of the architecture as it was expressed in that age of just proportions and elegance of embellishment. The ceilings are lofty, in accordance with the manner of the day, and when the house was a-building the members of his family remonstrated and assured John Livingston he would freeze. Fortunately, he kept right on undaunted and maintained the ceilings at their proper height—and did not freeze.

At Oak Hill is preserved one of the firebacks from the original Manor House, marked R. M. L., the initals of Robert and Mary Livingston, third Lord and Lady of the Manor. Here, also, are many of the originals of the family portraits as well as much of the old silver and furniture, exhibiting in design and workmanship the best traditions of the periods in which they were fashioned.

XI.

PELHAM MANOR

ERECTED THE 25TH. OF OCTOBER, 1687

O N THE 14th. of November, 1654, Thomas Pell, of Fairfield, Connecticut, entered into a treaty with the Indians for the land that was subsequently to become Pelham Manor, in the Province of New York. This treaty and the purchase of land from the Indians the Connecticut authorities instigated with the aim of extending Connecticut territory westward into the land claimed by the Dutch. Pell's treaty with the Sachems was signed under an oak tree, known in after years as the Treaty Oak.

In 1666, Governour Nicolls confirmed this grant of the land purchased from the Indians and, in October, 1687, under Governour Dongan the tract was erected into the Lordship and Manor of Pelham. This last confirmation of the grant and patent for the manor are issued in the name of John Pell, the nephew and heir of Thomas Pell.

John Pell was the son of the Reverend and Right Honourable John Pell, Doctor of Divinity, and when he learned of the death of his uncle Thomas he set sail for America, landing at Boston whence he journeyed to Fairfield and claimed his inheritance, his letters of identification being duly acknowledged by a certificate of recognition, issued by the Governour and Secretary of the Colony of Connecticut.

John Pell, disposing of his property in Fairfield, lived on his manor, building there a suitable house for himself. In 1688 he was appointed Judge of the Court of Common Pleas and, in 1691, was the first member of the Provincial Assembly for Westchester County. In 1684, he was commissioned Captain of Horse, and Major in 1692. For a long time he was a Vestryman and Warden of Saint Peter's Church, East Chester. In 1689 he sold the land now covered by the City of New Rochelle to Jacob Leisler as a colony for the Huguenot refugees driven from Rochelle in France by the revocation of the Edict of

Nantes; he also gave an hundred acres of land to the French Church for its support.

The Manor House of Pelham Manor was demolished many years ago and the property passed by marriage into the Bartow family. The Bartow house stands near the site of the Pell Manor House and is now used as the headquarters of the Garden Club of America.

XII.

THE MANOR OF PHILIPSBOROUGH

ERECTED THE 12TH. OF JUNE, 1693

"FROM carpenter-shop to a barony!" Thus, in all likelihood, might run the headlines of a newspaper account of the career of Frederick Philipse, were it written in these days of professed democracy and actual snobbery. Frederick Philipse did, indeed, begin life in the New World as a carpenter and ended as proprietary of one of the greatest manors in the Province of New York, but in the story of his life we find far more than the mere successful acquisition of wealth such as the bootlicking chroniclers of plutocratic domination like to set before an emulous public as the highest goal of human achievement. Furthermore, besides his native qualifications of energy, industry, and sound commercial judgement, Frederick Philipse had back of him, to fit him for the rôle of responsible leadership, the inherited driving force of family tradition and gentle instinct—call it, if you choose, the sense of *noblesse oblige*—an intangible but very real factor whose potency the pseudo-democratic worshippers of mercenary self-help, with its ultimate reward of material prosperity, are too prone to ignore.

**PHILIPSE MANOR HALL,
YONKERS, EAST FRONT**

**PHILIPSE MANOR HALL, YONKERS,
EAST AND SOUTH FRONTS**

Not a few there are who seem to fancy that the Lords of Manors, to whom were granted domains oftentimes the equivalents of principalities in extent and in the powers conferred with them, were either the favoured darlings of the mighty or the astute manipulators of political influence and that they were showered with privileges and wealth, at the expense of the public good, far beyond their deserts or the bounds of common justice.

The manorial estates were great and the powers of civil administration on those estates were also great, it is true, but the responsibilities and burdens—about which we hear comparatively little—were fully commensurate with whatever advantages were derived by the grantees. The business of founding a manor, or administering it after it was founded, was not like putting a penny in a slot machine and drawing out a definite quantity of success. There was just as much possibility of things going *wrong* as there was possibility of their going *right*.

The Lords of Manors were by no means idle parasites sucking profit out of the community and, in return, merely acting as decorative figure heads. Neither were they sly, unscrupulous politicians, laughing in their sleeves, and battening on the public pudding from which they had pulled out all the plums, albeit there are those who delight to pourtray them in the one character or the other. They were, on the contrary, workers, earning their salt and labouring just as truly to get their own living and to do their duty "in that state of life unto which it had pleased God to call them," as were the humblest hinds on their estates.

Frederick Philipse, the first Lord of the Manor of Philips-borough, was an excellent example of the industrious, diligent and capable grantee. The scion of a noble Bohemian family that had sought asylum in Holland two generations earlier, he came to the Colony of New Amsterdam as a young man of but slender means, some time prior to 1653. "The resources by which he became the foremost merchant and one of the foremost citizens of his generation were his craft as an architect and builder, his industry and shrewdness as a business man, and his substantial character."

At an early date his name appears in the official records and he is there designated as a "carpenter." He was appointed carpenter to the West India Company and, in that capacity had not only the supervision of the Company's buildings then in use, but also the planning and erection of their new structures, together with the oversight of any public works undertaken by their direction.

The duties of this post took him from time to time into different parts of the Province. In 1658, for instance, he accompanied Governour Stuyvesant to Esopus—the settlement that was later to become Kingston. Upon Stuyvesant's decision to fortify that place for protection against the Indians, Philipse and others set straightway to work to put the plans into effect. In his report to the Company, Stuyvesant wrote:

> "On the 13th., 14th., and 15th., we were busy making the east side of the palisaded enclosure and Frederick Philipsen erected, with the help of Claes de Ruyter and Thomas Chambers, in the northeast corner of the enclosure a guard house for the soldiers, 23 feet long and 16 feet wide, made of boards which had been cut during my absence."

Here we see two future Lords of Manors—Frederick Philipse and Thomas Chambers, who became Lord of Fox Hall

Manor—engaging in manual labour and thinking no scorn of it. Further on in the same report the Governour mentions employing some carpenters to build him a small house and barn at Esopus, and then notes:—"I referred the carpenters' work to the opinion of my carpenter, Frederick Philipsen."

Putting two and two together, it is quite evident that Frederick Philipse was what could properly be called an architect-carpenter. Even long after his official connexion with the West India Company had terminated, his architectural services were sought in various quarters so that, in a double sense he must be reckoned amongst the builders and makers of New York. His advice as a consulting architect, too, was frequently required. Although we have no direct evidence to prove it, it is not unlikely that Philipse had pursued some architectural studies before leaving Holland.

In April, 1657, Philipse acquired the Small Burgher Right of New Amsterdam, which rendered him eligible for appointment to minor public offices and gave him the privileges of trading. Thence onward, apparently backed by the favour of the Governour, his progress was rapid. Gradually, but steadily, he accumulated houses, town lots and other real estate holdings and pursued a course of judicious investments. Besides his numerous dealings in real estate, he launched forth into various branches of trade.

"Lands, mills, foreign trade, river trade and Indian trade, all brought wealth to his coffers. The records of the period are full of allusions to his dealings, and from them we learn the wide range of his transactions. Pipes of Spanish wine, brandies, 'rom,' Indian coats, horses, grain, wampum, bed pillows and bolsters, were among the articles in which he dealt, to which we may safely add all the staple goods of the period, including beaver skins and other furs received from the Indians in barter. His commerce extended to Esopus and Albany on the north and to the South, or Delaware, river on the south. He took his pay in wheat, wampum, beaver skins, or whatever came most convenient. He also loaned money. When his customers could not pay, he would accommodate them by taking as security their notes, silverware, or clothing, or a mort-gage on their houses. In a law-suit in 1664, Anneke Ryzen testified that she had a gown and petticoat in pawn with Frederick Philipse for a debt of 160 guilders. He also let out farms and draught cattle for hire and he received money on deposit."

In 1638 Philipse was *"my carpenter* Frederick Philipsen," in Stuyvesant's report; in 1666 he had become *"Sieur* Frederick Philipsen," to the Mayor and the Aldermen; in 1686 Dominie Selyns speaks of him as *"De Heer* Frederick Philipse." By these terms in which he was alluded to we may trace the increasing esteem in which he was held by his fellow-citizens. This increasing esteem bore fruit in the appointment to divers public responsibilities and honours, during both the Dutch and English *régimes.* As an evidence of the general trust reposed in him, both by the Government and by the people at large, we may note that during the Leisler Rebellion the Governour's Council recommended that the Government funds should be placed in Philipse's strong-boxes for safe-keeping. Under both Governour Dongan and Governour Fletcher, Philipse was a member of the Provincial Council.

From his marriage, in 1662, with Margaret Hardenbrook, the widow of Peter Rudolphus de Vries, Philipse derived no small advantage. She was both beautiful and well educated and, furthermore, blessed with exceptional business ability. She had been the companion of de Vries on his fur-trading expeditions and had her own ships in which the peltries were sent back to Holland, thus reaping all the profit without the charges and commissions of middle men.

In November, 1672, Philipse and two partners purchased a large part of the old Yonkers Plantation that had formed the Patroonship of Colen Donck. All of this interest Philipse subsequently acquired. To this beginning he added other extensive purchases until his possessions extended from Spuyten Duyvil Creek northward to the Croton River, a distance of about twenty-two miles along the east bank of the Hudson. Thus grew the estate that was to be erected into the Manor of Philipsborough by royal charter and letters patent, on the 12th. of June, 1693. At the mouth of the Neperhan, on that part of his domain now occupied by Yonkers, Van der Donck had established a mill. Owing to the presence of the mill, and also doubtless influenced by the eligibility of the site, Philipse here established his residence.

The exact date at which the first part of the house was built— the house that is now the Philipse Manor Hall at Yonkers—has long been a matter of controversy, but we are reasonably safe in assuming that it was not later than 1682. It may have been some-what earlier. Philipse also established a mill at the mouth of the Pocantico, near Tarrytown, and there, about 1683, built another house, still standing and known as Castle Philipse. The house at Neperhan, however, was always his chief place of residence when not in New York City. The Yonkers house was often referred to by Philipse himself as the "Lower Mills," while the Pocantico settle-ment was known as the "Upper Mills."

**PHILIPSE MANOR HALL, YONKERS,
OLD ENTRANCE, SOUTH FRONT**

The Manor Hall, as it was in Frederick Philipse's day, con-sisted of what is now the southern end of the building; the northern part, whose addition created the long east front, was not erected till 1745. Its walls were of grey stone rubble masonry, while the door and window openings were squared up with brick. The south front, in which direction the house then faced, is sixty-two feet long and the composition is symmetrical. There can be little doubt that Frederick Philipse designed the house himself, and in doing so he was evidently influenced by the style of house then fashionable in England. Of this the structure itself is sufficient evidence. In his interpretation of the Classic mode, however, he exhibited his preference for—or, at least, his greater familiarity with—contemporary Dutch mannerisms rather than predilection for literal adherence to English precedent. While the composition is both urbane and restrained, it is strongly marked in every detail by the sturdy vigour characteristic of contemporary design in both England and Holland. At the time of its erection it was unquestionably one of the most distinguished examples of domestic architecture to be found throughout the length and breadth of all the Colonies.

The fixed interior decoration of the original part of the house was apparently enriched and somewhat altered when the addition of 1745 was built, but where the earlier work remains it shews that the rooms were finished with far more elegance than was usual in the Colonies at that period and that they were of a character quite capable of holding its own with modern practice.

In 1691, Dame Margaret, the wife of Frederick Philipse, died. In 1692 he married again, this time taking to wife Catherine Van Cortlandt, the widow of John Derval. "She was," we are told, "young and pretty, had a sweet disposition and charming manner, and soon ingratiated herself with the tenants of the great Philipse estate by her generous benevolence." She it was, in all likelihood, who influenced her husband to what appears to have been their joint undertaking—the building of Sleepy Hollow Church, in 1699. The records of the church attest the virtues and interest of Catherine Philipse in these words:

SLEEPY HOLLOW CHURCH, ALBANY
POST ROAD, TARRYTOWN

"First and before all, the right honourable, God-fearing, very wise and prudent My Lady Catherine Philipse, widow of the late Lord Frederick Philipse of blessed memory, who promoted service here in the highest, praiseworthy manner."

By the same royal charter that erected Philipse's possessions into the "Lordship and Manor of Philipsborough in free and common soccage according to the tenure of our Manor of East Greenwich . . . rendering and paying therefor, yearly and every year, on the feast day of the Annunciation of the Blessed Virgin Mary, at our fort in New York, unto us, our heirs and successors, the annual rental of £4. 12s. current money of our said Province," the Lord of the Manor was granted the right to build a toll-bridge across the Spuyten Duyvil Creek, to be called Bang's Bridge, and to levy a fee upon everyone using it. The rates of toll were as follows:

"Three pence current money of New York for each man and horse that shall pass the said bridge in the day time, and three pence current money aforesaid for each head of neat cattle that shall pass the same; and twelve pence current money aforesaid for each score of hogs, calves and sheep that shall pass the same; and nine pence current money aforesaid for every boat, vessel or canoe that shall pass the said bridge and cause the same to be drawn up; and for each coach, cart or sledge or waggon that shall pass the same, the sum of nine pence current money aforesaid; and after sunset, each passenger that shall pass said bridge shall pay two pence current money aforesaid; each man and horse, six pence; each head of neat cattle, six pence; each score of hogs, calves and sheep, two shillings; for each boat, or vessel, or canoe, one shilling and six pence; for each coach, cart, waggon, or sledge, one shilling and six pence, current money aforesaid."

With the income from this valuable concession, and with his revenue from investments and other sources, the fortunes of Frederick Philipse throve apace and were appropriately reflected in the mode of life at the Manor House over which Catherine Philipse presided with genial and courtly grace. In his admirable little book, *Philipse Manor Hall*, Edward Hagaman Hall tells us that "sometimes the Manor House was the scene of elaborate hospitality, and in summer, Governours and their satellites and the leading citizens of New York, gayly attired, might have been seen riding a-horseback along the old Post Road up and down the hills and valleys of Manhattan and Westchester County, bound for the country house of the First Lord."

"It is not difficult to imagine how Philipse appeared on occasions like these as he moved among the guests and exchanged dignified salutations. He was a tall and well-proportioned man; had a quiet grey eye, a Roman nose, and a firm set mouth. Dressed with punctilious care in the costume of the period with full embroidery, lace cuffs and stock, and his head surmounted with impressive periwig and flowing ringlets, he moved with a slow and measured step, which gave him an air of dignity. In temperament, he was grave and melancholy, and so reticent as to be regarded dull; and while intelligent, shrewd almost to craftiness, and the possessor of remarkable abilities in many directions, he did not possess the culture which his successors manifested.

But however reserved and taciturn the Lord of the Manor might have been, his vivacious Lady and the cheer which she served from cellar and pantry made ample amends; and the melancholy of the Master of the House was conspicuously absent from the demeanour of the guests when they set forth on their return to the city."

Frederick Philipse died in 1702 and was succeeded as Lord of the Manor by his grandson, Frederick, the child of his eldest son Philip, who had died in 1700. The young Lord of the Manor was only seven years old when he fell heir to this vast estate. As his mother also had died, soon after he was born, by the terms of his grandfather's will, he was entrusted to the upbringing if his step-grandmother, Catherine Van Cortlandt; in the words of that document, the widow of the first Lord was to "have ye custody, tuition and guardianship of my grandson Frederick Flipse and his estate to use, until he comes to ye age of one and twenty years, who I desire may have ye best education and learning these parts of ye world will afford him, not doubting of her care in bringing him up after ye best manner possibly shee can."

Catherine Philipse, according to the expressed desire of her late husband, continued to occupy the town house also, and there she maintained a manner of living in the height of Colonial style, as became her station, with an entourage of seven negro slaves, and such equipment of plate and furniture as one might expect of one of the wealthiest and most cultured women of her day. Her wardrobe, too, is said to have been of the most elegant fashion of the time; mention is made of red silver-laid petticoats, red cloth petticoats, silk quilted petticoats, and two black silk quilted petticoats. "Furthermore," we are told, "like the ladies of old, she presented her most notable article of Sunday outdoor ostentation in a splendid Psalm Book, with gold clasps, hanging upon her arm by a gold chain."

The educational facilities offered by New York at the dawn of the eighteenth century may or may not have been as good as "these parts of ye world will afford," but they were not, to the thinking of Madame Philipse, of a quality likely to fit her grandson to fill with distinction his state in life as Lord of the Manor of Philipsborough. She deemed it best, therefore, to take him to England where he could be educated in a becoming manner. To

England, accordingly, they went, and there young Frederick studied law and was thoroughly imbued with "the best traditions of his day."

Frederick Philipse came of age and entered into his inheritance in 1716, and three years later married Joanna, the daughter of Lieutenant-Governour Anthony Brockholls, who also had been brought up in England. A more genial and cultured atmosphere now pervaded the Manor Hall, for the second Lord of the Manor, in marked contrast to his grandfather, had strongly developed social inclinations and none of the painful shyness and reticence of the first Lord. Besides possessing a fertile mind and being intellectually a man of distinguished parts, he was courteous, generous, affable, and a good conversationalist. His engaging personality and his companionable qualities won him hosts of friends and the favourable regard of all who came in contact with him, so that a visit to the Manor Hall was always an esteemed privilege to those who crossed its threshold. Nor was the mistress of the Hall less estimable, in her way, than the master. Together they made an exceptional pair and were, in the best sense, both highly useful members and ornaments of society.

Frederick Philipse, the second Lord of the Manor, played a conspicuous and active rôle in the public life of the Province, a part for which he was well fitted both by natural disposition and training. He was a Justice of the Peace and an Alderman of the City of New York, being regularly re-elected to the latter post for fourteen successive years at the Michaelmas balloting. At the same time, he was a member of the Provincial Assembly, for Westchester County, and from 1721 to 1728 he was Speaker of that dignified body. In 1733 he became Baron of the Exchequer, and in the same year he was also appointed Second Judge of the Supreme Court, the Honourable James De Lancey being then Chief Justice. This latter dignity he held during the remainder of his life.

In 1745 he enlarged the Manor Hall by an addition much greater than the original building, making the eastern side its principal front. The enlargement was wholly of brick, although the outward style, in other respects, was made to conform to the earlier structure. One feature that gives the house a most unusual appearance is its great length with the methodical iteration of the rows of windows. The east front is ninety-two feet long and has eight bays, that is to say, there are eight divisions of penetration. On the ground floor there are six windows and two doors and, on the first floor, eight windows. The length is emphasised, too, by the absence of any central feature of composition; the two doorways are alike and neither of them is in the centre. The doorways, and the porches before them with settles at each side, are identical in design with the south doorway of the earlier part of the house, that is to say, the doorway of the south front.

Inside, the rooms both downstairs and up are finished not only with the most elaborate fireplaces, doorways, panelling and other items of decorative woodwork, but also discover intricate plaster embellishments on a number of the ceilings— such enrichments as Frederick Philipse must have been familiar with in England, composed of scrolls, arabesques, musical instruments, wreaths, mythological figures and medallions containing heads. The heads in several of the medallions are said to be likenesses of members of the Philipse family.

Between the east front of the house and the Albany Post Road was the garden, laid out in formal parterres, the borders edged with low-growing boxwood and filled with the choicest flowers. During the lifetime of the second Lord of the Manor and, indeed, so long as the Philipse family remained in possession of the Manor of Philipsborough, the garden was always an object of solicitous care and must have made a brave appearance.

Life in the Manor House passed with courtly elegance and every circumstance of refinement and comfort that a truly patriarchal amplitude could contribute. The maintenance of the establishment required the services of no less than fifty household servants—thirty whites and twenty negro slaves. There was every opportunity for endless and lavish hospitality and, needless to say, the performance did not lag behind the opportunity. Besides the many distinguished guests who sought the master and mistress, the beautiful daughters of the house attracted an host of suitors and friends. One of these was Colonel Beverly Robinson who married the eldest daughter,

Susannah Philipse. Colonel Robinson and his wife Susannah we shall meet meet again in the accounts of Mount Morris and Beverly House.

Frederick Philipse died in 1751, at the age of fifty-six, as deeply regretted as he was highly esteemed by his contemporaries. The New York *Gazette*, in a notice printed at the time of his death, tells us:

> "His Indulgence and Tenderness to his tenants, his more than parental affection for his Children, and his incessant liberality to the Indigent, surpassed the splendour of his Estates and procured him a more unfeigned regard than can be purchased with opulence or gained by Interest. . . .There were, perhaps, few men that ever equalled him in those obliging and benevolent manners which, at the same time that they attracted the Love of his Inferiors, gained him all the respect and veneration due to his rank and station."

He was succeeded by his son Frederick, the third and last Lord of the Manor of Philipsborough.

This Frederick was a man of literary tastes and domestic inclinations, more disposed to the management of his estate than to mixing much in public affairs. Nevertheless, he held a commission as Colonel of Militia, whence he was generally known as Colonel Philipse to distinguish him from his father, the Judge, and he was also a member of the Provincial Assembly. The court leet and court baron of the manor were held in a building near the Manor Hall and over these he commonly presided in person, dispensing justice in both civil and criminal matters. The Reverend Timothy Dwight, of Yale, wrote of him, "Col Philipse. . . . I knew him well. He was a worthy and respectable man, not often excelled in personal and domestic amiableness." John Jay, too, said of him, "This Frederick I knew. He was a well tempered, amiable man; a kind, benevolent landlord. He had a taste for gardening, planting, etc., and employed much time and money in that way." Judging from these contemporary characterisations, and also from other sources, Frederick Philipse appears as a scholarly and courtly gentleman of the old school, much esteemed for "the qualities of his mind and the generous disposition of his heart."

PHILIPSE MANOR HALL, YONKERS, DOORWAY, EAST FRONT

In 1756 he married Elizabeth Williams, the young widow of Anthony Rutgers and daughter of Charles Williams, Naval Officer for the Port of New York. The bride was an "handsome and pleasing woman," according to the clerical estimate of Timothy Dwight. "Handsome," "pleasing" and "excellent," she was also vivacious and dashing, and seems to have had a well-earned reputation as a fearless and skillful horsewoman. Doctor Hall tells us that "the tenants of the Manor often stood agape in wonder at the sight of her ladyship setting forth with four spirited jet black horses and driving her dashing quadriga along the roads of Westchester county at what appeared to be a reckless pace." In this connexion, it is amusing to note that Colonel Philipse and his wife rarely appeared together in the same carriage—for a very good reason. Colonel Philipse was inclined to be fleshy and, in course of time, "attained such large dimensions that there was not room for both in the family chariot." Mrs. Philipse's manner of driving, too, may have had something to do with this habit on the part of each of "going it alone," for, as Doctor Hall further observes, "if the Colonel's temperament was at all nervous, perhaps the inconvenience of his size was not entirely without its compensations, for it probably saved him from many a nervous shock which he might have received had he gone driving with the adventurous Lady Elizabeth."

Colonel Philipse and his family were staunch Church of England people and were generous in their support of ecclesiastical affairs. They built Saint John's Church in Yonkers, a substantial stone building dating from 1752, and met the greater part of the parish expenses at their own charge. In addition to this benefaction, they built a rectory and likewise gave two hundred and fifty acres of arable land for a glebe by way of endowment.

When he became Master of Philipsborough, besides indulging his bent for gardening by greatly improving and extending the adjacent grounds, Frederick Philipse added to the embellishments and appointments of the Manor Hall and, ably seconded by his wife, who was fond of society and all the courtly amenities of life befitting their station, kept up all the brilliant social traditions of the period. The Philipses' house continued to be, as it had been in the past, an hospitable centre of all that was best in the life of the Province.

Mary Philipse, the second sister of Frederick, had remained single till after the death of her father and the marriage of her brother. Washington had once experienced an ardent attachment for her, but Roger Morris had successfully wooed her and won her hand. We may, therefore, pass on to the scene of her wedding which took place in the Manor Hall on the 19th. of January, 1758. It was not only one of the great social events of the Province that brought together a distinguished assemblage made up of the foremost families and the officers of the British army; it was also an occasion of deep interest and genuine rejoicing to all the manor tenantry. Mary Philipse was an admirable horsewoman and rides of fifty miles through the manor, where she was known and welcomed by all, were by no means uncommon with her. "Her semi-annual visits to the numerous tenants of the Manor were religiously made; and her arrival at the homes of the humble cottagers, by whom she was greatly beloved, was an event of no small importance to them." Hence the bountiful feast set forth for the tenants and their families, on the day of Mistress Mary's wedding, brought from all parts of the estate a vast concourse of those who truly wished her well.

It was a mild day, but the sleighing was good, and by two o'clock the parties of guests, "with jingling bells and merry shouts," began to throng the grounds and Hall. At three o'clock came the Reverend Henry Barclay, the Rector of Trinity Church, New York, accompanied by his curate, Mr. Auchmuty. The parlours were now crowded with guests arrayed in all the sumptuous and gaily-coloured habiliments of the mid-eighteenth century. At half past three entered Mary Philipse and Roger Morris, attended by the bridesmaids and groomsmen. The bridesmaids were Miss Barclay, Miss Van Cortlandt and Miss De Lancey; the grooms-men were Mr. Heathcote, Captain Kennedy and Mr. Watts, while Acting Governour De Lancey, the son-in-law of Colonel Heathcote, Lord of Scarsdale Manor, also assisted at the function. The ceremony took place under a crimson canopy embellished with the family crest in gold—a demilion crowned issuing from a coronet—the Lord of the Manor, richly clad and wearing the gold chain and jewelled insignia of the ancestral office of Master Ranger of the Royal Forests of Bohemia, giving his sister away.

Afterwards there was a lavish banquet. In the midst of the wedding feast, so the story goes, when all was merriment and joy, there suddenly appeared at the door a tall Indian in a scarlet blanket. His voice in measured syllables broke the amazed silence—"Your possessions shall pass from you when the Eagle shall despoil the Lion of his mane!" Having uttered these cryptic words of ill omen, he vanished as suddenly as he had come. Although the bride and her family, and all who were present, puzzled much to divine the meaning of this strange apparition and his sinister utterance, it was not until years after that the full significance became clear. It was really a prophecy of the misfortunes that were to befall the Philipse family for their adherence to the Crown in 1775.

When the struggle with the Mother Country became acute, and it was no longer possible for men of weight and position to refrain from declaring their attitude, Colonel Philipse saw his duty in loyalty to the established Government, however much he might personally disapprove certain measures which he believed to be mistaken. His sympathies were known to be with the old order and in opposition to the Whigs. When the Whigs of Westchester county met at White Plains, in April, 1775, to elect representatives to the next Continental Congress, the Loyalists held a meeting and adopted the following protest:

"We the subscribers, freeholders and inhabitants of the County of Westchester, having assembled at the White Plains in consequence of certain advertisements, do now declare that we met here to express our honest abhorrence of all unlawful congresses and committees and that we are determined to the hazard of our lives and properties, to support the King and Constitution, and that we acknowledge no representatives but the General Assembly, to whose wisdom and integrity we submit the guardianship of our rights."

Three hundred and twelve men signed this declaration and Colonel Philipse, then a member of the Provincial Assembly, was the first to set his hand to it. After this there could be no doubt regarding his attitude.

In June, 1776, the New York Provincial Congress, acting upon the recommendation of the Continental Congress that every person whose going at large might endanger the liberties of America should be placed under restraint, appointed a committee to summon and try suspected persons regarding their loyalty to the American cause. Those found guilty of hostility or equivocal neutrality were to be imprisoned, or allowed restricted liberty under bonds and parole, or else removed from their "present residence to some other place in this or a neighbouring Colony" where their presence would be less dangerous. Frederick Philipse's name was on the list prepared by this committee and although, for the time being, he was allowed to remain at the manor, in consideration of his ill health, he was arrested in August, upon Washington's order, and conveyed first to New Rochelle and then to Hartford, where he was given permission to live in Middletown under parole.

In December of the same year the Governour and Council of Safety, of Connecticut, granted Colonel Philipse and others permission to return home under parole "not to give any intelligence to the enemy; not to take up arms; not to do or say anything against the United States of America; and to return to Connecticut when requested." Having signed this parole, Colonel Philipse was allowed to go home. In 1777, leaving the Manor House in charge of his steward, he went to his town house in New York City. When a summons was sent for him to go back to Connecticut he never received it. He was, thereupon, adjudged guilty of breaking his parole. In October, 1779, the Legislature of New York, sitting at Kingston, passed an act of attainder against fifty-eight persons for "adhering to the King with intent to subvert the government and liberties of this State and the said other United States, and to bring the same into subjection to the Crown of Great Britain." The act further pro-scribed them, adjudged their real and personal estates confis-cate, and declared that "each and every one of them who shall at any time hereafter be found in any part of the State shall be and are hereby adjudged and declared guilty of felony, and shall suffer Death as in cases of felony without Benefit of Clergy."

Frederick Philipse, his sisters Susannah and Mary, their husbands, Beverly Robinson and Roger Morris, and fifty-three others specifically mentioned by name fell under this ban. Thus by one act the Manor of Philipsborough was dissolved and the family's estates confiscated. In 1783, when the independence of the United States was confirmed by treaty, Frederick Philipse, bereft of his title and great estate, "humiliated in spirit, blind of sight and broken in health," removed with his family to England where they lived in Chester. Colonel Philipse died in 1786 and was buried in Chester Cathedral.

During the greater part of the Revolutionary War the Manor Hall was in the Neutral Ground and after the family left it, in 1777, it was occupied for the most part only by care-takers, save when General Sir Henry Clinton made it his headquarters for a brief period in the latter part of May and early part of June, 1779.

When the Manor Hall was sold in 1785 under the act of attainder and confiscation, it was bought by Cornelius P. Low, of New York City. From Mr. Low it passed from one owner to another until it was purchased by the village of Yonkers, in 1868. It served as the Village Hall until 1872, when it became the City Hall and continued to be used as such until it was acquired by the State in 1908. In 1911 it was turned over to the custody of the American Scenic and Historic Preservation Society and this praiseworthy organisation has since then maintained it in an admirable manner.

CASTLE PHILIPSE

CASTLE PHILIPSE, UPPER MANOR HOUSE, PHILIPSBOROUGH

Castle Philipse, near the mouth of the Pocantico, has passed through so many vicissitudes and been so altered and, needless to say, spoiled by successive owners that it bears little semblance to the structure erected by Frederick Philipse in or about 1683. It is a stone building, now coated with roughcast stucco, of ample dimensions and covered by a gambrel roof. Its outward proportions and the lines of its roof remain unchanged, but the alterations made in the windows, the addition of sundry irrelevant features, and the ruthless treatment accorded many of the original details, have completely effaced the pristine character of the house and robbed it of nearly every shred of architectural interest.

Fortunately, the Colonial Dames of the State of New York have done what they could to perpetuate the memory of its origin by placing upon the walls a bronze tablet which reads:

"Castle Philipse. / This House was built / about 1683 by Frederick Philipse / First Lord of the Manor of / Philipsborough. / The Manor Was Granted in / 1693 / by Governour Fletcher. / Placed by the Colonial Dames / of the State of New York / MCMVI"

Soon after his purchase of this tract of land, later to become a part of the Manor of Philipsborough, Frederick Philipse built mills near the mouth of the stream which came to be known as the Upper Mills in distinction from the earlier mills near the house on the Neperhan (in what is now Yonkers) which were generally called the Lower Mills. To both of these mills the tenants of the manor brought their grain to be ground. Here they got such flour and meal as they needed for themselves, the surplus being sent to New York City for domestic use or export. The house Philipse built near the Upper Mills he occupied occasionally, but his usual place of residence, when not in New York City, was the house at the Lower Mills, afterwards the Manor Hall. It seems not altogether unlikely that Castle Philipse was built in such a manner that it might be used as a fort, should need arise for a place of defense.

When Frederick Philipse, the first Lord of the Manor, died he left to his son Adolphus all that vast tract of land known as the Upper Plantation. Adolphus made his home at Castle Philipse and the house became the centre of jurisdiction for the domain under his control. When Adolphus Philipse died in 1750, his nephew Frederick, the second Lord of the Manor, inherited the Upper Plantation and thus the whole of the original domain was brought again into the hands of a single proprietor. Thereupon the Manor Hall at Yonkers became once more the seat of the entire jurisdiction and Castle Philipse sank into a distinctly secondary position. As a matter of fact, the social splendour and political importance of the Manor Hall always overshadowed the claims of the Castle.

XIII.

THE MANOR OF MORRISANIA

ERECTED 9TH. OF DECEMBER, 1694,

PATENTED MAY, 1697

PERHAPS there is not in the annals of American history a family more interesting than the Morris family. Remarkable in the accomplishments of each branch, from the first Lord of the Manor down to the numerous survivors of the present day, the Morrises have ever been people of quality and true worth. For this reason there is no single portion of the country which can boast of as intimate a connexion with the early political history of the State as Morrisania and it therefore should command a foremost position in the affections of all true Americans.

The Morris family was originally of Welsh descent. The first evidence of the presence of the Morris family in America may be attributed to Colonel Lewis Morris and his younger brother, Captain Richard Morris. Both of these gentlemen had distinguished themselves in the military field, Colonel Lewis Morris having a troop of horse under Cromwell, and Captain Richard Morris having served with distinction in the Parliamentary Army. In addition, Lewis Morris, according to English State Papers, served under Admiral Penn from 1654 to 1655, and took an active part in the attack on the Island of Jamaica. He acquired a magnificent estate in the Island of Barbadoes where he was later joined by his brother in the guise of a Quaker, who did not think it advisable to remain in England after the Restoration.

Richard Morris married in the Barbadoes and shortly thereafter removed to New York, while that settlement was still in the possession of the Dutch.

Shortly after his arrival in New York, Richard Morris purchased for himself and for his brother land granted by the Dutch, in 1639, to Jonas Broncks who was subsequently flayed alive by the Indians. The title reads "William or Wilhelm Kieft, the Dutch

---

109

Governour, by patent October 20th., 1644, granted to Arent Van Curlear the land formerly in the tenure of Jonas Bronx, called by the Indians Ranachque, and by the English Bronck's Land, lying on the main to the east over against Harlem Town near Hell Gate, and a greater creek or river which divides it from Manhattan Island, containing over 500 acres or 250 morgens of land." There are numerous other titles and deeds and the sum total made up the nucleus of that estate which was later to be known as Morrisania.

MORRISANIA MANOR HOUSE, MORRISANIA

Only two months after the birth of her son Lewis, Mrs. Morris died and was followed two months later by her worthy husband. Colonel Lewis Morris and his brother had agreed in writing that in the event of the death of either his estate should be inherited by the other. Now, unfortunately, although Colonel Morris had agreed to make his residence in New York, he did not reach New York till after his brother's death in 1672. The small Lewis Morris now became the ward of the Dutch Government, which apparently dispossessed Colonel Morris and it was not until some time after that the latter was able to regain his property, complete his business in the Barbadoes, and return to make his home in Bronck's Land.

In 1676 Colonel Morris received a patent from Governour Andros which increased his original estate to about nineteen hundred and twenty acres; in the autumn of the same year he had granted to him and his associates a tract of land in New Jersey which amounted approximately to three thousand, eight hundred and forty acres, and in 1680 he received through the will of Nathaniel Silvester a portion of Shelter Island. Colonel Morris died the 14th. of February, 1691, leaving an estate of considerable value which, in time, after numerous legal difficulties had been settled, was granted to Lewis Morris, son of Richard and nephew of Colonel Lewis Morris, who was destined one day to be the first Lord of the Manor.

As a child Governour Lewis Morris was inclined to be wild and somewhat ungovernable and, needless to say, he received little enough attention from his Puritanical uncle. The story is told of him that one day, having climbed a tree, under which his Quaker tutor was accustomed to pray, he called out "Hugh Copperthwaite, Hugh Copperthwaite!" "Here I am Lord. What wiliest Thouf!" was the answer. "Go preach the Gospel to the Mohawks, thou true and faithful servant." The tutor soon discovered the prank played upon him by his young charge, and as a result, the lad was so severely chastised that he ran away from his uncle's roof. They were later reconciled.

The estate of Lewis Morris was officially erected into a manor on the 9th. of December, 1694, but it was not until May, in 1697, that Morris actually received the patent. Morrisania ceased to be a manor during the Revolutionary War. It had but three Lords, Governour Lewis Morris, Judge Lewis Morris and Lewis Morris, the signer of the Declaration of Independence.

It would seem that the members of the Morris family were justly famous for their intrepidity, a dominant characteristic with which they were imbued from generation to generation. To cite an instance. When General Lewis Morris, the third Lord of the Manor, who realised fully that his entire worldly possessions were at stake, was about to sign the Declaration of Independence, he received a letter from his brother begging him to consider the consequences. In reply to his brother's sentiments, Morris, as he was about to sign, said "Damn the consequences, and give me the pen!" It was the same spirit which was later to be developed by Gouverneur Morris at a time when he was the only foreigner to keep his post in Paris during the Reign of Terror.

This latter Gouverneur Morris was a man in whom all the noble characteristics of the family culminated. One has but to read the fascinating *Diary and Letters*, edited by Anne Cary Morris, to realise vividly the true nature of the man. Throughout, his letters and diary are marked by that charming and candid naïveté and brilliance of perception which made him the genius he was. An example, one of many, may be noted:

> "First the Gobelins, which after all that has been said in their favour, are an idle kind of art, because they produce pieces which are more costly and less beautiful than paintings, and though in one sense they last long, yet in another they do not, because the colour fades. For the rest, it is a wonderful operation. From the Gobelins, in the gallery of which there are some excellent paintings, we go to the King's botanical gardens. Having no knowledge of botany, except to distinguish onions and cabbages from oak trees, I can pretend to no judgement of this garden, which is, I dare say, excellent."

Gouverneurr Morris was born the 30th. of January, 1752. He was the son of Judge Lewis Morris, the second Lord of the Manor, and the brother of Lewis Morris, the signer. Besides General Lewis Morris, Gouverneur had two brothers, Scott Long Morris, a true Loyalist and an officer in the King's Army, who died in 1800 the Governour of Quebec, and Richard, Judge of the High Court of the British Admiralty and Chief Justice of New York. Gouverneur, the fourth and youngest son of Judge Morris, was given his mother's name. At the time of his youngest son's birth, Judge Morris made the following entry in his diary concerning Gouverneur; "He was born on the 31st. of January, about half an hour after one of the clock in the morning, in the year 1752, according to the alteration of the style by Act of Parliament, and was christened the 4th. of May, 1754." This notation of the exact time of day in a birth record is interesting because it brings to mind the almost universal habit, that continued till well into the nineteenth century, of keeping such data for the purpose of casting horoscopes. Doubtless many who made entries in this fashion, had no idea whatever of the cause that had induced this custom.

Judge Lewis Morris must have realised that his son was destined to enjoy a brilliant career, and he did not propose to have any pains spared on the boy's education. Consequently we find this clause in his will:—"It is my desire that my son, Gouverneur Morris, may have the best education that is to be had in England or America."

Morris acquired a comprehensive knowledge of French at an early age, graduated from King's College in 1768, and realising that the law was unquestionably the profession suited to his talents, he entered the office of William Smith, a lawyer, and later Chief Justice of New York. Morris's brilliance, application and intense ambition, gained for him an enviable reputation, and, in 1771, fully three months before he was twenty, he was admitted to the bar. Having completed his education, and been admitted to the bar, he was desirous to "rub off in the gay circles of foreign life a few of those many barbarisms which characterise a provincial education." Fortunately, financial circumstances prevented and Morris temporarily had to be content with making a brilliant name for himself in his native country before he was permitted to acquire that foreign culture and polish of which he was so covetous.

The conditions of the country at this moment were admirably suited to provide a stage for Morris's activities. The need was urgent for the man with the ability to formulate a satisfactory financial system Morris draughted a report which was sent to Congress and adopted without amendment. Of this report Morris wrote to a friend, shortly before his death:—"The first bank in this country was planned by your humble servant." A man of force and honest conviction, it may easily be imagined that Morris made his presence felt, in the third New York Congress, when he said, "Why should we hesitate? Have you the least hope in treaty? Will you trust Commissioners? Trust crocodiles, trust the hungry wolf in your flock, or a rattlesnake near your bosom, you may yet be something wise. But trust the King, his Ministers, his Commissioners, it is madness in the extreme. Why will you trust them? Why force yourself to make a daily resort to arms? Is this miserable country to be plunged in an endless war? Let each revolving year come heavy laden with those dismal scenes which we have already witnessed? If so, farewell liberty, farewell virtue, farewell happiness."

To Morris is due the wording of the Federal Constitution, and to him was entrusted the task of draughting the first instructions ever sent to an American Minister abroad, that is, to Benjamin Franklin who, at that time, was stationed at the Court of Versailles.

During Morris's financial activities in the newly formed republic, he became known to M. de Chastellux through two letters written to France in connexion with the commercial relations existing between the two countries. Of these letters Chastellux says, "Your letters have been communicated to M. le Maréchal de Castries, Minister of Marine, who is delighted with them: he told me he had seen nothing superior or full of more powerful thought on the subject of government and politics." Little did Morris know that this slight, nay almost chance acquaintance with M. de Chastellaux was later to mean so much to him.

In the autumn of 1788 Morris decided to go to France in order to superintend the commercial interests, namely the exporting of tobacco to France, in which he and Robert Morris were involved. Incidentally, he was entrusted with a number of commissions, including the purchase of a gold watch for Washington, who specified that it be, "not a small, trifling, nor a finical, ornamental one, but a watch well executed in point of workmanship, large, flat, and with a plain, handsome key." It is difficult for those of a more modern generation to appreciate the trials and hardships which the transatlantic voyage of the eighteenth century must have entailed, a trip which often took considerably longer than a month and, in the case of Morris, lasted from the 18th. of December, 1788, to the 27th. of January, 1789, and taken all in all, was an extremely tempestuous voyage.

Morris's entrée into the social life of Paris and environs seems to have been almost instantaneous, known as he was to M. de Chastellux, who apparently possessed the key to the entire situation. It was, therefore, only a short time before he found himself in the midst of the vortex of that brilliant and degenerate social activity whose equal has never been known. Morris was not a little surprised at the manners and customs of the ladies of the French Court, and although he frequently mentions particular instances in his diary, yet it is always with that tolerance and broad-mindedness which characterised his every word, and which was so unusual in a man of his strength of character and firm convictions. In this connexion, one of the entries in the diary reads as follows:—"What would have induced one of my countrywomen to place herself in such a position?" and again,

> "the waiter comes to tell me that two ladies are without who wish to speak to me. These, I find, are Madame de Boursac and Madame d' Espanchall, whom we had met before at the Tuileries. A good deal of light, trivial conversation in which these ladies intimate to me that their nuptial bonds do not at all straighten their conduct, and it would seem that either would be content to form an intrigue. As they can have no real want of lovers, and as they can have no prepossession in my favour, this conduct evidently resolves itself into some other motive—probably a view to some *jolis cadeaux*. As I have a vast fund of indifference on the subject, I say a number of handsome nothings, and as the ladies are relieved by my presence of the scandal of being alone, and the *ennui* of a female *tête-á-tête*, I shall have the credit with them of being more agreeable *et plus homme d'esprit*, than I am by a great deal."

Morris, all in all, stayed in Europe a little over ten years, as an entry in his diary made at Morrisania, the 15th. of January, 1799, indicates:—"To-day I dine at home and go, after dinner, to my house at Morrisania, where I arrive at dusk after an absence of above ten years." Morris spent his time travelling through many of the countries of Europe and made several trips to Britain, until the time when he was appointed Minister Plenipotentiary from the United States to France. From then on he was the only foreigner to keep his post in Paris. His diary and letters at this period of his life present a vivid picture of the frightful conditions in Paris and the hardships of living, which old and young alike, regardless of their station, had to undergo. Of these conditions Morris writes:—

> "While I am visiting M. de Coulteux, a person comes to announce the taking of the Bastille, the Governour of which is beheaded, and the Prevôt des Marchands is killed and also beheaded. They are carrying the heads in triumph through the city. The carrying of this citadel is one of the most extraordinary things I have met with. It cost the assailants sixty men, it is said. The Hôtel Royal des Invalides was forced this morning, and the

cannon and small arms, etc., brought off. The citizens are, by these means, well armed; at least there are the available materials for about thirty thousand to be equipped with, and that is a sufficient army. I feel that the information received last night as to the arrest of the Assemblée National is not correct. They have only declared that the last administration carried with them the regret of the chambers that they will persist in insisting on the removal of the troops, and that his Majesty's advisers, whatever their rank and station, are guilty of all the consequences that may ensue. Yesterday it was the fashion at Versailles not to believe that there were any disturbances in Paris. I presume that this day's transactions will induce the conviction that all is not perfectly quiet. . . . I learn through and from them (the Duc d'Aquillon and Baron de Menon) the secret history of the revolution of this day. Yesterday evening an address was presented to the Assembly, to which his Majesty returned an answer by no means satisfactory. The Queen, Comte d'Artois, and the Duchesse de Polignac, have been all day tampering with two regiments, who were made almost drunk, and every officer was presented to the King, who was induced to give promises, money, etc., to these regiments. They shouted 'Vive la Reine! Vive le Comte d'Artois! Vive la Duchesse de Polignac!' and then came and played under her Majesty's windows. In the meantime the Maréchal de Broglie was tampering with the artillery. The plan was to reduce Paris to famine and take two hundred members of the National Assembly prisoners, but they found that the troops would not serve against their country. Of course these plans could not be carried into effect. They took care, however, not to inform the King of all the mischief. . . . This morning (July 17th.) my coachman tells me there are placards up forbidding any carriages to run, as the King is in town this day, between ten and eleven. Here is another day in which nothing will be done. Dress immediately and go out. Get a window through the aid of Madame de Flahaut [one of Morris's most intimate friends] in the Rue Saint Honoré, through which the procession is to pass. In squeezing through the crowd my pocket is picked of a handkerchief which I value far beyond what the thief will get for it, and I should willingly pay him for his dexterity could I retrieve it. We wait from eleven till four. It seems that his Majesty was escorted by the Militia of Versailles to the Pont du Jour, where he entered the double files of Parisian Militia which extend from thence to the Hôtel de Ville. Our friend, La Fayette, elected General of the

Militia of Paris, precedes his sovereign. They move slowly amid acclamations of "Vive la Nation." Each line is composed of three ranks, consequently it is a body six deep extending that distance. The Assemblée National walk promiscuously together in the procession. The King's horseguards, some of the Garde du Corps, and all those who attend him, have the cockades of the city, *viz.*, red and blue. It is a magnificent procession in every respect."

In early life Morris was thrown from his phaeton by a pair of runaway horses and fractured his left leg so badly that amputation below the knee was deemed necessary to save his life. For the rest of his life he wore a wooden leg "of primitive simplicity, not much more than a rough oak stick with a wooden knob on the end of it." Soon after the operation a friend called to condole with him and philosophised upon the possible temptations of which the accident had relieved him. To him Morris replied: "Sir, the loss is much less than you imagine; I shall doubtless be a steadier man with one leg than with two." "During one of the years of his ministry in Paris, when carriages were abolished as being aristocratic, and the chances were against the escape of any person discovered driving in one, Morris, who seemed always to have despised the mob, though by no means averse to saving his life, drove through the streets followed by hoots and cries of, 'An aristocrat,' and quietly opening the door of his chariot, thrust out his wooden leg, and said, 'An aristocrat, Yes, truly, who lost his leg in the cause of American liberty,' whereat followed great applause from the mob."

Returning to America in January, 1799, and taking up his residence at Morrisania, Morris hoped to be allowed to live in peace and retirement from public life. This, unfortunately, so he said, was not vouchsafed him, for in 1800 he was elected Senator, and from that time on was compelled to take a more or less active part in public affairs. "With apparently no regret for the gay life of foreign courts, in which he had moved so long, Morris threw himself with all his natural energy into the affairs of his farm. He rebuilt his house, which he found in an unfit condition to receive the many articles of furniture he had brought home with him, and personally inspected the stones for the house, as they were taken from the quarry on his farm. He laid out roads, superintended their construction himself, and in the course of the summer made himself quite familiar with the large farm of fifteen hundred acres which he sometimes said he had 'rashly' undertaken to improve." This process of rehabilitation of his birthplace undertaken by Gouverneur Morris left the Manor House at Morrisania in virtually the condition in which it has subsequently remained.

In 1809, Morris, learning of the reduced circumstances of the daughter of Thomas Mann Randolph, an old friend, he offered to marry her. "His offer was accepted by Miss Randolph in the spirit in which it was made, and the spring of 1809 found her duly installed." Morris makes little mention of the affair in his diary, except in connexion with a family party on Christmas Day. The entry in his diary is as follows: "I marry, this day, Ann Cary Randolph, no small surprise to my guests."

The latter part of his life, as indeed his entire life, seemed to be very happy and when he died on the 6th. of November, 1816, he died as cheerfully as he had always lived.

There is a story about the wife and heir of Gouverneur Morris which is rather interesting and is, perhaps, worth while noting as a type of legend which so frequently surrounds the life and death of a great man.

"It is the first night of the year, 1817, the servants are asleep, and the widow sits late before the fire, her baby in her arms, listening betimes to the wind in the chimney, the beat of hail on the shutters, the roaring of the Bronx and the clash of moving ice upon it; yet thinking of her husband and the sinister look his promise had brought to the faces of his cousins, when the tramp of horses is heard without, and anon a summons at the door. The panels are beaten by a loaded riding whip, and a man's voice cries, 'Anne Morris, fetch us our cousin's will, or we'll break into the house and take it.' The woman presses the infant to her breast, but makes no answer. Again the clatter of whips; but now a mist is gathering in the room and a strange enchantment comes over her, for are not the lions breathing on the coat of arms above the door, and are not the portraits stirring in their frames!

"They are, indeed. There is a rustle of robes and clink of steel and one old warrior leaps down, his armour sounding as he alights, and striking thrice his sword and shield together, he calls on Gouvernour Morris to come forth. Somebody moves in the room where Morris died; there is a measured footfall in the corridor, with the clank of a scabbard keeping time; the door is opened, and on the blast that enters the widow hears a cry, then a double gallop, passing swiftly in the distance. As she gazes, her husband appears, apparelled as in life, and with a smile he takes a candelabra from the mantel and, beckoning her to follow, moves from room to room. Then for the first time, the widow knows to what wealth her baby has been born, for the ghost discloses secret drawers in escritoires where money, title deeds, and gems are hidden, turns pictures and wainscots on unsuspected hinges, revealing shelves heaped with fabrics, plate, and lace; then, returning to the fireside, he stoops as if to kiss his wife and boy, but a bell strikes the first hour of morning, and he vanishes into his portrait on the wall."

XIV.

THE MANOR OF CORTLANDT

ERECTED THE 17TH. OF JUNE, 1697

I N 1638 Oloff Stevense Van Cortlandt left his home at Wyk, by Durstede, near Utrecht in Holland and, as a soldier in the West India Company's service, accompanied Director-General William Kieft in the ship *Haring* to New Amsterdam. Arrived there, his native abilities and sterling qualities of character soon brought him to a position of wealth and influence so that he became one of the foremost figures in the little city on the southern end of Manhattan Island.

Not long after his arrival in the New World, he married an heiress, Annetje Loockermans, of Turnhout in Belgium, who, with her brother, Gouvert Loockermans, had come to New Amsterdam to make enquiries about the success of considerable investments they had ventured in the Dutch Colony and to see for themselves how affairs were being conducted.

The eldest child of this union, born in 1643, was Stephanus, who was later to become the first Lord of the Manor of Cortlandt. He was carefully educated under competent tutors and, at an exceptionally early age, entered into the public life of the city, his first appointment being to the Court of Assizes. When he was only thirty-four years old he was elected Mayor, the first native-born American to occupy that post in New York. In 1693 he was commissioned Colonel, commanding the King's County Militia. Besides rendering services in these capacities, he was appointed by Governour Sir Edmund Andros the first Judge in Admiralty and was likewise, an Associate Judge of the Colonial Court. Furthermore, he was chosen in rapid succession Chancellor, then Collector of the Revenues and, last of all, Chief Justice of the Supreme Court. Apart from the time devoted to the performance of public duties, he not only pursued an active mercantile career but also found opportunity to serve the interests of the Church as Senior Warden of Trinity Parish.

In 1677, agreeably to the law of the Province regarding such matters, Stephanus Van Cortlandt obtained from Governour Andros a licence to purchase lands from the Indians, and for a number of years thereafter he gradually increased his holdings, especially in Westchester County, until he owned the east bank of the Hudson from the mouth of the Croton River to a point north of Anthony's Nose. This tract extended into the interior as far as the Connecticut boundary line and, in all, constituted an unbroken area of about eighty-seven thousand acres. When he had bought from the Indians this wide domain, and completed its symmetry and the continuity of his river boundary by a purchase from Governour Dongan, he applied for a Royal Charter confirming his title to the territory. The successive steps by which he became possessed of his lands afford an illuminating instance of the way in which the New York manors were gradually formed before they were officially, by letters patent, erected into manorial entities with all the sundry prerogatives and responsibilities attached to them.

The Royal Charter creating and erecting the Manor of Cortlandt was granted to Stephanus Van Cortlandt on the 17th. of June, 1697. In addition to conferring the usual privileges, with the faculty of holding Court Leet and Court Baron, and "all the advowsons and rights of patronage over all churches that may be built on the Manor," it assured to the "Lords of Cortlandt the extraordinary privilege of sending a representative to the Provincial Assembly." This unusual privilege was bestowed upon only two other manors in the Province—the Manor of Rensselaerwyck and the Manor of Livingston—and was not granted them until eight and eighteen years afterwards respectively.

The original document creating the manor, and setting forth in due detail the faculties with which the Lord of the Manor was invested, is still preserved in perfect condition at the Manor House. It is beautifully engrossed, with the best scrivener's art of the day, upon two skins of vellum, and has attached to it by faded ribbons the Great Seal of the Province. The decorative scrollwork is elaborately wrought, and the highly ornamented initial letter encloses a skillfully executed portrait of King William the Third.

In the very early years of the manor's history, the white settlers on the manor lands were comparatively few in number and there were a great many Indians, for although the red men had sold their original title to the land and had acknowledged their sale of it to Stephanus Van Cortlandt, "they still considered that their ancient right to hunt, fish, and plant corn held good," and they were not molested. It was not long, however, before colonists came with increasing frequency to tenant the farms laid out for them and to pursue the various industries incident to colony building.

VAN CORTLANDT MANOR HOUSE, CROTON-ON-HUDSON, SOUTH FRONT

Unlike most of the other Hudson Valley manors, the Manor of Cortlandt retained its original Manor House throughout its history, and although the existence of the manor as a political, administrative and judicial entity ceased at the end of the Revolutionary War, the old Manor House at the mouth of the Croton River still preserves all the characteristics it displayed when it was the administrative centre of a wide domain over whose inhabitants the Lord of the Manor exercised the headship and control previously explained at length.

The Manor House is known to have been standing in 1681 but, in all likelihood, it was built at a considerably earlier date—perhaps as early as 1665. It was erected originally for a fort, and besides its thick stone walls pierced with loopholes, all of which remain just the same to-day, it had at first a flat stone roof and was similar in appearance to the Mohawk Valley forts constructed about 1640. At the beginning, it was a place of refuge for the settlers in the neighbourhood whenever the Indians became dangerously excitable upon the occasion of their various tribal feasts and dances which they were wont to hold on the sandy point where the waters of the Hudson and Croton met, congregating there in large numbers from all of the surrounding country. When all danger from the Indians was past, the stone roof was removed and an upper storey with dormers was added.

Although additions have been made from time to time, as the growing needs of the family demanded, the house presents to-day substantially the same aspect it assumed in the eighteenth century. To anyone approaching by the Albany Post Road, from Ossining, and crossing the long bridge over the Croton, its first appearance strikes the eye with a compelling appeal, an appeal which becomes more and more potent upon closer acquaintance.

Low-eaved and long of body yet full of gentle dignity, this ancient dwelling, instinct with all the real but indefinable atmosphere of an home, nestles comfortably under the lee of a steep, protecting hill at the back, and its front windows look out over the mouth of the Croton and across the Tappan Zee to the hills on the opposite side of the Hudson. The view from the verandah is one not soon to be forgotten. As far as the eye can see, the Hudson stretches away to the south, bounded on either side by wooded hills. Immediately below the house the ground slopes rapidly to the reedy margin of the river and, just beyond, to the southeast, thick-grown sheltering hills rise up abruptly. To the left the gardens, with rose-grown walks, stretch away to the old Ferry House, now a dwelling but once the quarters for the keeper of the ferry, the control and emoluments of which belonged to the Lord of the Manor.

On looking at the front of the Manor House, one is somewhat at a loss to know which is downstairs and which is up, and whether there are two floors with an half-storey in the roof or whether there is one storey and an half with a basement underneath. The latticed and vine-covered lower verandah, with its arched and hooded entrance, forms a substructure for the balustered verandah above, to which a flight of steps, broken by a landing, ascends at the side. The lower storey is now virtually the basement, and what is in effect the ground floor—its position is like the *piano nobile* of many old Italian villas—is reached by going up the steps which bring one on a level with the ground at the rear, owing to the slope of the hill under which the house is built.

Directly above the upper verandah, the peaked and dormered roof descends with its flaring kick-up at the eaves so that, at first glance, it is not apparent of what material the walls are built. Closer inspection, however, shews that they are of tawny reddish sandstone with wide mortar joints, relieved by quoins and window facings of old yellow brick, and of unusually thick and massive structure. High up, between the windows, are the narrow slits or loopholes, already mentioned, through which the defenders of the house could shoot at assailants, in case of attack. The shutters are stout enough to resist a good deal of battering, and the Dutch door, divided into upper and lower sections, is a piece of exceptionally robust panelling. At the top it is lighted by two roundels or bulls-eyes set obliquely in the small upper panels, slanting just like the eyes of a Chinaman.

Above the lintol of the door, a pair of antlers supports the bow of the old Indian chief from whom a part of the manor land was purchased and, just beneath it, in the middle of the frame, is nailed a tiny horseshoe which, like nearly everything else about the house, has an interesting association. This shoe was the footwear of a cherished pony, once the pet of the children of the household, which, by virtue of its position in their affections, was now and again allowed the privilege of coming indoors and going upstairs.

Within, the hallway runs clean through to the back of the house. There the woodwork is of oak, now darkened by age but not co-eval with the rest of the structure as it was put there to replace the earlier woodwork that was hopelessly damaged and, indeed, partially torn away during the Revolutionary War. In the rest of the house much of the original seventeenth century panelling remains although, in more than one room, eighteenth century mantels and mantel shelves were installed without disturbing the surrounding woodwork.

To the right, on entering, is the parlour, panelled on one side, with a capacious round-headed cupboard to the left of the fireplace containing a rare treasure of old china and glass. Within the fireplace, and projecting somewhat beyond the surrounding woodwork, is a small iron hood—put there for the sake of improving the draught—which may have inspired Benjamin Franklin with the idea for the famous Franklin stove. Certain it is that the great philosopher, on one occasion when he spent the night at the Manor House, slept in this room which was used as a bedchamber, the parlour being then on the lower floor. As the Franklin stove appeared not long subsequently, the natural presumption is that the Manor House fireplace planted the seed of an invention.

Beyond this room there is still another parlour to the east, while back of this latter, and reached through it, is the "far bedroom" with its high-posted, becurtained bedstead, its samplers, its old wood-stove, and its ancient mirrors and chests exactly as they might have been a century or more ago. There, too, is the little writing table at which De Witt Clinton died. But the chief association of this room is not with De Witt Clinton, but with a ghostly lady, related to the family, whose appropriation of some of the family plate that she claimed, but which was not rightfully hers, has caused her uneasy spirit to walk from time to time in this chamber, so it is said.

To the right of the hall, in the rear of the house, and back of the first parlour, is the library. Across from it is another bedchamber, still rejoicing in all its seventeenth century panelling, while, to the left of the hall as you enter the house, is the dining-room, on the wall of which, opposite the fireplace, hangs a portrait of the Indian Chief Joseph Brandt and, above it, his scarf, which he gave as a token of friendship to an ancestor of the family. It is interesting to know that Brandt dined at the table in this room and that, at one time or another, every Colonial governour as well as nearly every person else of consequence in the Colonies dined at it also. Quite apart from historic association, this table is a most interesting piece of furniture. It is of the gate pattern and the top is a perfect oval of mahogany. As Oloff Van Cortlandt brought it with him from Holland, along with one or two other treasured family possessions, when he came out to New Amsterdam in 1638, it is, therefore, as well as an exceptionally fine example of its type, one of the earliest pieces, if not indeed the *earliest* piece, of mahogany furniture in America, for mahogany was not used by British nor Colonial cabinet makers before the eighteenth century, save in very rare instances and then only in minute quantities, usually as inlay.

The Manor House is typically Dutch in every line and detail of its architecture. In fact, no better nor more faithfully preserved specimen of Dutch Colonial house can anywhere be found. There are, indeed, houses at Old Hurley, near Kingston-on-Hudson, other houses in Kingston itself and still others in various localities of Dutch New York that are, perhaps, more Dutch, but they are so thoroughly Dutch and such exact and faithful copies of their prototypes in the Low Countries that they have practically no Colonial features. The Manor House, on the other hand, while altogether Dutch in feeling, has enough Colonial modification about it to make it especially interesting to those who are attracted by the Dutch Colonial type, which unquestionably has many features to recommend it for use in suburban and rural America. It is unusually flexible, compact, and replete with the element of solid comfort, and is by no means devoid of either dignity or grace.

In the Van Cortlandt Manor House we see an excellent exemplification of all the best and most characteristic features of Dutch Colonial contour. There is the long, low, brooding roof line, broken, it is true, by dormers but not in an uneasy, restless manner. There is the unmistakably Batavian pitch to the roof and the piquant flare or kick-up at the eaves, which softens the contour remarkably and gives the gable ends the lines of a bell or a fairy godmother's hat. There is the rough rubble texture of the walls of native stone, with the wide, raked mortar joints. The paint is white and all the woodwork is exceedingly simple and strong in its mouldings. Ceilings are low, and the main part of the house is oblong in shape and it sits close to the ground so that its intimacy with its surroundings contributes materially to its general air of repose and restfulness. Last of all, there is the spacious verandah which is a purely Colonial development.

The upper part of the Manor House, as one approaches by the bridge over the Croton, would appear to be only a small attic. When you enter and go upstairs, however, this notion is quickly dispelled for you find a goodly number of comfortable rooms. The secret of it all seems to have been that the old Dutch builders were consummate economists of space and knew how to construct houses without any waste room, a problem that we to-day have apparently not altogether mastered.

The long, narrow yellow Dutch bricks used in the quoins and surrounds for the doors and windows harmonise agreeably with the tawny reddish sandstone and create a thoroughly pleasing combination. For a long time the walls were coated with roughcast stucco, but a number of years ago this coating was removed and the original face of the masonry was carefully restored. What faint traces of the plaster remain have imparted a wonderfully soft, mellow tone to the whole fabric.

Having mentioned Dutch bricks, it might be well to call attention to the popular fallacy regarding so-called Dutch and English bricks. As a matter of fact, some bricks sent over from Holland and England, but the vast majority of Dutch and English bricks, which certain mistaken folk vigorously maintain were fetched overseas, were made in America and were termed *Dutch* or *English* because of their Dutch or English shapes and sizes. If even a small fractional quantity of the bricks called Dutch or English had really been imported, great fleets would have been kept perpetually busy carrying cargoes of bricks and nothing but bricks, and this we know was not the case. It is doubly interesting, therefore, to know that the bricks in the Manor House quoins were really made in Holland.

HALLWAY

For a time after the Manor House ceased to be necessary as a fort it seems to have been used by Governour Thomas Dongan as a sort of hunting lodge, whither he went for occasional holidays, and there are traditions of "gay house parties of gentlemen, for he never went alone, quartered under its roof at one time and another." When Stephanus Van Cortlandt acquired the house and surrounding lands to round out his domain, the place became a summer home for the Van Cortlandt family, or really an home kept open all the year, "and with slaves always there to wait upon the family" whenever they chanced to go there, which they seem to have done very frequently.

Stephanus Van Cortlandt died in 1700 and his eldest surviving son, Philip, succeeded him as second Lord of the Manor. The "Lady Mayoress," as Gertrude Schuyler, the wife of Stephanus, is usually called to distinguish her from the later Ladies of the Manor, long survived her husband and she and her large family of children appear to have occupied the Manor House with increasing frequency and for longer periods of time than had been their custom at first. There was much business to be attended to and all the family were highly susceptible to the many charms of the place. Sometimes they went thither from New York by the Post Road and we are told that "the coach of Lady Van Cortlandt, with its outriders wearing badges of mourning, made frequent trips between the Manor House and the City, though the ladies might also be seen wending their way through the woods on horseback." The "ladies" alluded to were the seven daughters who "were distinguished for their decision of character, good sense, personal beauty and warm affection for each other."

The younger members of the family usually went in the saddle, very naturally preferring that wholesome and pleasant mode of progression to the jolting of the coach which must have been trying when we consider the state of the roads. The records of constant repairs to "coache" and harness shew the severe strain to which both were subjected.

PARLOUR

On still nights, it is said, the coach of the "Lady Mayoress" now and again can yet be heard drawing up before the door of the Manor House; the wheels grind on the gravel, the hoof beats of the four coach horses and the mounts of the outriders cease, the coach door opens, then slams, and—there is nothing there!

On these visits to the manor, the Countess of Bellomont, wife of the Governour, and other close friends of the family often made part of the entourage. Notwithstanding the discomforts of travel in wheeled vehicles over roads that were far from good, visitors to the Manor House were numerous and the Van Cortlandts, well knowing how much they depended upon the roads for the society they so much enjoyed, did all they could to better them. "Have the rift hill made passable before we come" was the order given in a letter when the family were returning after a short absence, and this was only one of sundry allusions to road mending.

When the journey between Manhattan and the Croton was not made by coach or on horseback, the Van Cortlandts travelled by the river, going in their sloop or in a *periagua* and landing at their own dock at the foot of the Manor House grounds. Some of the timbers of this old dock have recently been dug up in the course of making repairs to the Post Road bridge across the Croton. Indeed, this seems to have been their favourite way of going to and from the city and likewise of visiting kinsfolk and friends living along both banks of the Hudson. Sometimes the voyage from New York to the manor consumed nearly two days. In a journal kept by young John Van Cortlandt, that same John whose portrait we shall meet anon, he tells, in 1747, of what was then considered an average trip: "Went to Croton's river in the sloop, with brother Pierre, May 27th. and arrived there the next day after a pleasant passage." But if the voyage to or from New York was an undertaking to be planned for, the longer trip to Albany was full of peril and adventure, and the amount of provision to be laid in before sailing was simply amazing. Moored at the dock, the sloop could be overlooked from the house and the preparation and loading were of interest to the whole household. An unusually quick passage is described in a letter from Albany:

> "We came here in the sloop Ann about 5 o'clock in the afternoon, without coming to anchor once the whole passage. We left after breakfast, dined that day at the Horse Race, Anthony's Nose. Drank tea at New Windsor, and so on next morning we were at the Manor of Livingston, and at 5 o'clock were here in Albany. All was joy and gladness to see us so well."

Philip Van Cortlandt, the second Lord of the Manor, married Catharine, the daughter of Abraham De Peyster. Besides being a great landowner and an eminent merchant of New York City, he took an active part in the public affairs of his time and, at the request of Governour Montgomerie, he was appointed a member of the Provincial Council in 1729. He was also a commissioner of Indian affairs and was concerned in settling the boundary disputes with Connecticut. Philip died in 1747 and was succeeded as Lord of the Manor by his fifth and youngest son, Pierre, who was born in 1721.

In the hall of the Manor House hang two full length portraits, two little boys arrayed in the court dress of the period with high-heeled, silver-buckled shoes, long, full-skirted coats, lace at their wrists, and flowing lace stocks. The right hand of one lad, John Van Cortlandt, rests upon the head of a pet fawn. It was taken upon an island in the Croton, near the house, and long survived its young master for whose sake it was cherished as long as it lived, although it developed a most unruly and savage temper.

Its antlers now hang above the door nearby. The other painting is a portrait of John's younger brother, Pierre, who later became the third Lord of the Manor. The picture was painted when Pierre was about ten years old and the accompanying decorative attribute of which he seems to have made choice is a vase of flowers from the Manor House garden—roses, lilies, flowering almonds and hare-bells—a fore-promise of interests that he was afterwards to envince in far ampler manner, for it was during his lordship that the garden became an important feature of the place. Although the garden was an object of care and some pride when Philip Van Cortlandt became Lord of the Manor, in 1700, it was his son Pierre who brought it to a state of hitherto unknown excellence, and it was Joanna Livingston, his cousin and bride, who brought with her many flowers that she loved. An old letter says she made of the Manor House and its garden "an earthly Paradise."

Pierre Van Cortlandt and his wife Joanna gave up New York City as a place of partial residence and, in 1749, came to make their permanent home at the Manor House all the year round. Thence onward the stream of distinguished guests increased; apart from the wide family connexion and the hosts of personal friends who always found a warm welcome and generous hospitality awaiting them, there came now also nearly everyone who bore an active or important part not only in the affairs of the Province but of the whole country as well, for Pierre Van Cortlandt played a conspicuous public rôle. From 1768 to 1775 he was a member of the Provincial Assembly, sitting for the Manor of Cortlandt. As the struggle with the Mother Country became imminent, his sympathies were strongly upon the side of the Colonies and when Governour Tryon came to the Manor House one night in 1774, and told his host "the great favours that would be granted to him if he would espouse the royal cause and adhere to King and Parliament, Van Cortlandt answered him that he was chosen a representative by unanimous approbation of a people who placed confidence in his integrity to use all his ability for their benefit and the good of his country." This course of conduct he was determined to pursue. In November, 1775, he was chosen deputy to the Second Provincial Congress, and sate also in the third and fourth congress, till May 1777, when he was elected President of the

Council of Safety. In 1777 he became also Lieutenant-Governour of the State of New York, fulfilling the duties of both Governour and Lieutenant-Governour during the Revolutionary War since General George Clinton, the Govemour, was busied with his military duties. The office of Lieutenant-Governour he occupied until 1795, and in 1787 he was likewise President of the State Convention that ratified the Federal Constitution.

Thus, as may readily be imagined, the public capacity of the Lord of the Manor as well as purely personal considerations drew to the old house every person of note who came within the neighbourhood, the foreign officers who served with the Continental Army being numbered amongst the guests along with American officers and visitors of civil and administrative conse- quence. Hither came the Count de Rochambeau, the Marquis de la Fayette, the Due de Lauzun and many more of equal fame, while the name of the Baron von Steuben especially stands forth in a long list of eminent foreign personages because of his huge enjoyment of roasted oysters in the Manor House kitchen, a form of gastronomic frolic in which he had never before indulged. The catalogue of American officers and civil worthies would be too long to give, for it is virtually all-inclusive, so we must content ourselves with chronicling that General Washington and his aides many times enjoyed the Manor House hospitality.

Not all the guests of the Revolutionary period were of exalted station or well-known name. At one time there were three hun- dred of them for supper, a night's shelter and breakfast—the men of Colonel Hammond's Regiment who came in November 1775. They were heartily welcomed and made as comfortable as might be under the circumstances. From the family chronicles we learn that "they spread themselves over the lawn; they consumed two hogsheads of cyder and twelve were put to bed in the barn."

It would have been strange had there not been clergymen, now and again, in all the unceasing stream of visitors. One of the most notable guests of the cloth was the great evange- list, George Whitefield, who came on horseback a few years before his death in 1770. Messengers were sent in all directions to announce his arrival and the crowds that came in response to the summons sate upon the lawn as Whitefield preached to them from the upper verandah. This visit is commemorated by a little brass plate let into one of the verandah posts. Franklin, who heard him preach in Philadelphia, said of him that "his voice was so powerful, rich and sweet that it was perfectly distinct in the open air to thirty thousand people," and on this occasion at the Manor House the sermon was plainly heard on the opposite bank of the Croton.

So accustomed were the good people of the Manor to entertaining the clergy that the little bedroom across from the library and back of the dining room, which was usually given to them, received the name of the "Prophet's Chamber." The "Prophet's Chamber" has a ghost, but it is not a clerical ghost. During the Revolutionary War, while some of the British officers were quartered in the house in the absence of the family, one poor fellow was stricken with brain fever and died raving mad, chained to the floor, in this room, and the dank of his chains may now and again be heard—*it is said!* Another British officer ghost, in his red coat, has sometimes been surprised in one of the upper rooms bending over a chest of papers, with what object has never been known.

Only once in its history was the old house left desolate. In 1777, when the men of the family were constantly called away in the service of their country, the unsettled conditions of the neighbourhood made it no longer safe for the mother and her young children to remain in the house, and with flocks, herds and household gear they removed to a farm they had taken near Rhinebeck. Only a few slaves were left in charge, and they lived in constant dread of the hated "Row-galley Men," who spared neither friend nor foe. Once when the slaves were crouched in their hiding place under the roof they overheard a band of raiders, seated on the verandah, discussing plans to burn the house. Fortunately the advance of Generals Greene and Knox at this juncture sent them flying and brought their plans to naught.

DINING ROOM

More than three years elapsed before it was considered safe to return, and then, in 1780, with glad hearts the exiles came back to their own again. Much wanton damage had been done in their absence, but by diligent measures the destruction was soon repaired and the house had assumed its wonted appearance when, in July 1781, Washington stopped for a short rest on his way to Peekskill after he had "crossed the new bridge over the Croton," directly in front of the house, and visits were paid by the Due de Lauzun, the Marquis de la Fayette, Count Rochambeau, Barons von Steuben and de Kalb, General Philip Schuyler and many others of lesser renown. In 1783, when Washington made his triumphal entry into New York City, after the evacuation by the British Army, he was accompanied by Pierre Van Cortlandt, who has left an account of the progress in his diary.

With the return of peace Pierre Van Cortlandt was at liberty to spend most of his time at the Manor House once more and there, in 1814, at the age of ninety-four, he died. A contemporary notice of his death says: "The simplicity of his life was that of an

Ancient Patriarch. He has descended to the grave, full of years, covered with honour and grateful for his country's happiness." He was succeeded as head of the family by his eldest son, General Philip Van Cortlandt, who had fought with distinction during the war and received from Congress the rank of Brigadier General for his gallant conduct at Yorktown.

FAR BEDROOM

From the day Philip Van Cortlandt threw his royal commission into the fire and joined the Continental Army his career was an eventful one. He was the close friend of Washington, Rochambeau and la Fayette, and was one of the original members and founders of the Society of the Cincinnati. On intimate terms, as he was, with all the foreign officers belonging to the Society, there was a double attraction that drew these eminent soldiers to the Manor House, for they came to see him as well as to pay their duties to his distinguished father. When the Marquis de la Fayette made his tour through the United States in 1824, General Van Cortlandt accompanied him. For sixteen years he was a member of the United States Congress, and in other ways also rendered valuable public services to his State and country as long as he lived. He died in 1831 and was succeeded in possession of the Manor House by his brother, General Pierre Van Cortlandt.

LONG WALK IN GARDEN

Pierre Van Cortlandt, like the rest of his family, carried on the tradition of unselfish public service and held sundry posts of honour for the discharge of whose duties he was well equipped. He had studied law in the office of Alexander Hamilton and his legal training under a most able and inspiring preceptor stood him in good stead throughout his subsequent career, part of which embraced a term of two years in Congress. Curiously enough, in view of his early connexion with Alexander Hamilton, his first wife was the daughter of Governour George Clinton—the "Caty" Clinton whose portrait still hangs in the Manor House. At his death the Manor House descended to his only son, Colonel Pierre Van Cortlandt, a man of whose exemplary life and kindly ways the elder people of the neighbourhood still cherish many recollections. Colonel Van Cortlandt died in 1884 and the manor property descended to his one surviving son, Captain James Stevenson Van Cortlandt—a son who nobly observed the honoured traditions of his forefathers. Captain Van Cortlandt died in 1917, the last descendant of the name in the direct male line. He was survived by two sisters, Mrs. John Rutherford Matthews, who died in 1921, and by Miss Anne Van Cortlandt, who resides at the Manor House. Rich in historic associations, surrounded by its gardens with their brooding spirit of ancient peace, it stands to-day wrapped in the priceless serenity of dignified age and, all unchanged by the surging onrush of modern life on every side, bears silent witness to the manners of those ampler days when the course of the country's future had its first shaping.

XV.

SCARSDALE MANOR

ERECTED THE 21st. OF MARCH, 1701

THE Manor of Scarsdale, in Westchester County, was the last manor to be created in the Province of New York. In fact, it was the only manor erected in the eighteenth century, all the rest being creations of the seventeenth century.

Owing chiefly to the tortuous course of the Mamaroneck River, which formed a great portion of its eastern boundary, the Manor of Scarsdale was of irregular shape. By the terms of the patent, the manor grant covered a tract embracing the present towns of Mamaroneck, Scarsdale, a small part of Harrison, with White Plains and a portion of Northcastle.

To Colonel Caleb Heathcote, of New York, on the 21st. of March, 1701, this broad tract, embracing divers purchases previously made by him, was patented as a manor, with all manorial rights and privileges and, we may add, manorial responsibilities, and named the Manor of Scarsdale after the birthplace of the grantee, the Hundred of Scarsdale in Derbyshire. The transference of the name was particularly appropriate owing to the similarity in the character of the land in both the old Scarsdale and the new.

Colonel Heathcote married the daughter of William Smith, of Saint George's Manor, Long Island, sometime Chief Justice and President of the Council of the Province of New York. He himself at sundry times held public posts of trust and was a valuable and highly esteemed personage in the Colony. He was at one time Surveyor-General of His Majesty's Customs for the Eastern District of North America, Judge of the Court of Admiralty for the Provinces of New York, New Jersey and Connecticut, and a member of His Majesty's Council for the Province of New York. Curiously enough, he was Mayor of the City of New York from 1711 to 1714, during a part of which time his brother, Sir Gilbert Heathcote, was Lord Mayor of London.

Upon an eminence at the head of Mamaroneck Harbour, over-looking the two peninsulas that form its eastern and western sides, and the distant hills of Long Island—a spot called after him, to this day, Heathcote Hill—Colonel Heathcote built himself a large brick manor house, in the prevailing English style of that period, with all the customary offices and outbuildings. In addition to these there was the purely American feature of quarters for the negro slaves, set at a convenient distance from the master's dwelling.

Here, at Heathcote Hill, the Lord of Scarsdale Manor lived for a great portion of his time during the rest of his life. He never appointed any steward for the manor but attended personally to the many onerous duties that his position entailed upon him. There are papers still in existence that shew how his tenants were wont to come to him for aid and counsel in their most private affairs, especially the settlement of family disputes. Furthermore, he was often called upon to draw their wills. In addition to all these services which he rendered in a paternal manner, there were the many administrative matters, not only of his immediate personal demesne, but of the whole country round.

Colonel Heathcote died suddenly of a stroke of apoplexy, in New York City, on the 28th. of February, 1721. Besides all his many other interests, he was deeply devoted to the welfare of the Church of England, of which he was a staunch and faithful adherent. To him, more than to any other one man, was the Church of England in New York City and in Westchester County indebted for its support and growth, so long as he lived.

XVI.
APTHORPE HOUSE

ALTHOUGH the Apthorpe house, which stood near what is now Ninth Avenue and 90th. Street, in New York City has long since been demolished, it is included in this volume because of its claims to architectural recognition. New York once boasted many old houses of great architectural interest and merit, but they have been so rapidly and so ruthlessly destroyed to make room for the pressing requirements of swarming city life that the very recollection of them seems in danger of being lost. Many, nay most, of them have gone without any pictorial record of their appearance. Fortunately, in the case of the Apthorpe house, this is not true.

APTHORPE HOUSE, NEW YORK CITY

It was built about the middle of the eighteenth century, or a little after the middle, and was typical of the better sort of suburban house that New Yorkers of affluent circumstances erected for themselves within easy distance of their business in town. The illustration of the Apthorpe house speaks so eloquently for itself that it is unnecessary to enter into a detailed description of its characteristics. While the easily recognised Middle Georgian mode may be spoken of as typical of the style of country house belonging to well-to-do merchants, attention should be called to the arrangement of the portico which, in this case, is rather unusual. The other features might have been found repeated in dozens of other instances. It only remains to add that all the details are most justly proportioned and executed with exquisite finish and refinement.

Mr. Apthorpe, the owner of the house, was well known and had many friends in official circles at the time of the outbreak of the Revolutionary War. He was generally believed to lean toward the Loyalist side in his sympathies but both sides ascertaining that he was disposed to pursue a neutral and inactive course, he was allowed to live in comparative peace without serious molestation. At one time or another, as he managed through his neutrality to keep on friendly terms all round, the officers and other prominent personages of both sides were, or had been, entertained in his house.

XVII.

THE GRANGE

142nd STREET AND CONVENT AVENUE

BUILT BY ALEXANDER HAMILTON, 1801

O N THE 2nd. of August, 1800, Alexander Hamilton bought fifteen acres, at what is now 142d. Street and Convent Avenue, from Jacob Scheifflin, determined to build himself a country house. On this land he began to build "The Grange," in 1801, and he went there to live in 1802. Here he passed two of the happiest years of his life.

THE GRANGE, BUILT BY
ALEXANDER HAMILTON, 1800

New York Public Library Digital Collections

All the timber for the house was furnished by his father-in-law, General Schuyler, and came from the General's Saratoga estate. Hamilton was intensely interested in the building and watched and superintended every step of the construction. General Schuyler, apparently, was no less interested than his son-in-law, and was constantly making useful presents. In 1802, Schuyler writes of some cedar posts he has ordered, half for himself and half for Hamilton. Again, in the same year he writes:—"I very much wish to see your improvements at the Grange. Your task and my dear Eliza's exertions, I am persuaded, will make it a desirable residence. Be assured I shall make it mine when I leave this for a visit to my children."

Another instance of his very helpful interest in the new house occurs in April, 1803, when he writes to Mrs. Hamilton, saying, "Dear Child: This morning General Ten Broeck informs me that your horses, which went from hence, were drowned, and that you had lost paint, oil, etc. to a considerable amount. Supposing this account to have been truly stated to the General, I send you, by Toney, my waggon-horses of which I make you a present. If you cannot recover the paint, purchase no more, as I will have the house painted. When the opportunity offers, send my bridle and saddle, which Toney will leave."

The style of the house, as the illustration indicates, was that which was most in favour at the beginning of the nineteenth century when the Neo-Classic influence and French bias were at their height. Hamilton, as we know, had excellent taste and was a discriminating person in the choice of everything concerning his surroundings. There was unostentatious simplicity from first to last, but there was also elegance, so that it is fortunate the house has been preserved—though moved from its original site and divorced from its wonted environment—both on account of its historic associations and as a national shrine to the memory of one of America's greatest men, and also for the testimony it bears to the architectural achievements of the time. It must be remembered, in this connexion, that Hamilton was not by any means a wealthy man and could not afford to build an expensive house. The Grange, therefore, is a good example of the *modest* house of that period.

Here Hamilton hoped to be able to indulge his tastes for gardening and also to get relaxation from the stress and strain of a busy public and professional life, and here for two brief years he did gain that satisfaction. When he first bought the land, he wrote whimsically in one of his letters, "A garden is a good place for a defeated politician, so I have bought a farm nine miles from town."

Hamilton brought his devotion to the principle of federalism into the adornment of his estate. He was intensely "devoted to the perpetuation of the new union of States. He conceived a design of establishing at his own home an emblem of the original thirteen States. He planted on the grounds of the Grange a circle of thirteen trees that would be symbolic of the thirteen stars in the blue field of his country's flag. These trees were set out a few years before his tragic death. "

It was from the Grange that Hamilton went forth on that fateful morning of the duel that brought his life to an untimely end. Hamilton's fourth son, John, was twelve years old at the time of the duel and, in later years, told of his father's last hours at home:—

> "The day before the duel," says the son, "I was sitting in a room when at a slight noise, I turned and saw my father in the doorway, standing silently looking at me with a most sweet and beautiful expression of countenance, full of tenderness and without any of the business preoccupation he sometimes had. 'John,' said he, 'won't you come and sleep with me to-night,' and his voice was frank as if it had been my brother's instead of my father's. That night I went to his bed and in the morning, very early, he awakened me and taking my hands in his palms, all four hands extended, he told me to repeat the Lord's Prayer. Seventy years have since passed over my head, and I have forgotten many things, but not that tender expression when he stood looking at me at the door, nor the prayer we made together the morning just before the duel."

Hamilton as we know, thoroughly disapproved duelling and in the statement he drew up he spoke of his wish to avoid the engagement with Burr, on "religious and moral" grounds, the possible loss to his family, his consciousness of obligation to his creditors, and yet, he says, "my relative situation, as well in public as in private, enforcing all the considerations which constitute what men of the world denominate honour, imposes on me (as I thought) a peculiar necessity not to decline the call."

The rest of the sorry story is well known—how Hamilton discharged his pistol in the air; how he fell mortally wounded, and was carried, in a dying condition to the house of his friend, William Bayard, where he was joined by his wife and family; and how he tried to console them.

What is perhaps, not so well known is the heartless way in which Burr went home, settled himself down to read in his library, calmly and unconcernedly ate his breakfast, and started about the day's business as though nothing whatever had happened.

Hamilton died on the day of the duel, the 11th. of July, 1804. He was buried from Trinity Church, of which parish he was a vestryman, on Saturday, the 14th. instant.

XVIII.
THE DYCKMAN HOUSE
BROADWAY, NEW YORK CITY

ALTHOUGH neither distinguished history nor exciting associations engage the mind or filip the imagination in connexion with the Dyckman house, at 204th. Street and Broadway, New York City, nevertheless, its appearance challenges attention and its character is so strongly and distinctively marked that it cannot be overlooked. The house was not built until 1783, when a great building boom seems to have taken place in the first assured calm after the war, but its fashion is thoroughly typical of a much earlier date.

DYCKMAN HOUSE, BROADWAY AT 204th STREET

It is a low house with steeply pitched roof, the lower slope of the front pitch projecting far enough beyond the house walls to form an ample covering for the slender-posted verandah that extends the full length of the building. The utter simplicity of the house is one of its most striking qualities. There is no elaboration of detail to be found anywhere. Indeed, there is a complete absence of any attempt at ornament, however modest, and the charm of the building depends wholly on the naïveté and straightforwardness of the composition and the interesting manner in which a number of divers building materials are employed.

To the student of the old Hudson Valley houses the Dyckman house is particularly valuable because it exhibits in peculiar perfection a type that prevailed all up and down both banks of the Hudson from the latter part of the seventeenth century till well past the middle of the eighteenth. It is an especially valuable example because it is unspoiled, while elsewhere there are comparatively few that have escaped mutilation at the hands of the nineteenth century "improver."

To make the house still further valuable as an object lesson, several members of the Dyckman family have equipped the rooms with the furnishings in use at the time the house was built and thrown the building open to the public at specified times so that one may go there and study the material accompaniments of daily life at the period of the nation's early infancy.

XIX.

MOUNT MORRIS

HARLEM HEIGHTS

O F ALL the historic houses in the vicinity of New York, none has had a more chequered career than Mount Morris, more commonly known as the "Jumel Mansion" situate on the King's Bridge Road in Harlem Heights. Fortunately it is now well preserved as an historic monument, and its days of ups and downs are past.

MOUNT MORRIS, KING'S BRIDGE, HARLEM HEIGHTS

(Generally known as the Jumel House)

It was built about 1765 (being, it seems, ready for occupancy in the summer of 1766), by Colonel Roger Morris who, in 1758, had married Mary Philipse, a daughter of Frederick Philipse, second Lord of the Manor of Philipsborough and sister to Frederick, the third and last Lord. Up to the time when Mount Morris was built, Colonel and Mrs. Morris had been living in their town house, at the southeast corner of Whitehall and Stone Streets, when not making prolonged visits at the Manor House in Yonkers. This town house they retained, making use of Mount Morris as a country seat whither they might go to escape the heats of the city summer.

Roger Morris, born in England in 1727, came out to the Colonies in 1755 as aide-de-camp to General Braddock, and then, for the first time, met George Washington, a young colonel also attached to General Braddock's staff as aide-de-camp. Morris was wounded in the action at the Monongahela, and when he was recovering from his wound, not long after, in New York, Washington was visiting at the house of Beverly Robinson, who had married Susannah Philipse, an elder sister of Mary Philipse, that "charming Polly" who "was to fascinate both of these soldiers and marry one of them." Whether Morris had paid serious addresses to Mary Philipse at this time, we do not know. He served with his regiment in a campaign under Lord Loudoun, in 1757, but was back in New York in July of that year.

Life at the Manor House in Yonkers must often have been somewhat dull for lack of adequate society, since Mary Philipse spent much of her time with her sister, Mrs. Robinson, in New York, where the gayety and stir of a garrison town added their spice to social intercourse. Mary Philipse was attractive and independently wealthy. Some time previous to the date of our story there seems to have been a division of the manor lands, of which Mary Philipse's portion was more than 51,000 acres. Nevertheless, she had stayed single till she was twenty-seven and remained mistress of her own heart till Roger Morris laid siege to her and captured it.

The engagement seems to have been short, for only six months prior to their marriage at the Manor House at Yonkers—on the 28th. of January, 1758—a close friend of the family, conversant with all their doings, refused to believe the rumour of the approaching matrimonial alliance.

Very soon after his marriage Captain (as he then was) Morris bought a major's commission in the Thirty-fifth British Foot and accompanied his regiment to Halifax. For the next six years, until he resigned from the service in June, 1764, an outline of his career is

given in the "Colonial History of New York." Taking his station now
in private life, with high honours conferred upon him in the administration of the Colonies, and blessed with an ample fortune, Colonel
Morris not unnaturally wished to establish a country seat as well as a
town house, and when the farm on Harlem Heights was offered to be
sold in 1765 he acquired this highly desirable property.

The Morrises spent the summers of eight or nine years of happy
domestic life at Mount Morris before the storm of the Revolutionary
War broke. As Mr. Shelton points out, in his fascinating history of
the house, "whatever opinion Roger Morris may have held as to
the justice of the cause of the colonists, he was not ready to enter
into revolt against the English Government, in whose service
he had spent most of his life. He was a man of large wealth and
it behooved him to look ahead and devine if possible what would
be the result of the war. His position as a member of the King's
Council jeopardised his property." He might be obliged to sanction measures at the next meeting that would bring upon him the
wrath of the hoodlum "Liberty Boys," who loved to burn the houses
of Loyalists. He had not yet taken sides. "His wife, now a matron
of forty-five, was quite capable of looking after the family estate.
She would have no political entanglements. He believed that it was
only a question of time when the home Government would regain
control of the Colonies. He could avoid taking sides by leaving the
country. He would not need to stay away very long." Accordingly
he sailed for England on the Packet *Harriet*, the 5th. of May,
1775, and remained until late in the autumn of 1777. It has been
suggested—and not without reason—that the prompt decision to
leave the country was rather "the decision of Mary Philipse than of
Roger Morris," and was taken at the instance of the Philipse family,
whose vast landed property made it expedient that "one member
of the family who was a retired British officer should exile himself
before he could be drawn into the British Army."

Mrs. Morris and the children, in all likelihood, lived at Mount
Morris during the summer of 1775, and possibly the spring of 1776,
after which proximity to the City of New York became too disquiet-
ing and they moved to the Manor House at Yonkers. When Colonel
Morris came back to New York in 1777 he was appointed Inspector
of the Claims of Refugees, in the discharge of which office it became

his duty to adjudicate the claims for Government compensation preferred by Loyalist refugees who had been despoiled of their property. This post he retained until peace was signed in 1783, when he
and his family returned to England to live.

Not long after the departure of Mrs. Morris and her children
from Mount Morris, General Heath made the house headquarters
for his pickets for a brief period. Following General Heath's occupancy, General Washington established his headquarters here—to
be exact, on the 14th. of September, following the evacuation of
New York City—and remained there for a space of thirty-three
days. This was a time of special stress and anxiety to the
Commander-in-Chief. In an encounter with the advancing British
troops in their progress through the city, the Connecticut troops
had exhibited the most cowardly behaviour and, though officers
and men alike were caned by Generals Washington, Putnam and
Mifflin, they fled in the most dastardly manner. As though this were
not sufficient cause for irritation, on Monday morning, the 15th.,
the British pushed out a reconnoitering party from Bloomingdale,
expressing their derision by blowing fox-hunting horns, as much
as to say they were out for a morning's sport. Old fox hunter as he
was, this was doubly galling to General Washington.

It is of some interest to note the usual programme carried out at
headquarters by the Commander-in-Chief. The post riders, bearing the mail through to the Convention at Fishkill or to Congress
in Philadelphia, set out at daybreak. As early as six o'clock, working parties detailed to the fortifications, paraded in front of headquarters. When there was a trial by court-martial, the court was
wont to assemble in the great parlour at nine o'clock, after which
the prisoners were fetched in from the guard-room.

This great parlour, thirty feet long by twenty feet wide, with
the corners clipped off so that it formed an octagon, has six large
windows. It was one of the comparatively few rooms of the time
hung with wall paper, consisting of panels of cool green bordered
with morning glories, the whole being backed on buckram hung
from the cornice. It was doubtless a source of genuine satisfaction
to Mrs. Morris, who was a person of discriminating taste.

At three o'clock the Commander-in-Chief dined, following the
custom then prevalent, and in all likelihood he maintained a generous

Virginia hospitality at his table, for he was most punctilious about such matters, be the stress of military conditions what it might.

On the 16th. of November, 1776, the British and Hessian troops, fourteen thousand strong, captured Harlem Heights and confined their prisoners in the barn at Mount Morris. For a time, this barn was used as the guardhouse of the new British headquarters but, in later years, while still under British rule, it was used for military church services. It is not certainly known whether any British General-Officer took up his quarters in Mount Morris at this time, but if any did it was Lieutenant-General Earl Percy who was then in the neighbourhood.

From the 14th. of July to the 9th. of November, 1777, Lieutenant-General Sir Henry Clinton occupied Mount Morris, and during that period it is more than likely that the ladies of the Philipse and Morris families were now and again honoured guests of the staff in the house that was really their own. So long as the house was used for military purposes by the army holding New York, the British Government paid rent for it, and all the rest of the Philipse and Morris property within the British zone was restored to its owners. General

HOUSE DOOR

Baron von Knyphausen had his headquarters at Mount Morris from the 23rd. of July till the 9th. of October, 1778.

From the end of the Revolutionary War till the time that Stephen Jumel bought the property in 1810, Mount Morris passed through divers vicissitudes and was in danger of falling into utter dilapidation. For nearly thirty years this stately mansion was by turns a tavern, posting house, farmhouse and suburban restaurant. In 1787 it was graced by the name of Calumet Hall and was maintained as a roadhouse and posting inn by Talmage Hall. Here the stages from New York to Albany made their stop to change horses. The following year it was offered for sale and seems to have been bought by a farmer. Not long after, it seems to have become a restaurant for the entertainment of parties driving out from the city, corresponding in status to many a tea-house of today.

In 1790, on the 10th. of July, when Washington was President and still resident in New York, he gave a dinner at Mount Morris to some of the ladies and gentlemen of his Republican Court, a dinner from

SIDE DOOR

which, for some reason or other, Mrs. Washington seems to have been absent. Of this dinner he writes in his Diary:

"Having formed a party consisting of the Vice President, his lady, son and Miss Smith, the Secretaries of State, Treasury, and War, and the ladies of the two latter, with all the gentlemen of my family, Mrs. Lear and the two children, we visited the old position of Fort Washington and afterwards dined on a dinner provided by

**SIDE DOOR OPENING INTO PASSAGE
CONNECTING WITH GREAT PARLOUR**

a Mr. Marriner at the house, lately Colonel Roger Morris's, but confiscated, and now in the possession of a common farmer."

This dinner at Mount Morris was presumably served at the time customary in those days for such functions—half-past two or three o'clock in the afternoon—and we can picture Washington and his distinguished guests, in the mellow light of the summer evening, driving back to New York in gilt coaches and chaises, or making their way on horseback.

From this time on to 1810, when the Jumel *régime* began, there is nothing of note to record of Mount Morris. When Stephen Jumel bought the estate in 1810 to please his capricious wife, everything was done to put it in perfect repair again and no expense was spared in furnishing the house with the most elegant and handsome appointments that money could buy. The stage was set with punctilious care for the guests who never came and the feasts that were never eaten. The trap and the bait were there, and the pipers were ready to pipe, but gentle-born New York folk of that day—albeit they loved gaiety well enough—declined to be snared by gilded enticements and would not dance to the piping of an hostess whose past was more than questionable and whose bearing had never been aimed to mitigate the vivid recollections of her unsavoury behaviour.

It mattered not that she was now the wife of a wealthy French merchant and that the means at her disposal were amply adequate to create for her all the brilliant surroundings of a distinguished *salon*, of a sort hitherto unknown in the New World, or to embark on a career of lavish hospitality which they might have shared without limit at no greater cost to themselves than a friendly nod. Betsy Bowen; Madame de la Croix; Eliza Brown; Madame Jumel! The series of kaleidoscopic changes of name and station rose too fresh in the memory of New York society. Everybody knew the history of the new mistress of Mount Morris, and what they did not know they more than suspected, with very plausible grounds for their suspicions.

The lady of four names—and a fifth was still later to come— first appeared on the stage as little more than a common strumpet; then, profitting by the unusual brilliance of her personal charms, she became the acknowledged beauty of the hour and received no little homage from the gay beaux of the city; she might have become the Aspasia of the Republican Court, when New York was the seat of the Federal Government, but, unfortunately for her ambitions, she had no brains, no education, and no tact. Her only intellectual accomplishments, if intellectual they can be called, were a certain sort of elemental cunning and a modicum of histrionic aptitude when the feigning of emotions might serve her purpose. By employing these two accomplishments in conjunction she finally captured a legitimate and eligible husband, M. Stephen Jumel.

And this was the manner of the capture. About 1795 Stephen Jumel arrived in New York from San Domingo. He was a merchant and wealthy; in fact he was one of the richest merchants in New York at a time when wealth was increasing with astonishing rapidity. About 1800, being a person of independent spirit and given to following his inclinations regardless of the opnions of others, he elected to set up a mistress as head of his household. And that mistress was Betsy Bowen, or Eliza Brown as she was at that particular period of her career. In a small, church-going American city, and in an age that was distinctly straight-laced, at least so far as the outward observance of conventions went, this was a daring step and a deliberate challenge to public sensibilities. But what was an even greater affront to the social proprieties was giving his mistress a carriage and horses, all quite equal in the elegance of their appointments with the equipages of the most aristocratic persons in the city. Eliza was beautiful and she knew it, and she was not in the least shy in challenging all competitors in display and extravagance. Her carriage and horses were useful adjuncts in her campaign of ostentation.

But somehow the desired recognition did not come in response to all this display of magnificence. People gazed, it is true, but they did not smile nor unbend, and they held themselves frigidly aloof. Eliza at last conceived the plan of consummating a legitimate union with Jumel by way of remedy for the withering scorn that greeted her when she drove abroad or went afoot in the streets. Perhaps, then, some of the haughty dames, whose acquaintance she so much desired, might condescend to speak to her; perhaps, even, one or two might be brave enough to cross her threshold and see in what elegance and luxury she lived, if only she could call herself Madame Jumel, with the sanction of law and the blessing of the Church. Besides, if anything should befall her, and she were honourably married, she might go straight to heaven—an eventuality scarcely to be expected so long as the irregularity of her relations continued. In consequence of Eliza's determination to become Madame Jumel, she and Stephen were married in old Saint Patrick's on the 9th. of April, 1804. But somewhat went before that culmination of her manoeuvres.

One day when M. Jumel came home from a short absence he found Eliza very ill a-bed, attended by a physician and nurses, and apparently fast approaching her dissolution. He was deeply distressed and, in genuine agony of mind, begged to know what last thing he could do for her. The physician, who was an accessory to the plot, assured Jumel Eliza could not live till morning. Now the longed-for opportunity was within Eliza's grasp and she promptly seized it. With tears coursing down her cheeks, and voice choked with sobs, she told Jumel her one wish was to die a married woman. There is no need to enter into all the harrowing details of this fictitious death-bed scene, sincere on one side and adroitly acted on the other. The upshot of it all was that Eliza had her way and they were married. Matrimony had an amazingly restorative effect upon her condition. In less than two days she was driving about town in her carriage, wreathed in smiles. Years later, Henry Nodine, an old servant of Jumel and his wife, told how M. Jumel on occasion chided the designing Eliza for her deception. "My Eliza, you tell me one story," complained the duped husband. "You never, never tell Mr. Jumel you had one little boy down in Providence. Else Mr. Jumel would not marry you." The truth of this accusation Madame Jumel admitted; she also cursed and swore at her spouse, and threatened to shoot him with a pistol that she kept and carried. The same witness thus recounted the manner in which Jumel was tricked into marriage, repeating the victim's own words as he upbraided his shrewish partner: "You tell Mr. Jumel you very sick and going to die and you want to die one married woman. The doctor tell Mr. Jumel marry you, you die before morning. The doctor tell Mr. Jumel one story, too. Mr. Jumel he marry you. In two days you ride around town in your carriage. You tell Mr. Jumel one big story. "

But though Eliza may have landed a legal husband by her histrionic *tour de force* and "the one big story she tell Mr. Jumel," she had reckoned without her host in counting on a triumphal entry into the ranks of society. The Jumels were still just as much ostracised as ever. At last, in 1810, came the purchase of Mount Morris. Perhaps some few of the less meticulous respectabilities might relent far enough to allow themselves to be decoyed thither—out of curiosity, at any rate, if for no better reason. At all events, there would be the diverting task of doing over and furnishing a large house, This venture was attended with slightly more success. A few of the less scrupulous slipped out surreptitiously—to gratify their curiosity; a very few repeated the visit. Madame Jumel was a little encouraged, but not satisfied, and she was beginning to be bored by the companionship of one or two members of her own family whom she had induced to come now and again and share her gilded loneliness; Mr. Jumel, apparently, did not care.

In 1815 the Jumels went to Paris, and they went to many places besides Paris. Madame Jumel's success was as complete as she could have wished. She had wealth, she had beauty, her husband's family more or less accepted her, and society was gracious, not knowing her past, or not caring when it did. The nobility of the Old World held out its hand to Betsy Bowen, and she was even smiled upon by royalty. She could do in Europe what she could not do in New York.

Then came the separation from her husband, the subsequent return to Mount Morris, a few years later the death of Mr. Jumel, later still the marriage with Aaron Burr, then his death, followed by a period of partial recognition—half condoning, half indifferent—and then the long years of loneliness, living on the memories of past grandeur, amidst the present squalour of carelessness, and the heart-breaking emptiness of recollection, when a mind, stored for the most part with barest frivolities, fed upon reminiscences of glittering ephemeral success in the ball-rooms and *salons* of Europe.

Madame Jumel's latter years were spent in a pathetic atmosphere of cobwebs, dirt, faded, shabby finery, and slatternly quasi-indifference to her present environment. In the autumn of 1862, a young lady with keen powers of observation and a facile pen was taken, in company with several others, to see Madame Jumel as a kind of local curiosity. Her description of the visit, and of the semi-tragic, semi-comic state of Madame Jumel's existence at that time, so vivid and so faithfully pourtraying an extraordinary personality in the evening of life, when all remaining mental activity seemed a strange compound of lynx-eyed shrewdness, vanity and tottering reason, when a weary, disordered mind begot fantastic hallucinations that passed for realities, is given at length in Mr. Shelton's *Jumel Mansion* and is well worth reading.

Poor Betsy Bowen! She had begun life destitute of the shelter of a real home and the love of parents, destitute of any tenderness and accustomed from infancy to stony harshness, destitute of any mental training, and equipped only with the bloom of youth and a beautiful body, along with a dash of innate shrewdness that was her only weapon with which to turn the selfishness and lust of others to her own preservation. With her limited assets and her limited outlook, who can blame her for the course she pursued! It was not only the easiest way; it was the *only* way she knew.

She was adroit enough to achieve the fulfillment of certain ideals she had the cleverness to form, and to acquire at last the long coveted cloak of respectability and recognised legal status. She was not clever enough to understand the fearful odds against which she was pitted, nor to turn the successes for which she had striven to good account when they came.

We can view her at the close of her career only as an empty derelict, once gaily painted and joyous with the exuberance of youth and ambition, and now, after all the buffettings of human hardness and heartlessness, reduced to purposeless old age, with all the bravery of colour and gilding battered and tarnished. Knowing her history, who is there to blame and point the pharisaical finger of scorn! We can only pity her and her folly, and forgive.

Mount Morris, more happy in its old age than its erstwhile mistress, is now carefully preserved and cherished, and is adequately provided for under intelligent direction as an historic monument.

XX.

CLAREMONT

RIVERSIDE DRIVE, NEW YORK CITY

CLAREMONT, on the Riverside Drive, north of Grant's Tomb, must not be confounded with Clermont in the Livingston Manor. The similarity of names sometimes leads to confusion in the minds of those who are not familiar with both places—and a surprisingly small number are familiar with even the sites of these old houses, let alone their actual appearance.

Claremont is one of the comparatively few old houses still left within the limits of New York City and for that reason, if for no other, deserves to be cherished. There is, however, some history attached to it, and associations with notable people, so that it has a double claim on our regard.

The house was built in 1783 and is a good example of the large, square late Georgian house with the usual complement of urbanely designed details without and within. The rooms are lofty and spacious, and of well proportioned dimensions. The property now belongs to the city and for a number of years past has been let for a restaurant. The addition of glassed-in verandahs, to provide the necessary additional room for patrons, has, of course, greatly altered the appearance of the house from its original state and obscured its architectural character.

George Pollock, a wealthy linen merchant, bought the land from Nicholas de Peyster and built the house, in 1783 as we have stated, naming the place "Strawberry Hill." His five-year-old son, St. Clair Pollock, fell off the cliffs and was drowned, on the 15th. of July, 1797, and unable to stand the associations of the place after that, the father removed to New Orleans. Reserving a burial place containing the urn that held the ashes of his boy, Mr. Pollock sold Strawberry Hill in 1803 to Joseph Alston, the husband of Aaron Burr's daughter, Theodosia. Alston in turn deeded the property to Michael Hogan.

Hogan, who had been the British consul at Havana, when he acquired Strawberry Hill renamed it Claremont, after Claremont in Surrey, the seat of Prince William, Duke of Clarence, later to become King William IV. Hogan had served as a midshipman in the Royal Navy along with Prince William, of whom he was very fond, and he renamed the house out of compliment and for the sake of old associations.

The Earl of Devon, while living at Claremont in 1807, witnessed the trial trip of Robert Fulton's *Clermont* up the Hudson.

In 1815, Joseph Bonaparte, the ex-King of Spain, went to New York to live and occupied Claremont. Bonaparte was meticulous about the furnishing of his house and doubtless equipped Claremont sumptuously, according to the best taste of the day, with handsome movable and fixed decorations he had brought with him from France.

XXI.
CORTLANDT HOUSE
VAN CORTLANDT PARK, NEW YORK

C ORTLANDT HOUSE. / Built by Frederick Van Cortlandt / MDCCXLVIII. / Placed in the custody of the Colonial Dames of the State / of New York MDCCCXCVI. / Opened by them as a public museum / MDCCCXCVII. / This large estate has been held / continuously by the descendants / of Jacobus Van Cortlandt who was born in 1658.Mayor of the City 1719. Until Purchased for a Public Park MDCCCLXXXIX. / Virtutes Majorum Filiæ Conservant."

So reads the tablet affixed to one of the outside walls of Cortlandt House, set there for the edification of the thousands who yearly pass by this stately old dwelling of the Colonial period with its clustering memories of the broad days when State and Nation were in the making.

CORTLANDT HOUSE, VAN CORTLANDT PARK

Library of Congress, Prints and Photographs Division

Jacobus Van Cortlandt, a younger brother of Stephanus Van Cortlandt, the first Lord of the Manor of Cortlandt, married Eva Philipse in 1691 and eight years later, in 1699, his father-in-law, Frederick, the first Lord of the Manor of Philipsborough, conveyed to him fifty acres of land near Spuyten Duyvil Creek. This land was part of the old Patroonship of Colen Donck which, after the death of the Patroon Adriaen van der Donck, had passed through the possession of Elias Doughty and Joseph Heddy to Matthias Buckhout. From the latter Frederick Philipse bought it in 1694 when he was completing his land purchases just after the creation of the Manor of Philipsborough. This tract was generally known as "the old Younckers," and was so called because of its first ownership by the Jonkheer or Younker, Adriaen van der Donck. Subsequently it was spoken of as "Little or Lower Yonkers."

Eva Philipse, the wife of Jacobus Van Cortlandt, was really not Eva Philipse at all, except by adoption, but Eva de Vries. Born in 1660, she was the daughter of Pieter de Vries and Margaret Hardenbrook. When the latter, in 1662, in her early widowhood, gave her hand in second marriage to Frederick Philipse, the future Master of Philipsborough adopted his wife's infant daughter by her first husband and she was always known as Eva Philipse.

The marriage of Jacobus Van Cortlandt and Eva Philipse was the first link of the connexion between the Van Cortlandt and Philipse families; the marriage of Catherine Van Cortlandt, the sister of Jacobus, to Frederick Philipse a year after the death of his first wife was the second link in the chain of intimacy and affectionate relationship that bound the two houses together. There seems to have been an especially devoted attachment between sister and brother, for when Frederick Philipse, the newly created Lord of the Manor of Philipsborough, and his wife were building Sleepy Hollow Church, in 1699, we are told that Mrs. Philipse, deeply interested in the progress of construction, was wont "to ride up from New York or from Yonkers mounted on a pillion behind her favourite brother, Jacobus Van Cortlandt." It needs but a little putting of two and two together in a matter of dates to track down a double romance.

SOUTH FRONT

Frederick Van Cortlandt, the son of Jacobus and Eva Philipse, built Cortlandt House in 1748. In his will, dated the 2nd. of October, 1749, he speaks of the new house he was then "about finishing," and the date stone bears the figures "1748." The structure is built of grey stone, in rubble masonry, with brick facings for the doorways and windows, the materials being disposed in much the same way as at the Philipse Manor Hall in Yonkers. Like the Manor Hall, too, the house is L-shaped, the main portion facing south and the shorter frontage facing east. The south front is fifty-five feet in length and the east front is a little more than fifty-one feet from end to end; the depths of the two parts are respectively twenty-four and twenty-two feet. The lines of the hipped roof and the general arrangement of mass contribute to a singularly pleasing composition. Several details of the interior woodwork, as well as the features already noted are reminiscent of the Philipse Manor Hall which seems to have supplied much of the inspiration embodied in Cortlandt House, although the latter is by no means an imitation. On the contrary, it possesses a strong individuality of its own and affords many indications of the distinctive architectural manner peculiar to the period of its building. One of these earmarks may be seen in the masques which adorn the keystones above the windows.

WINDOW DETAIL

Both because of proximity and the bonds of relationship between the families, the connexion between the history of Cortlandt House and the Manor Hall at Yonkers was peculiarly close and intimate. Whatever events took place in one house generally evoked an echo in the other. There was endless visiting back and forth and most of the guests who crossed one threshold were more than likely to pass the other also.

When the Revolutionary War came, Cortlandt House was in the midst of the contested zone, although it was virtually within the British lines a great deal of the time. The family was again in undisturbed possession, however, long before the British forces evacuated New York City. General Washington stopped there to visit the family and spend the night while on his way to make his triumphal entry into New York at the termination of the war. An allusion to this progress, with attending friends, is found in Pierre Van Cortlandt's diary. He writes:—

> "I went from Peekskill Tuesday, the 18th. of November, in company with His Excellency, Governour Clinton, Colonel Benson and Colonel Campbell—lodged that night with General Cortlandt, Croton River, [this was his son, General Philip Van Cortlandt of Revolutionary fame,] proceeded and lodged Wednesday night at Edw. Couwenhoven's where we met His Excellency General Washington and his aides. The next night lodged with Mr. Frederick V. Cortlandt at the Yonkers, having dined with General Lewis Morris. Friday morning in company with the Commander-in-Chief as far as the Widow Day's at Harlem, where we held a Council. Saturday I rode down to Mr. Stuyvesant's, stayed there until Tuesday, then rode triumphant into the City with the Commander-in-Chief."

We catch an amusing glimpse of Washington, on his way to Cortlandt House, from the description written by a little girl of ten, penned with all the delightful naïveté of a child. In his fascinating and valuable book on the "Jumel Mansion", Mr. Shelton gives the summary of the youthful observer's impressions. Little Sarah Adams, it seems, lived in the village of Pleasantville, near White Plains. As Washington was passing through on his way to New York, Sarah ran down to the gate to see him, for in her childish enthusiasm she regarded the Commander-in-Chief as being almost superhuman. A drizzling rain was falling, and what she saw was the General seated in a sulky driving the horse. "His uniform was covered by a greatcoat with capes, and his powdered hair was protected by a bandana handkerchief bound around his head under his cocked hat. She distinctly saw that his nose was red and his face pock-marked. This was a glimpse of Washington at fifty-one. Incidentally, we can see that he had no intention of meeting the Van Cortlandt ladies that evening with a water-soaked uniform and a face streaked with powder."

INTERIOR WITH PARLOUR FIREPLACE

Library of Congress, Prints and Photographs Division

For a short time, in the latter part of the Revolutionary War, Cortlandt House was Sir Henry Erskine's headquarters. Amongst its noted guests, at a later date, were the Duke of Clarence, afterwards King William IV, and Admiral Digby, of the Royal Navy.

XXII.
THE ODELL HOUSE
GREENBURGH, PHILIPSBOROUGH MANOR

THE home of Colonel John Odell, in the Manor of Philipsborough on the high ridge of the Greenburgh hills, west of Hartsdale, was an ordinary country farmhouse at the time of the Revolutionary War and yet, for a little while on two successive occasions, it was the centre of important events. In all the years since the Revolution the dwelling has changed but little in outward aspect. It is an unpretentious structure of two storeys with clapboarded sides and a shingled roof, of long slope in the rear to cover the low kitchen wing, overshadowed by tall trees and half-concealed by luxuriant shrubbery.

**ODELL HOUSE, GREENBURGH,
PHILIPSBOROUGH MANOR**

In the summer of 1776, the newly organised "Convention of Representatives of the State of New York" was in a migratory condition. On the 10th. of July, just after the tidings of the Declaration of Independence in Philadelphia, the members had resolved to take steps towards forming a new State Government on the 16th. instant, but when that date arrived affairs had become too alarming for calm deliberation and they were obliged to content themselves with passing only such enactments as were most urgently required for immediate administration. Washington was considering the abandonment of New York City, and British ships were anchored in the Hudson opposite Tarrytown.

On the 27th. of July the Convention found it expedient to remove to Harlem. From Harlem they soon transferred their sittings to King's Bridge, and from King's Bridge to the Odell house where they continued to sit until the 29th. of August, when they rose again to resume their sessions a few days later at Fishkill. For a brief period, therefore, the Odell house was the seat of the State Government. At Fishkill the members of the Convention "supplied themselves with arms and ammunition, and thereafter legislated with their swords by their sides, literally building the peaceful fabric of constitutional government in the very presence of the alarms, the perils, and the carnage of war."

John Odell, later to win military distinction, was the eldest son of Jonathan Odell, of Irvington, and Mary Dyckman, his wife. Born in 1756, he led an exciting life during the war as we may find by the memorial of his public services set forth for the legislature of the State of New York, in 1839. In 1776, when not yet twenty years old, he enlisted as a private and in that same year he was reduced almost to destitution by the British forces encamping on his farm and destroying his property. His taste for excitement and active service found full scope in his work as one of the famous Westchester Guides. From 1780 to the end of the war "he was a member of the Horse Guard of Westchester County, ranking as lieutenant and as captain in the line, and in this capacity he did remarkable work for the patriot cause." So well known did he become, and so annoying were his activities that the British authorities offered a reward of £100 for his capture. Although he had several narrow escapes, in consequence, he managed to elude his would-be captors. After the war he became Lieutenant-Colonel of a regiment of the Westchester County militia.

The next appearance of the Odell house on the stage of Revolutionary history was when it became the headquarters of the Comte de Rochambeau, Commander-in-Chief of the French forces, from the 6th. of July till the 19th. of August, 1781. It then became the scene and centre of not a little military gaiety and entertaining while the French army lay encamped on the Greenburgh hills from White Plains to the Neperhan, the American army lying to their right and extending to the banks of the Hudson.

Albeit these parallel encampments lasted for a few weeks only, both commands embraced the occasion to indulge in social and military festivities. Visits were exchanged between the French and American officers and a continual round of functions seemed in progress. The diaries and letters of the officers of both armies are full of allusions to these exchanges of courtesies. Doctor Thacher speaks of a dinner given by some of the French officers to the officers of the regiment to which he was attached. The American officers were received, he tells us, "in an elegant marquee; the dinner served in the French style, consisted of soups, roast beef, etc. The officers were accomplished gentlemen, free and affable in their manner." It would have been strange, indeed, had the *haute noblesse* of the *ancien régime*—to which most of the officers under Rochambeau's command belonged—been otherwise!

It is amusing to note, however, that M. Blanchard, the French Commissary, did not express so much pleasure with a dinner he took with Washington. "The table," he wrote, "was served in the American style—vegetables, beef, potatoes, lamb, chickens, salad, puddings and pies, all being put on at the same time. They gave us on the same plate beef, potatoes, lamb, etc." One can easily imagine a sensitive Frenchman's annoyance, especially if he were something of a *bon vivant* with a meticulous regard for the unalloyed flavour of each successive viand, at what must have seemed to him a barbarously profuse array of simultaneous victuals that did not admit of the separate appreciation of dishes in duly ordered sequence.

During the time of the encampment numerous banquets were given, and not infrequently were the tables spread "in the big barns adjoining the farmhouses where the generals had their headquarters." The young French officers, we are told, "ingratiated themselves into the favour of the country belles, dances in whose honour enlivened the summer evenings."

The Odell house still bears much of its original aspect. As a reminder of its occupancy by Rochambeau there have been found not far away the remains of the bake ovens constructed by the French army cooks. They are built into the side of a knoll and were about six feet long by two and a half feet wide. They appear to have been constructed for the most part underground with the sides and ends formed of cobble stones.

XXIII.

THE VAN CORTLANDT HOUSE
PEEKSKILL

NOT far to the north of Peekskill—less than three miles, as a matter of fact—is the Van Cortlandt house. Although situated within the limits of the Manor of Cortlandt, it is not a manor house and must not be confounded with the only Van Cortlandt Manor House which, as we have already seen, is at the mouth of the Croton River. It was one of the homes of Pierre Van Cortlandt, third Lord of the Manor, who occupied it at various times when either his personal occasions or public affairs made it more convenient for him to be in the vicinity of Peekskill rather than at the Manor House farther down the river. It was also a place well known to the officers of the Continental Army.

On the east front of the house, affixed to the wall, is a bronze tablet that reads:

"General George Washington
with his Aides
Slept in this house many nights
While making Peekskill
Their Headquarters in 1776, 1777 & 1778.

It was the house of
Pierre Van Cortlandt
Member of Colonial Assembly,
Member of 2nd., 3rd. & 4th.
Provincial Congress,
President of the Committee
of Public Safety,
A Framer of the State Constitution,
First Lieut.-Governour
of the State of New York,
Col. of Manor of Cortlandt Regiment.

**Erected by Daughters of the Revolution
of the State of New York
January 19th., 1904.**

The house was once a comely dwelling of ample dimensions, designed in the Georgian manner and possessed of a good claim to architectural consideration. Now, it is shorn of all its comeliness and has nothing left to please the eye, so that it would be an unkind and ungracious thing to give an illustration shewing it in its fallen and mutilated estate. It was unfortunately sold out of the family about the middle of the nineteenth century and its new owner succumbed to the craze then prevalent for gables, fretted barge boards and jigsaw pendants at the eaves.

During a part of the Revolutionary War the house was occupied by Cornelia Beekman, a daughter of Pierre Van Cortlandt and wife of Gerard G. Beekman. She was a person of great courage and determination, and though her home was time and again within the danger zone, she remained there undaunted. Once, indeed, she took refuge some miles back in the country but stayed away for only a day and a night. When she came back she found that the raiders had left not an article of furniture save one bedstead, and of provisions in the larder naught but one ham.

This serious and annoying loss, we are told, she bore with such equanimity that when General Putnam paid her a visit shortly afterward he was deeply impressed and "immediately sent her woodenware and several other most necessary articles, and with these she recommenced housekeeping." She was a resourceful woman, as well as determined and courageous, and was not the sort to sit idly by when there were things to be done in the trying times of war. She displayed a marked degree of initiative, and was noted for her acts of benevolence and humanity, even to enemies.

General Patterson was at one time quartered in her house, and Washington visited her frequently when he was in the neighbourhood. When Washington made the house his headquarters there is a tradition that the scarcity of furniture at one time, owing to the recency of the raid previously mentioned, obliged his aides to improvise bedsteads by placing chairs together.

Cornelia Beekman, unconsciously and indirectly, played an important part in the capture of Major André. Lieutenant Jack Webb, acting aide to General Washington, came to the house one evening and left with Mrs. Beekman for safe keeping a bag containing a new uniform and some gold, asking her to send it to him "at Brother Sam's" when he sent word. One evening, about a fortnight later, Joshua Hett Smith appeared at the house and asked for the bag, saying that Jack Webb was in Peekskill and had asked him to come and get it. Mrs. Beekman was on the point of handing over the bag, but suddenly thought better of it and declined to do so. Smith was insistent and urged that as Mrs. Beekman knew him well it must be all right to let him have the uniform. To this Mrs. Beekman promptly replied that she knew Smith so well that she didn't trust him. There was nothing for him to do but go away greatly disappointed.

This was just at the time that Smith was trying to get Major André back within the British lines In some way he had learned of the whereabouts of Lieutenant Webb's new uniform and hoped to get it for André knowing that André and Webb were about of a size. Had he succeeded in persuading Mrs. Beekman to give it up, André, in all likelihood, would never have been captured.

XXIV.
BEVERLY HOUSE
GARRISON, PHILIPSBOROUGH MANOR

ALTHOUGH Beverly House was destroyed by fire, in 1892, it would be inexcusable not to give due attention in this volume to a place round about which centred events of such strikingly dramatic interest and importance in the history of the Revolutionary War. It stood at the foot of Sugar Loaf Mountain, in the Highlands, in Philipstown, near what is now Garrison, and was built about 1758 by Colonel Beverly Robinson when he and his wife, Susannah Philipse, came hither to make their chief abode on their lands in the Philipse Patent.

**BEVERLY HOUSE, GARRISON
(DESTROYED) SOUTH FRONT**

Courtesy Miss Haldane

Colonel Robinson himself described the dwelling as "a wooden house lined with brick; it was," he adds, "originally begun in 1758, but was added to afterwards." Architecturally it was unpretentious, but it was commodious, as houses built at that time, and comfortable and rich in that domestic quality which, after all, is more satisfactory and enduring than mere urbanity of style. Nor was it without a becoming degree of elegance inside, for a number of the rooms were panelled and the appointments were in keeping with the quality and means of the occupants, who here maintained an unostentatious but lavish hospitality, so constant that the house was rarely without a guest beneath its roof. The panelled dining-room, in which occurred Arnold's ill-fated breakfast party, is in the middle portion. This, along with the higher eastern part of the building, formed the Master's quarters, the low western end containing the kitchen and service accommodations.

Beverly Robinson, the son of John Robinson, sometime President of the Colony of Virginia, and Catherine Beverley, was born in Virginia early in the eighteenth century. He grew up as the contemporary and close friend of George Washington, and their friendship endured till the firm convictions of each drew them to opposite sides during the Revolutionary War. On the strength of their old intimacy it was that Robinson subsequently appealed to Washington in behalf of André. At an early date Robinson showed his loyalty to the country when, in 1746, "he raised a Company in the Service of the King and Government of Great Britain in an expedition against Canada, and was ordered with his Company to the Colony of New York; in the fortress of said colony he did duty (the greater part of the time) until the conclusion of that war, when the forces raised for the expedition were disbanded."

Attracted by the prospects the rapidly growing city offered to men of enterprise, Robinson determined to settle there at the end of the Canadian Expedition. "In colonial times the aristocrats were for the most part engaged in mercantile pursuits, and Beverly Robinson became one of the number, associating himself in business with Oliver DeLancey, who afterwards commanded a Loyalist brigade in the Revolution." At one time the firm of DeLancey, Robinson & Co. occupied what was afterwards Fraunce's Tavern, as we learn from an advertisement in the New York Mercury, in May, 1759, announcing that:—

"DeLancey, Robinson & Co.—have removed their store to the house where the late Colonel Joseph Robinson lived, being the comer house next to the Royal Exchange."

In the month of July, 1748, Colonel Robinson married Susannah Philipse, the eldest sister of Frederick Philipse, the third and last Lord of the Manor of Philipsborough. For a number of years following their marriage they continued to live in the city, and with them Mary Philipse, who later married Roger Morris, spent much of her time. It was during one of these city sojourns that George Washington is said first to have met and fallen in love with Mary Philipse, to whom, also, according to current report, he is said to have offered his heart and hand, only to learn that Roger Morris had been before him and won the prize.

Not long after the middle of the century Colonel and Mrs. Beverly Robinson "retired into the country and settled in the county of Dutchess where their estate lay." The house was called Beverly House although, so far as the country people were concerned—and many other people, for that matter—it was commonly referred to as "Mr. Beverly Robinson's house." The estate embraced a tract of some sixty thousand acres, Mrs. Robinson's share of the Philipse lands, and Colonel Robinson's wealth and character together combined to make him the most considerable resident of the southern part of Dutchess County. The exterior of the house, as may be seen from the pictures still in existence, was exceedingly simple and unpretentious, although ample and eminently comfortable. The interior was executed in a far more urbane manner than the simplicity of the exterior might lead one to expect and as previously mentioned was furnished with such attention to the elegancies and amenities of polite life as the means and station of the occupants rendered appropriate.

Colonel Robinson was himself a practical farmer on a large scale. There were over 1500 acres in the home farm alone, besides mills and other features requiring constant personal supervision. He was an admirable and kindly landlord and treated his tenants with the greatest consideration. In 1785, when Colonel Robinson had preferred claims for compensation to cover part of his losses due to his adherence to the Crown, Captain Duncan Campbell testified before the Royal Commissioners that "Mr. Robinson was not only beloved and respected by his tenants, but was also universally respected and esteemed by all in the County in which he lived."

Throughout his career he was a loyal and devoted supporter of the Church of England. He was really the founder of Saint Philip's Chapel in the Highlands, for which he gave the land whereon the chapel is built and also enough besides for a glebe. Of the united Parish of Saint Peter's (Peeks-kill) and Saint Philip's he was the first church-warden and to his generosity were due many benefactions by which the Church profitted and the fruit of which it still continues to enjoy. It was doubtless due to Colonel Robinson's active support of Saint Philip's Chapel that it was later on spoken of as a "Tory Church." The story is told that, on one occasion during the Revolutionary War, when General Washington was riding past Saint Philip's Chapel in company with one of the higher officers of his staff, the officer, pointing with his crop, said "That is a Tory church, Sir." To which Washington, who was a vestryman in his own parish in Virginia, replied, "It is *my* church."

Although the active Whigs of the County, esteeming Robinson's position and personality, were anxious to secure his interest on the American side, he staunchly supported the cause of the King from the moment the conflict became acute, both from conviction and from his sense of loyalty. For a time, local considerations of respect and gratitude saved him from some of the serious annoyance to which other Loyalists were subjected, but at last, on the 20th. of February, 1777, the Commissioners for Dutchess County summoned him before them and required him to take an oath of allegiance to the American cause. Such an oath, of course, Colonel Robinson could not conscientiously take. The Commissioners gave him till the following May to make up his mind whether he would take it or not, but he declared "he would never take it."

"Remain in the country without subscription he could not; all he could do for the King he had done, and 'finding he had made himself obnoxious to the Leaders, and that he could no longer be of service to the King's cause in the County,' on the 5th. of March, 1777, he left his Family (except his eldest Son who had made his Escape some months before) and repaired to the City of New York." When he arrived there he addressed a letter to John Jay, "President of the Commission before which he had been summoned," and in this communication he presumably set forth his reasons for his loyal adherence to the Crown. Jay's letter to Mrs. Robinson, written in reply to Colonel Robinson's letter, expressed the deepest regret that his convictions did not permit her husband to support the American cause and informed her that, under the circumstances, it was impossible to avert measures for the confiscation of the family estate. Mr. Jay added the hope that Mrs. Robinson might influence her husband to reconsider his decision. That, however, was not to be thought of, and Colonel Robinson was already raising a regiment for the service of the King. It is interesting to know that many of the recruits for this regiment were his own tenants, and nearly all of them were men from his own county. This fact is an illuminating index to the strength of the Loyalist sentiment in the Province of New York, not only amongst the families of rank and wealth but also amongst those of the plainer sort.

Some of the Loyalists were merely passive and negative in their attitude of adherence to the Crown and abstention from assistance to the American programme. Thanks to this semi-neutral behaviour, not a few of them enjoyed comparative immunity from persecution and inconvenience, at least for a season. But Beverly Robinson was utterly incapable of any such anomalous position. He not only declared his stand unequivocally, but set actively to work with all his might and main to render useful service where he honestly believed it due. Consequently, "the powerful influences which had hitherto shielded him from pecuniary loss were of necessity withdrawn. Immediately on his departure" from Beverly House, "his personal property was seized by the Commissioners of Sequestration and ordered for instant sale. A strong but vain appeal was made by Mr. Samuel Verplanck to James Duane" to stay the proceedings against him. On the 21st. of April, 1777, the Commissioners held a sale which included household furniture, live stock, slaves, farming implements and the growing crops of fruit and grain. Mrs. Robinson and her children were turned out of house and home and obliged to remove to the shelter of New York City along with other Royalist refugees.

Colonel Robinson's war record was honourable and distinguished. He served under Sir Henry Clinton, Lord Rawdon,

General John Vaughan and Govemour Tryon, and bore an active part in the capture of Forts Clinton and Montgomery, in the Highlands, in the Pennsylvania campaign, at Stony Point, and in the South under Lord Cornwallis. At Fort Montgomery, when Lieutenant-Colonel Campbell was killed, the command devolved upon Colonel Robinson and he finally captured the position. Sir Henry Clinton testified:—"He distinguished himself on many occasions, particularly at the taking of Fort Montgomery where he behaved not only with Spirit and Courage but with the utmost Humanity." Besides commanding the Loyal American Regiment, he had under his command the Royal Guides and Pioneers, who were attached to that Regiment and were of great use in the department of military intelligence. He was Chief of the Military Information and Secret Intelligence Service, and in that capacity was conversant with all the details of the unhappy André tragedy.

Upon the evacuation of New York City by the British Army, at the end of the war, Colonel Robinson and his family removed to England where, after such unavoidable delays as are generally incident to the adjustment of matters of that sort, he was partially compensated for the loss of his estate in America, and was thus able to live in comfortable retirement in his advancing years. He died at Bath, survived by a family who sustained the honourable traditions in which they had been reared and achieved distinction in one direction or another. The descendants of Beverly Robinson and Susannah Philipse are now to be found in both England and America, and Beverly Robinson's Christian name and surname have been perpetuated, in several generations, in the land of his birth which his convictions and loyalty to his oath compelled him to leave under such unhappy circumstances. He was a man of parts and sterling worth, and was distinguished by a fortunate combination of energy, initiative, good common-sense and executive ability that qualified him to play successfully the role he did as one of the builders of a new country. The motives that actuated his conduct were above suspicion and though his candid honesty dictated a course of personal action contrary to the hopes and wishes of many of his former associates and friends, his fair name and fame have never been tarnished by the cheap and rancorous efforts of penny-whistle patriots to besmirch the memory of the Loyalists.

Close following upon the confiscation of Colonel Robinson's estate, begins the dramatic chapter in the history of Beverly House. There Generals Putnam and Parsons made their headquarters upon several occasions in 1778 and 1779, and in 1780, when General Benedict Arnold was appointed to the command of West Point, he chose to make his headquarters in the house of Beverly Robinson. Mrs. Arnold was with him to add her gracious presence during the brief period of their residence. Washington's orders appointing Arnold to the station of West Point are dated at Peekskill on the 3rd. of August, 1780, and shortly after that date the General and Mrs. Arnold took up their abode in Beverly House, the General using the old house on Constitution Island as his office. Between his house or his office and West Point he was accustomed to go back and forth in his barge.

Washington was puzzled at Arnold's desire to have the command at West Point, a desire for garrison duty which seemed strangely inconsistent with his previous anxiety always to serve in the most dangerous and conspicuous places. The wound in his leg from which he suffered considerable inconvenience, however, furnished a good excuse for avoiding the rigours of campaigning in the field and, as his heart seemed set on the post, the Commander-in-Chief assented to Arnold's wishes in the matter. There can be little doubt that Arnold's negotiations with Sir Henry Clinton had already been of long standing when he sought the control of the key to the American position on the Hudson. With West Point gone not only would the American hold on the Hudson become untenable, but the line of communication between New England and the rest of the country would be seriously jeopardised if not wholly severed; the coveted appointment to the command of this important stronghold would give Arnold his long-wished-for opportunity to consummate his schemes and ambitions, hence his anxiety to obtain it.

Directly the prize was within his grasp, events began to move rapidly toward a climax. No time was to be lost. Arnold knew that Washington was preparing to go to Hartford to hold a conference with the newly-arrived French officers, and he was convinced that the most proper time to carry out his plans would be during the absence of the Commander-in-Chief, more especially since several incidents in connexion with his attempts to hold inter-course with the British authorities had caused embarrassments and necessitated explanations, explanations which, however, Arnold had been ingenious enough to contrive very plausibly.

It was Arnold's first plan to have an interview with Major André, to whom the negotiations had been entrusted, at his own headquarters. This would have been perfectly safe for Arnold. He wrote to André assuring him that if he could make his way safely as far as the American outposts above White Plains he would encounter no obstacles thereafter. He also wrote Colonel Sheldon ordering a safe conduct for "John Anderson", the name by which André was to be known, once he had come within the American lines. This plan, however, was not at all agreeable to André, "for he was not disposed to go within the American lines and assume the odious character of a spy. He accordingly wrote the following letter to Colonel Sheldon, signed 'John Anderson,' which he knew would be placed in Arnold's hands. It proposed a meeting at Dobbs Ferry, upon the Neutral Ground:—'I am told that my name is made known to you, and that I may hope your indulgence in permitting me to meet a friend near your outposts. I shall endeavour to obtain permission to go out with a flag which will be sent to Dobbs Ferry on Monday next, the 11th. Instant at twelve o'clock, when I shall be happy to meet Mr. G—. Should I not be allowed to go, the officer who is to command the escort—between whom and myself no distinction need be made—can speak of the affair. . . . .'"

This letter puzzled Colonel Sheldon; it also puzzled Arnold to explain it. On the 10th. Arnold went down the river in his barge to King's Ferry and early the next morning continued to Dobbs Ferry, where André and Colonel Beverly Robinson had already arrived. Not having a flag of trace, his barge was fired upon and he was obliged to withdraw. This made it necessary to arrange for another meeting; not only that, but as he had gone down the river quite openly in his barge, Arnold had to find an appropriate explanation for Washington. All of this was extremely awkward and increased his anxiety to bring things to a head and have the business over with.

Arnold next sent word to André that a person would meet him on the west side of Dobbs Ferry on Wednesday, the 20th. instant, and that he would conduct him to a place of safety, where the writer would meet him. "It will be necessary," he said, "for you to be in disguise. I cannot be more explicit at present. Meet me if possible. You may rest assured that, if there is no danger in passing your lines you will be perfectly safe where I propose a meeting." By way of response to this letter, Sir Henry Clinton sent Colonel Robinson and André up the river on board the *Vulture* with orders to proceed as far as Teller's Point. Arnold was then made acquainted with the fact. How he got André ashore by the aid of Joshua Hett Smith, and how he virtually tricked poor André into passing within the American lines against his will, is set forth at length in the account of the "Treason House" at Haverstraw. We now return to Beverly House and take up the narrative of what occurred on the morning when Arnold discovered to his discomfiture that André had been captured and all the incriminating documents found.

On the 24th. of September Washington came back from Hartford by the upper route through Dutchess County to Fishkill, and thence along the Highland road towards Philipstown. Just after leaving Fishkill, he met the French Minister, the Chevalier de la Luzerne who, with his suite, was on his way to visit the Count de Rochambeau. The Chevalier persuaded the Commander-in-Chief to turn back with him and spend the night at Fishkill. Washington, with his party, however, was in the saddle next morning before dawn for he was anxious to reach Arnold's headquarters by breakfast time, and Beverly House was eighteen miles away. The men with the baggage had already been sent ahead some time before and told to tell Arnold that General Washington would breakfast with him.

When they came opposite West Point, Washington turned his horse down a lane toward the river. There upon la Fayette, who was riding beside him said, "General, you are going in the wrong direction; you know Mrs. Arnold is waiting breakfast for us, and that road will take us out of the way." Washington answered good-naturedly "Ah, I know you young men are all in love with Mrs. Arnold, and wish to get where she is as soon as possible. You can go and take your breakfast with her, and tell her not to wait for me, for I must ride down and examine the redoubts on this side of the river, and shall be there in a short time." The officers, however, stayed with Washington except two of his aides whom he sent on to tell Mrs. Arnold to go on with breakfast.

Breakfast was waiting when the aides reached Beverly House and they sate down with the General and Mrs. Arnold. Arnold was silent and moody. The British forces had not appeared to attack West Point, according to the plan agreed upon, and Washington had come back full two days ahead of the time he was expected. Evidently something had gone agley. While they were at breakfast Lieutenant Allen came in with a letter from Colonel Jameson. Instead of bringing welcome news, the letter informed him that Major André was a prisoner in his custody. Arnold controlled himself, made his excuses to his guests and asked them to say to General Washington when he arrived, that an unexpected message had called him immediately to West Point but that he would be back soon. He ordered his horse, and then went up to Mrs. Arnold's room and sent for her. When she came he told her quickly what had happened, bade her good-bye and leaving her in a swoon, rushed downstairs, flung himself into the saddle and made off toward the dock by a precipitous short-cut—ever since known as Arnold's Path—whither he had hastily summoned his rowers. Driving them into the barge when they were but half prepared, with mingled threats and promises he urged them down the river at top speed, evidently labouring under great nervous tension, as the men afterwards testified, and handling his pistol which lay across his knees. As they passed Verplanck's Point his white handkerchief answered for a signal to Colonel Livingston, in command there, and also to Captain Sutherland of the *Vulture* which lay at anchor a few miles downstream. Coming alongside, he was taken aboard and was safe from the consequences of his misdoings. He then dispatched a letter to General Washington, apprising him of his defection, and enclosing another for Mrs. Arnold.

When Washington arrived at Beverly House, soon after Arnold's precipitate flight, he was surprised not to find him there, but learning that he had been hastily summoned to West Point, the Commander-in-Chief set out thither expecting to find him. As his boat approached the West Point landing there was no salute, a circumstance that amazed Washington, and nettled him, too, for he was always a stickler for the proprieties, whether in military or civil life. Just as he started up from the dock he met Colonel Lamb coming down. The Colonel apologised for the apparent neglect of courtesy, explaining that he knew nothing of Washington's intended visit. "Sir, is not General Arnold here?" said Washington. "No, sir," said Colonel Lamb, "he has not been here these two days, nor have I heard from him within that time." Washington's dismay at this unlooked for revelation may well be imagined; his suspicions were aroused and he was sorely puzzled. Nevertheless, he inspected all the works, and about noon crossed the river again to Beverly House.

On the way from the dock to the house, Colonel Alexander Hamilton, at that time one of Washington's aides, hastened up with an anxious face and told Washington what had happened. Colonel Jameson's messenger, despatched to Hartford with papers taken from André and bearing André's letter to Washington, hearing at Danbury of Washington's return by the upper road, had ridden post haste and reached Beverly House four hours after Arnold's flight. At that hour Washington was at West Point and the messenger had given the papers to Hamilton. As soon as the Commander-in-Chief realised what had happened, he sent Hamilton to Verplanck's Point to tell Colonel Livingston to intercept Arnold in his escape. But Arnold had already been safe aboard the *Vulture* for several hours and as Hamilton reached Verplanck's Point a messenger from the *Vulture* was approaching with a flag of truce. He brought Arnold's letter to Washington which, besides announcing his act, besought protection for Mrs. Arnold and his child. The letter, and the letter to Mrs. Arnold, Hamilton straightway forwarded to Washington at Beverly House, and then went on to carry out the rest of Washington's instructions.

From this point Washington's own despatches tell the story so well that it is best to let them speak for themselves, To Colonel Wade, at West Point, he wrote:

"Monday, the 25th. of September, 1780."

At the Robinson House:

"General Arnold is gone to the Enemy. I have just now received a line from him, enclosing one to Mrs. Arnold, dated on board the *Vulture*. From this circumstance, and Colo. Lamb's being detached on some business, the command of the Garrison, for the present devolves on you."

On Tuesday, the 26th. of September, he wrote to Governour Clinton:

"I arrived here yesterday on my return from an interview with the French general and admiral and have been witness to a scene of treason as shocking as it was unexpected. General Arnold from every circumstance had entered into a plot for sacrificing West Point. He had an interview with Major André, the British Adjutant-General, last week at Joshua H. Smith's, where the plan was concerted. By an extraordinary concurrence of incidents André was taken while on his return, with several papers in Arnold's handwriting that proved treason. The latter unluckily got notice of it before I did, went immediately down the river, got on board the *Vulture*, which brought up André and proceeded to New York."

On Wednesday, the 27th., he wrote to General Greene:

"I have concluded to send Major André of the British Army and Mr. Joshua H. Smith, who has had a great hand in carrying on the business between him and Arnold, to Camp [at Tappan] tomorrow. . . . I intend to return tomorrow morning."

Major André had been brought to Beverly House on the morning of the 26th. and was sent across to West Point on the evening of the same day.

With the sending of Major André and Joshua Smith to Tappan, and Washington's departure, closes this short but intensely dramatic episode in the history of Beverly House. After that it relapsed into its accustomed quietude and there is nothing further to command our interest in connexion with a dwelling that was the scene of so much history making. We can only regret the unfortunate accident of its destruction by fire. The site, however, will always be invested with haunting memories of Major André's pathetic figure and Arnold's black treachery. As to the latter, certain writers have pointed out extenuating considerations which reveal a strong character gone wrong under the continued irritations of a few narrow-minded and

virulent jingo officials, who utterly failed to understand the disposition of the man they were defiling with, or to see how more generous action on their part might have kept him as a veritable tower
of strength to their cause. Nothing, however, can palliate the con-
temptible meanness with which he duped Major André, nor excuse
his personal disloyalty to Washington and his other friends whom
he knew reposed implicit confidence in him.

After the first shock of his defection was over, it was useless
for his former friends and military associates to "cry over spilt
milk." One cannot help sympathising with the reputed attitude of
General Putnam towards the incident. They tell the story of the
lisping general that at his own headquarters there was an heated
discussion over Arnold's personal qualities and military ability
just after his treason had become known. Lamb, who had been
with him, declared he had much merit as a soldier. Others differed
with him and the dispute was becoming acrimonious. Thereupon
Putnam interrupted and ended the controversy with "Whath all
thith God cuth it, gentlemen, let the traitor go to hell! Hereth
Washington'th health in a brimmer."

XXV.

CONSTITUTION ISLAND OR MARTELAER'S ROCK

THE story of Constitution Island, or Martelaer's Book, to call it by its early Dutch name, is so intimately connected with the histories of Beverly House on one side of the river and West Point on the other that it cannot be separated from them. Although the greater part of the house, that has many important associations for other reasons, does not date from the Colonial period of New York history, the island itself figures so constantly in the annals of the Province and State that its claim to a place in this volume is beyond question.

Geographically speaking, in the strictest sense, Constitution Island or Martelaer's Rock is really an island, although it was never so considered in early Colonial times. Between it and the proper east bank of the river is a narrow waterway, called Crooked Creek, so concealed by reeds that there appears to be only an uninterrupted marsh growth between the uplands of the shore and the high ground of the point of land standing forth into the stream. This rocky islet originally was included in the extensive land possessions of the Philipse family on the east side of the Hudson. The name "Martelaer's Rock" has given rise to much discussion and some puzzlement, but so far as can be discovered the most likely derivation seems to be as follows. The early navigators of the Hudson, for the sake of convenience, divided the river into certain sailing distances known as "reaches" or, in the Dutch, "rachs." The short stretch of water from Gee's Point, northward bound, appears to have been one of the most difficult on the river to navigate, and was known as "Martelaer's Rach" which, being done into English, means "Martyr's Reach." "Rach" was easily corrupted into "Rock." The word "Martelaer," it seems, may signify either contending and struggling or else martyr, and the name was apparently given in allusion to the contending against wind and tide often required to weather this rocky promontory.

The name Constitution Island comes from Fort Constitution, established there at the time of the Revolutionary War. A Dutch engineer, Colonel Bernard Romans, began work on the fortifications on the 29th. of August, 1775, and early in November, of the same year, three companies were stationed there as a garrison for the fort. In his historical sketch of the island, Mr. Stuyvesant Fish calls attention to the fact that the name of the fort, and hence the present name of the island, must have been given with reference to the British Constitution, as the fort was built before the Declaration of Independence and before either the State of New York or the United States had assumed corporate existence, much less adopted constitutions.

It was recognised at the beginning of the Revolutionary War that at this place was the strategic point of control of the whole upper river—therefore the anxiety to fortify it thoroughly. Curiously enough, the original plan of defense did not include works at West Point, but it was soon seen that an hostile force seizing the high promontory overlooking Constitution Island and mounting artillery there could immediately render the island forts untenable. Consequently on the 23rd. of November, 1775, a committee was appointed to investigate the high ground west of the river with a view to erecting fortifications there also. "Because of its geographical situation with respect to the already garrisoned defenses on the east bank of the river, the site of the new defenses derived its present name—West Point." Thus Constitution Island may be regarded as the parent of West Point and all the developments that have taken place there.

In 1775, when the Continental Congress had determined to fortify various points on the river, the Committee of Safety communicated with Colonel Beverly Robinson relative to the purchase of the islet and asked him to set a price on "the whole point of dry land or island called Martelaer's Rock Island," for the erection of military works. Colonel Robinson replied that, although the place appeared to be a part of the tract pertaining to Beverly House, the point of land did not belong to him but another division of the Philipse estate. It seems that at that time the work of building the fort had already begun without waiting to determine the question of ownership or the price of the land. As a matter of fact, notwithstanding the presence of the fortifications and the military uses to which the island was put during the Revolutionary War, the actual title and ownership remained in the Philipse family until the 3rd. of November, 1836, when Samuel Gouverneur and his wife sold the whole island to Henry W. Warner of Long Island. Mr. Warner it was who built the house that is now one of the chief objects of care to the Martelaer's Rock Association. In building it he seems to have incorporated part or all of a smaller house already standing there prior to the Revolutionary War.

It was this older house that Benedict Arnold used as his office when he was in command of West Point, and here he is said to have written his letter announcing that he had removed a link from the chain that held the log boom stretched across the river at this, its narrowest point, in order to obstruct the passage of British war ships should they attempt to ascend the Hudson. Arnold's ostensible reason for removing the link was to repair the chain; his real reason was to assist the British ships on the occasion of his proposed surrender of West Point.

After Mr. Warner had bought the island and built the house he called "Wood Crag," he occupied the place as a country seat. As the home of the Warner sisters for many, many years, it has become a literary shrine. Here, in 1850, Miss Susan Warner wrote the "Wide, Wide World," a book that was read and re-read and left an indelible impress upon an older generation. Miss Warner also wrote "Diana" and "My Desire," as well as some thirty-odd other books, nearly all of which enjoyed wide popularity in their day. It was but natural that the literary character of such an home should collect about it numerous memories of an highly interesting nature, and such was the case with the Warner house on Constitution Island. It is a simple dwelling with white clap-boarded walls, yet rich in inestimable associations and that priceless atmosphere of a gentle home, in the best sense of the word. Miss Anna Warner's long life was dedicated to useful works and she gave much of her time to conducting a Bible class for the students at West Point and to other ministrations to the cadets, "by hundreds of whom her memory is most tenderly revered."

Through the generosity of Miss Warner, who wished the island ultimately to become a part of the Military Reservation of West Point and was willing to sell it to the Government at a price far below what it was really worth, and through the equal generosity of Mrs. Russell Sage, who gave the necessary funds to put the scheme into effect, Constitution Island was tendered as a gift to the United States in September, 1908, and by the Government accepted as "an addition to the Military Reservation of West Point and to be for the use of the United States Military Academy."

It is of interest to note that Washington was first officially mentioned by the Continental Congress in connexion with the defenses on Constitution Island; that the breastworks commenced here in 1775, by order of the Continental Congress, were later completed under the supervision of Kosciusko; and that here, on the 20th. of December, 1783, the members of Washington's body guard were mustered out.

XXVI.

VAN WYCK HOUSE
(WHARTON HOUSE)

FISHKILL

T O THE east of the Albany post-road, just a little before entering the old town of Fishkill, stands a long, grey wooden house facing south. The lower eastern end, farthest from the road, is the original portion of the dwelling and was built early in the eighteenth century. It is now chiefly taken up with the kitchen and servants' quarters, since the larger and more commodious addition in the late eighteenth century affords more comfortable accommodations for the owner's use. Both parts of the house plainly shew the period of their erection—the low east end characteristically simple and unpretentious, while the larger western part bears evidence of the restraint and urbanity that prevailed when it was reared.

**VAN WYCK ("WHARTON")
HOUSE, NEAR FISHKILL**

About the house cluster many historic associations of undoubted authenticity and, at the same time, some other associations of agreeably romantic flavour that may or may not have a background of truth. They have been called in question, but since documentary evidence is lacking either to substantiate or disallow them, we may as well take them for what they are worth, as contributing to the aura of romance attaching to the place. Fenimore Cooper, in his delightful invention, "The Spy," in which fact and fiction are skilfully blended, is chiefly responsible for the elements of local fame that cannot be proved to have their foundation upon indubitable incidents.

Cooper calls this house the "Wharton House," and pictures it as the home of a family of that name who had removed thither during the Revolutionary War, after their home in Westchester County had been destroyed by fire. He also represents Harvey Birch, the American spy, as piloting Captain Wharton of the British army thither to visit his family, next relating how Captain Wharton was there captured by the Americans and held prisoner until, by Birch's aid, he made his escape through the neutral ground to the British lines near New York.

The original of Harvey Birch in the novel was Enoch Crosby in real life. Crosby led a most exciting life during the War as a spy. Curiously enough, he seems to have been able to insinuate himself into the confidence of both the British and American authorities, so that, whenever he was captured, influence was always brought to bear from high quarters to secure his immediate release. As a matter of fact, though frequently serving the purposes of the British military command, he was in reality in the American secret service, and always carried credentials that procured his release whenever captured by American troops.

Crosby's actual connexion with the Van Wyck House was this:— He lured thither a company of Loyalists, where they were seized by the Whigs and tried by the Committee of Safety in the autumn of 1776. On another occasion, he decoyed a group of Loyalists to Fishkill where they were all arrested and tried together and were then confined in the old Dutch church, which now and again served as a military gaol. Here he was not long imprisoned, however, his escape being connived at by the authorities who apparently received some intimation that Crosby's detention was not desired.

During most of the Revolutionary War Fishkill was the scene of large encampments. It was really a gathering place and base of supplies, and some military manufactures were there carried on. The barracks extended along the post-road south of the village of Fishkill and were in close proximity to the Van Wyck House, which General Israel Putnam and other distinguished officers from time to time used as their headquarters. It was also the scene of several courts martial. Not far distant from the house is the plot in which many of the Revolutionary soldiers who died in the encampment were buried.

Fishkill was such an important centre of activity that it was natural that the Convention of the State of New York, after being obliged to remove from the vicinity of the city, should establish themselves at this point. They first met in Trinity Church which at that period, had fallen into a sad state of dilapitation because of the ill feeling of the country people against the Church of England. The services had long been discontinued, the windows were broken and the building was defiled. One may gather some notion of its condition by the following extract from the minutes of the convention:

> "This Church being very foul with the dung of Doves and fowls, without any benches, seats or other Conveniences whatever, which renders it unfit for the use of this Convention, therefore they unanimously agreed to adjourn to the Dutch Church in this village, and adjourned to the same accordingly."

Here, in the Dutch Church, they had at least some place to sit down and were not surrounded with filth, but the weather was getting cold, and they were subject to great discomfort, of which they complained in no uncertain terms.

The members of the Convention, however, were not the only people in Fishkill subject to serious discomfort during this trying period. The soldiers suffered great hardships, and at one time clothing became so scarce in the Highlands that "a building was erected at Fishkill as a retreat for naked men. The soldiers had patched their clothes until patches and clothing both gave out and the garments dropped from their bodies," and the soldiers were sent to this refuge to save them embarrassment and avoid outrage to the sensibilities of the towns-people.

XXVII.
TELLER HOMESTEAD
FISHKILL

IN 1654, Francis Rombout, a Huguenot, born in the town of Hasselt in Flanders, sailed as a supercargo on a ship bound for New Netherland. A mere lad at the time, after discharging faithfully the responsible duties of his post, he was obliged to sue the captain for his wages. That he did so was indicative of the traits of character he subsequently displayed—energy, determination, and love of justice.

TELLER HOUSE, NORTH FRONT, FISHKILL LANDING (BEACON)

As a merchant trader he soon rose to a prosperous position, acquired a valuable property on what is now Broadway, and there built himself a substantial stone house, surrounded by an orchard and garden. In this house he placed such furniture as he had brought overseas with him, including a beautiful Dutch *kas* of ebony and rosewood, still carefully treasured by his descendants. He was evidently a man of taste, as well as an energetic merchant and man of affairs in the Colony, for he is said to have imported for his own satisfaction the first table linen ever used in America.

One important responsibility in the life of an enterprising colonist he did not neglect—matrimony. He entered into that "holy estate" early in life and may, in fact, be said to have continued a "persevering bridegroom."After the death of his first spouse, Aeltje Wessels, to whom he was wed in 1665, he married Anna Maschop, widow of Warnart Wessels, in 1675. Becoming a widower a second time, he made a third matrimonial venture in 1683 with Helena Teller Van Ball. She was his third wife, and he was her third husband!

Other matters than matrimony, however, had occupied Francis Rombout between 1665 and 1683. Besides diligently managing his mercantile interests, he was an active member and an elder in the Dutch Reformed Church, and found time to serve the city in sundry public offices—as Schepen under Dutch rule, and afterwards under English rule as Alderman. At the Dutch recapture of New York he was continued in office and, in 1679, after the English power had been restored again, he was Mayor, succeeding Stephanus Van Cortlandt in that post of honour.

As early as 1667 Rombout was associated in business with Gulian Verplanck, and in 1682 they jointly filed a petition for a grant of land and permission to purchase from the Indians the fertile tract on the east bank of the Hudson extending from Fishkill almost to Poughkeepsie, later known as the Rombout Precinct or Patent. This transaction, be it said, like most of the Dutch dealings with the Red Men, was peaceably and honestly carried out. It is told that Rombout bargained with the Indians for "all the land that he could see," which being agreed to, he thereupon climbed to the top of Mount Beacon in order to extend his outlook. Tradition also has it that during the negotiations the future Patentees sate at one side of a table while the Wappinger chiefs sate opposite. A round sum of Royalls—a Royal was equal to an half sovereign—was placed on the board as the purchase price, and this the

Indians repeatedly pushed back, saying "More, More," until the bargain was adjusted to their satisfaction. After this, the deed of sale, bearing date of record 1683, was duly drawn, executed and witnessed.

The licence for the Rombout Patent was granted by that genial bachelor, Governour Dongan, in 1682; the purchase was consummated in 1683; and in 1685, soon after the accession of King James the Second, came the confirmation or exemplification of the grant, about the same time that the Patroonship of Rensselaerwyck was constituted a Manor, and the Manor of Livingston erected. Prior to the exemplification Gulian Verplanck had died and his widow had married Jacobus Kipp, who was substituted as representative for the interests of Verplanck's children. Stephanus Van Cortlandt had also been admitted to a third share in the purchase. The exemplification was, therefore, issued in the names of Rombout, Kipp and Van Cortlandt.

By his third wife, Helena Teller Van Ball—daughter of William Teller, one of the four original Patentees of Schenectady—Francis Rombout had a daughter Catheryna, born in 1687, to whom he willed his house in Broadway and "his land in the Wappins," that is to say, his third share in the Rombout Patent or Precinct. Catheryna, destined to become famous as a colonial dame of pre-eminent character and pioneer achievement, in November, 1703, married Roger Brett, of Somersetshire, a young Lieutenant in the British Navy who had accompanied his friend, Lord Cornbury, when Queen Anne sent out that eccentric cousin of hers to be Governour of the Province of New York.

Determined to live in the country and develope her land in the Rombout Patent, Madame Brett and her husband, in the summer of 1708, mortgaged their city house "situated on the Broadway which leads from the English Church down to the Fort Anne, upon the west side of Broadway, for 240 pounds current money." In 1707 the Rombout Patent had been partitioned into "three long, narrow parcels, each containing a stretch of river front, and water privileges by adjointure to the two creeks, the Fish Kill and Wappingers. Lot Number One, in the drawing, fell to Madame Brett and her husband, while the Verplanck heirs obtained Lot Number Two, just to the north of them, on the river and on

Wappingers Creek "in the Middle"; the third or northernmost Lot, on the river and the upper part of Wappingers Creek, going to the Van Cortlandt heirs.

Roger Brett and Catheryna, his wife, by this division, found themselves possessed of the fertile valley of the Fish Kill, a broad stretch along the river, and "the north side of Wappingers Creek from its mouth to beyond the present site of Wappingers Falls." On the banks of the Fish Kill, which gave them a valuable water power, they built a mill and a dwelling, presumably with the proceeds of the mortgage raised upon the town house. The following year, April 9th., 1709, "Roger Brett of the Fishkills in the County of Dutchess, Gentleman, and Catheryna, his wife, sole daughter and heir of Francis Rumbout, late of the City of New York, deceased, conveyed to Wm. Peartrie, merchant of the said city, "all that Messuage or tenement and 300 acres of land adjoining, situated in Dutchess County, on the east side of Hudson's river, just above the highlands, and also that Grist Mill standing near said tenement, all of which being on the north side of a certain creek, called the Fishkill." It was then, in 1709, upon the sale of the mill and mill house, that the Bretts built the homestead that forms the subject of our enquiry.

It was staunchly framed of immense hand-hewn timbers, one storey and an half in height, with long, slanting dormers, of characteristic Dutch type, emerging from the slope of the roof. Outside, the walls were covered with long, red cedar shingles, their weather-ends cut in scallops, which impart a curious and unusual aspect to the structure. The kitchen wing, though of early date, is somewhat later than the body of the house. Entirely devoid of any architectural pretension, its naïve simplicity, its just proportions, and its ingenuous, homelike mien, nevertheless combine to produce a charm to which few can be insensible.

Since the house was built, many changes have taken place inside, but, for the most part, they have been only such as were needful to meet the growing demands of a large family and ensure comfort. All have been carried out with due regard for the character of the old house, and no violence has been done the spirit of its design. In the kitchen wing is a curious little room where the ladies of the family were wont to compound those mysterious delicacies that form a delightful part of the tradition of homes that have passed from generation to generation in uninterrupted sequence. The northwest room, that is now the library, was at one time the spinning room.

After selling the mill and the mill house, Madame Brett exercised a woman's privilege of changing her mind, and the next year she bought them back along with the land pertaining to them. From then until 1743, when she sold the mill property to her kinsman, Abraham de Peyster, she managed the enterprise with energy and success, and for many years the people of Dutchess and Orange Counties "depended solely upon this mill for their daily bread." A local historian, writing in the *Fishkill Standard*, says:

"Madame Brett's mill was the central point where the roads from the interior converged on their way to the river. They ran to this place from Hackensack, from Wappingers, and from Wiccopee, formed by grading, widening and bridging the Indian trail into a waggon road. The Indians, after the sale of their lands, had retired beyond Fishkill plains, where they had a village of huts made of stakes overlaid with bark, with a castle consisting of a square, surrounded with palisades, used as an asylum for the old men, women and children, when they went out hunting or on warlike expeditions. At the request of the chiefs, with whom Madame Brett was a great favourite, she visited them in their villages. Until they removed over the mountains and joined the Mohegan nation, of which they were a tribe, they were in the habit of coming down to the mill with corn, beans and peltries to exchange for meal, and for years afterwards their young men crossed the mountain and continued their visits, to shoot pennies from between a split stick with their bow and arrow, at a distance of twelve or fourteen yards, which they would strike nineteen times out of twenty, much to the amusement of persons waiting for their grists."

One might very appropriately have made a local variation of the old adage, "All roads lead to Rome," by saying, "All roads lead to Madame Brett's Mill." Far and wide it was customary to quote distances and directions, "From Hackensack to Madame Brett's Mill," "From Wiccopee to Madame Brett's Mill," and so on, as roads grew more numerous. An old resident of Orange

County, across the river, was responsible for the following bit of graphic description:

> "The neighbours and settlers for miles would come with a bag of grain securely fastened upon the back of an horse. When they had all arrived the horses were tied to each other's tails and, mounting the foremost one, he wended his way to the river. With an Indian canoe he would carry over the grain and when ground, return home again in the same fashion."

Lieutenant and Madame Brett had three sons, Francis, Robert and Rivery, the last so named because he was born on the Hudson River when his parents were coming home from New York in their sloop. In 1726 Lieutenant Brett met a tragic death. Returning from New York in his sloop, he was knocked overboard by the boom, just as he was entering the month of the Fish Kill. Thence onward, all the burden of developing and administering a large estate fell upon the shoulders of Madame Brett, aided only by her sons. She was fully equal to the task, however. In addition to her other sterling qualities, she possessed clear-headedness, business acumen, and indomitable energy. She is said to have galloped daily on horseback over her lands, directing her slaves and superintending her varied affairs. Being a woman of peculiarly dynamic character, she was a veritable power in the development of the whole region round about and left impress of her personality in many quarters.

Activity and locomotion seem inseparable from the story of her life. We find her not only journeying back and forth to New York by sloop and making the rounds of her estate in the saddle, but, in 1710, when the first place of worship was established in the neighbourhood—the Lutheran church of the German Palatines who had settled at Newburgh—she was accustomed on Sundays to cross the river in a canoe to attend service. Madame Brett's progresses, however, were often made in a manner fully befitting a lady of quality. In his *Local Tales and Sketches*, Mr. H. D. B. Bailey describes her arrival at the wedding of the Dutch pastor who served the two congregations of Fishkill and Poughkeepsie:

> "As the hour of twelve drew near, the excitement became intense and what added more to the enthusiasm was the appearance of

Madame Brett, in her coach drawn by four horses, coming down Main Street [Poughkeepsie] with two negroes on the front seat and one on the rear of the coach, whose business was to open the door."

When the Dutch Reformed Church of Fishkill was founded, Madame Brett was a substantial benefactress. One of her benefactions was a gift of "225 pounds lawful currency," which was known as "Mistress Brett's legacy." Prior to her death, in 1764, she devised her property to her son, Francis, and the children of her son, Robert, predeceased—Rivery had died in early life—and in that part of her will touching the slaves, she left to her son Robert's children "the wench called Coban, and if sold she to have the liberty of Chusing her own master. I also order that if my wench Molly [whom she had willed to her son Francis] should be sold that she have the liberty of Chusing her own Master with whom she will live."

Besides those qualities that rendered her a potent force for good in the upbuilding of a new land, Madame Brett possessed a gentle, gracious and affectionate as well as a strong character so that all who came within the radius of her influence, even utter strangers, were sensible of the rare charm attaching to her presence. Her passing was the occasion of sincere mourning far beyond the circle of her immediate family and kin. Unusual executive capacity and the ability to manage successfully a wide diversity of interests, quite outside the domestic sphere, did not lessen her devotion to her home and its duties nor obscure her distinctly feminine graces; she was a shining example from whom some of the modern feminists might take pattern to their profit and the improvement of their manners.

Francis Brett and his wife, Catherine Margaret Van Wyck, with their eight children, continued to occupy the homestead and, in due time, their daughter Hannah married Henry Schenck, who became a major in the Continental Army and played an active part in the War for Independence. While he held the post of Quartermaster for the troops, the ample cellar of the house was stored with rations for the soldiers and, on one occasion, a detachment of exhausted men was ranged in rows on the floor of the east room to sleep off their fatigue. In 1791 Major Schenck was a

Member of the Assembly and up to the time of his death, in 1799, he fulfilled the duties of a useful and public-spirited citizen.

General Washington and Abraham Yates, while presiding at the Fishkill Convention, were entertained by the Major and Mrs. Schenck and later, when the Commander-in-Chief had his head-quarters at Newburgh, he was a welcome guest at Locust Grove. The Marquis de la Fayette likewise experienced the hospitality of the Schenck household, as did also Baron von Steuben, who had his headquarters at Mount Gulian, not far distant.

In 1790 Alice Schenck became the bride of Isaac de Peyster Teller and began housekeeping in the old mill house at the mouth of the creek, where she continued to live till her father, Major Schenck, died. Mr. Teller then bought the homestead from the "doweress," as Madame Schenck was called, who thereafter made her home with her daughter and son-in-law. Mr. Teller, "with the genius of wise farming, developed the property until it became locally renowne d for its grain and other farm products." The economic system of slave labour, however, apparently did not wholly commend itself to him, if we may judge from the following anecdote.

On one occasion, when the old Dutch Dominie came to call, Mr. Teller was just setting forth on his accustomed rounds of the farm and took the Dominie along with him. As they were returning to the house the Dominie, much impressed by what he had seen, said, "Mr. Teller, you must be a very rich man."

"No, Dominie," said Mr. Teller. "I'm not. I'm a poor man."

"But, Mr. Teller, with all these acres of corn land, all these fine, fat swine, and all these negro slaves, how can you be poor! "

"That's just it, Dominie. I'm a poor man."

"But I don't understand."

"Well, Dominie, it's this way. The hogs eat up all the corn, and the damned niggers eat up all the hogs! "

The Honourable Isaac Teller, as a member of Congress and a country squire, was highly esteemed and beloved. Kindly and generous by nature, he allowed the poor people on his mountain lands many privileges, and to this day their grateful descendants will tell you "he never charged us nothin' for wood, and he'd pay us money for the cuttin' of it."

Prior to this time there was no Church of England place of worship nearer than Fishkill Village and Miss Hannah Teller, aided by her sisters, established a mission in the "long room"—the dining-room—of the homestead. In order to procure a clergyman, Mr. Teller was in the habit, in winter, of driving back and forth on the ice to West Point to get the Reverend Mr. Hackley, then Chaplain of the Post. Later on, as the mission grew, a corner of the orchard was given for the purpose and a chapel erected. The mission was put in charge of the Reverend Robert Boyd Van Kleeck, the son of Doctor Baltus Livingston Van Kleeck, of Newburgh. This young parson found a wife in Miss Margaret Teller.

The Honourable Isaac Teller, through his associations in Washington City, had become a great admirer of Henry Clay and had a favourite old white horse which he named after the Southern statesman. In a buggy drawn by Henry Clay, Mr. Teller habitually made the circuit of his farm land. One day the horse stood so long quietly grazing at the edge of a grain field that "a farm hand came to see why the master tarried." Death had silently carried away one more link with the Colonial past.

So attached were they to the old home and its life that the remaining daughters and one son continued to live together and never married. Mr. and Mrs. Van Kleeck, after the former had grown old in the service of the Church elsewhere, came back to Locust Grove and made their home there, too. In time, one of the daughters, who had married the Reverend Robert Fulton Crary, the eldest grandson of Robert Fulton, came into possession of "Teller's Villa" and their children now live in this cherished home, built in what was then the wilderness by their revered ancestress, that notable Colonial dame, Madame Brett, whose presence still pervades the place.

A thousand memories cling about this abode of seven generations, hallowing it to its occupants and, to the world outside, yielding a faithful mental picture of the wholesome sort of life lived by those who made the thew and sinew of the country in its infancy. In houses like this, history was a-making, in an homely, quiet way, it is true, but no less surely than in those dwellings closely associated with more stirring and dramatic episodes. After all, we can easily err in setting too much store by the "trumpet and drum" events and ignoring the less spectacular, intimate features of the background.

If we would truly understand the countryside story in its entirety, and grasp its full spirit, it is meet that we foster a sensitive appreciation of the more delicate values as well as an appetite for martial heroics or the brilliance of social gaieties. The lavender and rose leaves of memory—the Canton jar on the "back pantry" shelf, with its perennial supply of fragrant-scented ginger-nuts; "Harry Clay," in the serene comfort of old age, jogging along country roads with a load of happy-hearted children behind him, ere that day when his faithful body was laid away in the glen; the youthful thrills of driving home the cows from distant pastures, on late summer afternoons; feeding the chickens from blue India plates, or sitting again round the fireside to munch red-cheeked apples in the light of the dying embers—all these things it is just as necessary to heed, for the truthful completeness of the picture, as it is, at other times, to fix our minds on some brave pageant, or catch the din and triumph of some hard-fought field.

XXVIII.

MOUNT GULIAN

FISHKILL LANDING (BEACON)

"K NOW YEE—that for and in consideracon of a Certain
Sume or Quantity of Money, Wampum, and divers other
Goods in a Schedull hereunto Annexed Perticularly
Menconed and Expressed to them the said Indians, in Hand Payed
by Mr. ffrancis Rumbouts and Gulyne Ver Planke, both of the
Citty of New Yorke, Merchants, the Receipt whereof they, the said
Indians Doe hereby Acknowledge, and therewith ownes them-
selves to be fully payed, Contented and Sattisfied, and thereof
and of every Parte and Parcell Doe hereby Acqnitt, Exonerate and
Discharge them, the said ffrancis Rumbouts and Gulyne V. Planke,
their Heirs and Assignes, have Given, Granted, Bargained, Sold,
Aliened, Enfeoffd, and Confirmed, and by these Presents Doe
Confirme unto the said ffrancis Rumbout and Gulyne Ver Planke,
All that Tract or Parcell of Land Scituate, Lyeing and being on
the East side of Hudson's River, at the north side of the High
Lands, Beginning from the South side of A Creek Called the fresh
Kill, and by the Indians Matteawan, and from thence Northward
along the said Hudson's River five hundd Rodd bejond the Great
Wappins Kill, called by the Indians Mawenawasigh, being the
Northerly Bounds, and from thence into the Woods fouer Houers
goeing, always keeping five hundd Rodd Distant from the North
side of said Wappinges Creeke, however it Runns, as alsoe from
the said fresh Kill or Creeke called Matteawan, along the said
fresh Creeke into the Woods att the foot of the said High Hills,
including all the Reed or Low Lands at the South side of the said
Creeke, with an Easterly Line fouer Houers going into the Woods,
and from thence Northerly to the end of fouer Houers goeing or
Line Drawne att the North side of the five hundd Rodd Bejoyand
the Greate Wappinger Creeke or Kill called Mawenawasigh,
together with all the Lands, Soyles, Meadows, both fresh and
Salt Pastures, Commons, Wood Land, Marshes, Rivers, Rivoletts,

Streams, Creekes, Waters, Lakes, and whatsoever else to the said Tract or Parcell of Land within the Bounds and Limitts aforesaid is Belonging, or any wise Appurteining, without any Reservacon of Herbage, Trees, or any other thing Growing or Being thereupon, To have and to hold the said Tract or Parcell of Land, Meadow, Ground, and Primisses, with their and every of their Appurtennces, and all the Estate, Right, Title, Interest, Clayme, and Demand of them the said Indian Proprietors, and each and every one of them, of, in, and to, the same, and Every Parte thereof, unto them the said ffrancis Rumbout and Gulyne Ver Planke, their Heires and Assignee, to the Sole and only Proper use, Benefitt and Behoofe of them, the said ffrancis Rumbout and Gulyne Ver Planke, *their* Heires and Assignes for Ever."

**MOUNT GULIAN, WEST FRONT,
FISHKILL LANDING (BEACON)**

New York Public Library Digital Collections

So ran the substance of the old deed of sale for the Rombout Patent, to which reference has already been made in the account of the Teller Homestead. It was dated the 14th. of August, 1683. The "fouer Houers Going" meant sixteen English miles, the person or persons walking off the bounds of the purchase being expected to walk at the rate of four miles an hour—a pretty stiff pace considering the untamed character of the country to be traversed. This sale by the Indians, afterward confirmed by royal letters patent, issued by the Governour of the Province, was the foundation of the estate of the Verplanck family on the shores of the Hudson. In the history of the Teller Homestead, a little to the south of Mount Gulian, we have seen how the original purchase was divided between the Verplanck heirs, Madame Brett and Stephanus Van Cortlandt.

The third part of the Rombout Patent or Precinct falling to the lot of the Verplanck family was somewhat later in its development than Madame Brett's portion. It was not until 1730 that another Gulian Verplanck, a descendant of Gulian or Gulyne the Patentee, came into possession of the estate on which the house whose history we are now considering was built. There is no date visible on the gable end or elsewhere, as there is so often on dwellings of the period, so that it is impossible to name the exact year in which Mount Gulian was erected. It is possible, of course, that there may have been a date on the north gable, but if there was, it was covered up when the addition was built in 1804. In all likelihood, however, Gulian Verplanck built Mount Gulian somewhere about 1735. The architectural features of the older portion of the house lend plausible colour to this conjecture and there are also other circumstances tending to confirm it.

Gulian Verplanck died on the 11th. of November, 1751, "at 3 o'clock in the morning very suddenly." In his will, one clause reads:

> "I give, devise and bequeath to my son Samuel and his heirs forever All that my farm in dutchess County called Mount Gulian, with all the Buildings thereon erected and all and every the slaves, stock, household furniture, farming utensils, etc."

From this it is quite evident that there was a well-appointed dwelling and farm at Mount Gulian and that it was a place occupied by the owner as a residence for himself and his family, at least during a portion of the year. The mention of "slaves, stock, household furniture, farming utensils, etc.," shews that Mount Gulian was not a place let out to a tenant farmer. If it had been merely a tenant farm, as some contend, none of these items would have been there. As Gulian Verplanck was married on the 8th.

of September, 1737, it seems highly probable that he built his country house either just before or just after that important event in his life. It is said that the dwelling was constructed largely by the labour of his own slaves. Whether that be true or not, whoever planned and superintended the structure succeeded in producing a building of dignified aspect, eminently homelike and comfortable character, and thoroughly representative of the Dutch domestic style that obtained at that period along the shores of the Hudson and in the Dutch parts of North Jersey.

The gambrel roof, flaring outward bell-wise at the foot of the lower pitch to form the roof of the verandah, on both the east and west fronts, is one of the best examples of this manner of construction anywhere to be found. It is peculiarly graceful in its lines, and the curve of the outward flare at the eaves is extremely subtle, as those who have attempted to reproduce it in modern dwellings have found. The higher portion at the north end, was added by Daniel Crommelin Verplanck in 1804 when it became necessary to enlarge the original homestead. The rooms in the old portion are spacious and comfortable but unpretentious in their general character. In the new part, on the other hand, there is a most urbane ball room exactly copied after the state dining room at the White House in Washington. To the east of this ball room is the present dining room which was, however, a bedroom at one time. It was occupied as such by the Marquis de la Fayette, when he visited Mount Gulian in 1824, and in memory of that event has since been known as the La Fayette room. To the north of this is the kitchen. The entrance is on the east front of the old house and admits one to a wide stair hall running through to the west. To the right is a broad hall, really a long room in its proportions and in the manner of its use, giving access to the Cincinnati room and also to the 1804 enlargement. In the Cincinnati room the original beamed ceiling has been laid bare, after a long period in which it was covered up with lath and plaster, and is now the same as it was when the Society of the Cincinnati was organised there. The upper floor, although from the outside apparently of limited proportions, is in reality amazingly capacious after the manner of the old Dutch houses.

Samuel Verplanck, to whom Mount Gulian was left by the will of his father, Gulian, as previously mentioned, married Judith Crommelin. Their town house was in Wall street, beside the old City Hall, afterwards turned over to the Federal Government and called Federal Hall, where Washington was inaugurated at the beginning of his first term. This building was later used as the United States Treasury. There are numerous old prints of Federal Hall shewing a portion of the Verplanck house with the family coach standing before the door. It is interesting to note that this was in the days when an exact municipal record was kept of all the families who maintained coaches.

During the Revolutionary War, when New York City was occupied by the British forces, Lord Howe was often entertained by Judith Verplanck at the house in Wall street and, as souvenirs of this episode in the life of their forebear, there are still preserved the tea set and some paintings by Angelica Kauffmann that Lord Howe gave his hostess to remember him by. Whilst Samuel and Judith Verplanck were living in their town house, for at least a part of the war period, Mount Gulian was occupied by General Baron von Steuben as his headquarters. It has been said that Samuel Verplanck was a Loyalist, but too good care was taken of Mount Gulian to make this seem at all likely, and, besides, there are no recorded proceedings against him under the Act of Forfeiture, as there almost certainly would have been if he had openly maintained his allegiance to the British Crown.

Whilst Baron von Steuben was at Mount Gulian it was an easy matter for him to cross the river to New Windsor or to Newburgh, when General Washington had his headquarters at those places, and easier still for him to supervise the tactical and disciplinary training of the American troops quartered in the vicinity of Fishkill. The record of some of the genial baron's visits to the Newburgh headquarters will be found in the account of the Hasbrouck house. It was doubtless from Mount Gulian that he set out with his aides in the torrid midsummer weather to go a-whale-hunting on the Hudson, an adventure of no small discomfort to the worthy gentleman.

Of all the memories connected with Mount Gulian the most notable is the institution of the Society of the Cincinnati. Within these walls, in the room on the ground floor, whose windows overlook the Hudson, now known as the Cincinnati Boom, on Tuesday, the 13th. of May, 1783, was organised this famous society which has been perpetuated ever since, despite periods of opposition and indifference.

"The first suggestion of the organisation into a society of the officers of the American Army of the Revolution appears in a paper, in the handwriting of General Knox, entitled 'Rough Draft of a Society to be formed by the American Officers, and to be called the Cincinnati.' " It is dated West Point, the 15th. of April, 1783.

"This paper, circulated among the officers of the army, then lying on the banks of the Hudson, in the neighbourhood of Newburgh (in the State of New York), is understood to be referred to in the preamble of the institution of the 'Society of the Cincinnati' as the 'proposals' which had been "communicated to the several regiments of the respective lines.' " It is printed as reported by the committee to which the proposals were referred, and as adopted May 13th. 1783.

"The original paper of General Knox, and the Institution as adopted, both aimed at some bond which would still unite those who for long years had shared the hardships of the camp and the dangers of many a battle field, now about to separate, many of them penniless, to find homes ruined, and families dispersed or dead . . . . They wished that their children should inherit and maintain the friendships which had bound them together. . . ."

As specifically set forth, in the wording of the Institution as adopted at Mount Gulian, the object of the Society was perfectly unmistakable, and the intent was obviously of a beneficent and patriotic character. Surely no society could be more benevolent and harmless in the intent of its organisation, and yet carping critics at the time found in its avowed objects—or what they imagined to be its avowed objects—sufficient ground for all manner of dark suspicions which they assiduously circulated until a very storm of vituperative abuse and acrimonious opposition broke loose. Truly, "jealousy imagines dangers and magnifies objects of its own creation. And those who had no words of censure, but all of praise and encouragement for the officers and soldiers of the army, so long as they stood between themselves and a power-ful enemy, not only forgot their promises, but became profuse in censure and in denunciation so soon as peace was ensured and the British forces were withdrawn."

The society had had the temerity to incorporate the principle of the descent of their dignities to the "oldest male heir." This was heinous and dastardly, in the eyes of the narrow-minded cav-illers, and apparently, also, provoked disapproval on the part of those whose unquestionable ability and judgement should have dictated different behaviour. The opposition, in its extreme viru-lence, came not so much from the "common people," or the fam-ilies of the file of the army, "who might have cherished hopes of impossible social equality, but from many civilians of the highest attainments, culture, refinement and position."

A Justice of the Supreme Court of South Carolina seems to have been the first to detect the lurking wickedness, profligacy and dangerous tendencies inherent in the Society, but was by no means the last. Count Mirabeau issued a pamphlet "predicting dire calamities that were about to befall America if the Society should be permitted to exist." Thomas Jefferson discovered in the organisation a spirit hostile to "the natural equality of man "— that fatuous will-o'-the-wisp of doctrinaire politics in which he had persuaded himself he believed—and he also detected therein "the germ whose development is one day to destroy the fabric we have reared." Samuel Adams wrote, in May, 1784—"This is as rapid a stride towards an hereditary military nobility as ever was made." To his watchful and suspicious mind the association presented "an odious hereditary distinction of families," "a plan disgustful to the American feelings." Considering the source of these latter vituperations, however, little else was to be expected; indeed, a more pyrotechnical display of splenetic rancour would not have been surprising.

Even as late as the 25th. of April, 1785, John Adams, whose good common-sense was usually in evidence, wrote:— "What is to be done with the Cincinnati! Is that order of chivalry, inroad upon equality, to be connived at! It is the deepest piece of cunning yet attempted; it is sowing the seeds of all that European Courts wish to grow up amongst us, viz., of vanity, ambition, corruption, discord and sedition." Nor was so fair-minded a person as John Jay free from the misconception that attended the institution of an Order that he thought "will eventually divide us into two mighty factions." "With characteristic honesty and consistency," in reply to a suggestion that he should become an honorary member of the Society, he said that "he was neither young enough nor old enough to desire that honour," and declared that if the Society obtained permanent foothold, he would cease to care whether the Revolution had succeeded or not. Benjamin Franklin railed at " an order of hereditary knights," and howled disapproval at those who "violate the united wisdom of our nation by establishing ranks of nobility, " but after pouring ridicule upon the "Chevaliers of Cincinnatus," and damning them for flaunting rank, privilege and primogeniture in the face of democracy, he subsequently accepted an honorary membership in the Society.

It is both interesting and amusing now to look back upon all this pother stirred up over the organisation of a society whose objects and principles were so manifestly harmless and amongst whose founders were numbered such men as Washington, General Knox, and Alexander Hamilton, not to mention a long list of others, whose honesty and probity of intention should have been above all suspicion and whose names alone should have been accepted as sufficient guaranty of the propriety of any movement with which they were associated.

After the declaration of peace and the restoration of established order, Samuel and Judith Verplanck returned to the occupancy of Mount Gulian and the setting of the place in order. Although the house itself had sustained no injury, there were many claims to be adjusted with reference to the farm, especially in the matter of getting compensation for the timber that had been cut. Eventually the place was got back to its old wonted aspect of peace and order and homelike comfort, and family life there resumed its accustomed placid routine.

In due time, Daniel Crommelin Verplanck, the son of Samuel and Judith Verplanck, inherited Mount Gulian. When he lived there he was a member of Congress and also Judge of the County. He kept open house, summer and winter, and the holidays were marked by the advent of hosts of visitors in whose minds the lavish hospitality dispensed left an impression never to be erased.

The old house was filled with beautiful furniture, fine paintings and other objects of elegance, many of which had been brought from Holland by the Judge's mother, Judith Crommelin. The Judge himself was a great collector of silver.

He was also a good judge of wine, and "as the fashion of that time was to drink Madeira, he imported in 1804, through his brother-in-law, James DeLancey Walton, a large quantity of that wine. It was the custom of Madeira to make several voyages before being taken from the vessel, for it was thought the quality was thereby improved. When the wine was finally bottled it was generally labelled with the name of the vessel in which it was imported." Some of the Judge's importation is still in existence— or *was*, only a few years ago—and in fair condition. It ought to be added that in latter years its use was for *weddings only*. Such things are far too precious for ordinary consumption.

From an old letter comes a vivid word picture of a Christmastide gathering, with its plentiful good cheer, beneath the hospitable roof-tree of Mount Gulian.

"I sate," says the writer, "on the right of the Judge, in front of whom was, a large saddle of venison, the finest I ever saw; opposite was a turkey, boiled with [word illegible], in the finest style. Partridges Rabbits, Geese, Ducks, Chickens, Brants, Chicken Pie, Oysters indeed every variety that could be desired. The dinner passed off very pleasantly and the dessert still more so, Pies, Puddings, Jellies, Fruits, and all kinds of wines, etc. We arose from the table at about eight o'clock . . . having sate down at five. . . . The ladies retired and the gentlemen closed around the fire and discussed the merits of a bottle of Skuppernong (wine made in South Carolina). It was said by Mr. Y. (the young gentleman who brought it) to be very fine for the kind, but the Judge and company thought it better to make Whiskey Punch of than to drink. About 9 we went into the drawing room and took coffee with the ladies, who were still more agreeable."

Before starting on the homeward drive, the parting guests were cheered and warmed with something more to drink by way of a stirrup cup. This was in 1826, before people had altogether forgotten the art and joy of living.

The Mount Gulian family were all much attached to the river and made constant use of it in summer as a source of unfailing pleasure. Besides row and sail boats, they kept "an oared barge which seated ten besides the oarsmen. In this boat they made visits to their friends along the river, even going to West Point, ten miles below, to attend balls and other entertainments there."

Daniel Crommelin Verplanck and his daughter Mary Anna were devoted to the art of gardening and they themselves laid out the gardens and grounds immediately about the place. Many of the box hushes, trees and shrubs they planted are still flourishing. It is one of the traditions of Mount Gulian that Daniel Crommelin planted all the streams in the neighbourhood with watercress, by seed brought from Washington when he was a member of Congress. James Brown, the black gardener, was one of the institutions of Mount Gulian. He was a runaway slave from Maryland, but Mr. Verplanck afterwards purchased his freedom from his former master. He presided over the garden from 1829 until 1864, when he died "full of years and honours." He had learned to read and write and during all this period he kept a diary in which it was his pleasure to note down the names of all the visitors to Mount Gulian and his comments upon them. This diary grew to the bulk of seven volumes.

For many, many years till the old customs were maintained at Mount Gulian, including the three o'clock dinner hour. For the retention of time-honoured usages and manners no more appropriate setting could be imagined than Mount Gulian with its rich store of domestic and historic memories. In conclusion we cannot do better than give the recollections of a lady whose happy childhood holidays were passed at the old house by the river. Her account of holiday life at Mount Gulian is valuable not only for the glimpse of child life at the period of which she writes, hut also for its depiction of the spirit that brooded over the home reared by Gulian Verplanck in the first half of the eighteenth century on his share of the lands in the Rombout Precinct, the old map of which now hangs in the library.

"I remember well the eager looking forward to the day and the drive to the homestead in our great Noah's Ark of a sleigh, which had a hood over the back seat with long green curtains looped back, which in case of a storm were let down while we children crowded in behind our parents, where there was ample room for a row of little folks to stand up. Arrived at the house, we took off our wraps in the room opposite the nursery, amidst an excited interchange of greetings. After the elders had gone down stairs, and our dinner had been served on a long, low table in the nursery, we amused ourselves in various ways till it was time to go to the dining room for dessert. Very often the principal amusement was the acting of improvised plays by the older children, while the younger ones, as spectators, were perched in the deep dormer windows or huddled in the two tent bedsteads which, with their long curtains, made admirable boxes. These plays, however, were oftener on the occasion of other family gatherings for children, for on Christmas day we were in a state of too excited expectation for anything but desultory amusements interspersed at intervals by an excited rush down the stairs singing: 'Christmas comes but once a year,' while the bolder ones pounded on the dining-room door, demanding admittance. It was great fun in the meantime to watch the dishes as they came from the table, among them the traditional Boar's head, with celery for tusks.

"After dinner, Mrs. William S. Ver Planck and her sisters mysteriously disappeared and we knew they were lighting the tree and that the crowning event of the day was soon to come.

"It is hard to realise in these days, when Christmas trees have become so universal and commonplace, how great was the interest of this homestead tree to the little band of children. So far as I know, it was unique at the time; at all events there could have been but very few in the country. We were far too excited to stay quietly with the grown people in the little drawing room as it was called (the Cincinnati room), which was all aglow with a bright wood fire and candle-light and adorned for Christmas, as indeed was all the house, with the trailing mountain pine over doors and pictures, with wreaths of laurel and the berries of the bitter-sweet in various places. These were brought to the house by the 'Mountaineers' a people who seemed almost like a separate race, and are now nearly extinct. They lived in huts of stone rudely piled together, or caves dug in the earth. They drank, ate opium, and supported themselves by basket making and begging, patronising the old families by taking their 'cold victuals,' and confidently expecting sympathy and aid in time of want, as for instance when a woman told Miss Ver Planck that her daughter 'had a spine in her back.'

Some of these people were always haunting the homestead, and years afterwards, when I went to see one old 'Meg Merilies' of a woman in her last days, it delighted her to talk of Miss Ver Planck and the old times. They were proud in their way, and had always the manner of conferring a favour by their visits. This is a long digression, while the children are romping out in the large unheated halls (furnaces were not thought of then) till the door of the large drawing-room was opened and the Christmas tree burst on our sight. It was lighted with little wax candles, as the modern trees are, but there were none of the stereotyped ornaments of tinsel and glitter. There were lady apples on the trees, and oranges, cornucopias and toys and the sugar plums. The tree was always of laurel, reaching nearly to the ceiling and yet it looked small in that great room, where a wood fire, blazing at one end, seemed to accentuate the cold of the remaining space, and the little girls with their bare necks and arms, and the boys with their bare legs, shivered as they danced about in glee and did not know they were cold.

"I wish I could give you any idea of our kind hosts, all of whom have passed away, and indeed, of the elder generation assembled at those Christmas parties, only my mother is living, and Miss Margaret Newlin, who seems rather to belong among the younger ones.

"Miss Harrison always danced the Spanish dance for our entertainment, the delighted applause inciting her to deeper courtesies and more elaborate swayings of her arms and figure.

"The Christmas tree was more expressly Mr. Ver Planck's treat to the children, but Miss Ver Planck very often invited us all to spend the day and always on Easter Monday, when eggs of every hue and shade made their appearance after dessert and were cracked to see who could win the most. On these occasions we wandered over the house from garret to cellar, made ourselves at home in the kitchen, and hunted upstairs and read from the bookcases which were all over the house as well as in the library."

XXIX.

CLEAR EVERITT HOUSE

POUGHKEEPSIE

BUILT *circa* 1770

THE Clear Everitt house, built of grey stone, and shewing an interesting blending of the local Dutch Colonial manner with certain Classic amenities of the Georgian mode—as the illustration indicates—stands on Poughkeepsie's chief thoroughfare. Fortunately, it is under the protection of the Daughters of the American Revolution, so that its destruction need not be feared.

CLEAR EVERITT HOUSE, POUGHKEEPSIE

The house, it seems, was built somewhere about the year 1770, though whether Clear Everitt, the former sheriff of the county, built it, or whether his brother Richard built it is not clear. Richard Everitt was a Loyalist. Whether Clear Everitt was a Loyalist, also, is not definitely known. He may not have been an open supporter of the King, but it seems highly probable that his sympathies were on the side of the Crown. There were a great many Loyalists in the county, men of humble station as well as men of substance and position, and consequently Poughkeepsie was a veritable hotbed of contention, especially after the State Legislature and the Governour took up their quarters there after the flight from Kingston and the brief sojourn at Old Hurley.

The Loyalists or "Friends of Constitutional Liberty," as they styled themselves, had the law and, at first, the General Assembly on their side, and they saw no reason for all the bluster over relatively small matters of taxation. They had no intention of binding themselves not to buy tea or other taxed articles brought over in British ships. A number of the Loyalists, indeed, held a meeting on the 15th. of January, 1775, and entered into an association, declaring:

> "That we will upon all occasions mutually support each other in the free exercise and enjoyment of our undoubted right to liberty in eating, drinking, buying, selling, communing and acting what, with whom and as we please, consistent with the laws of God, and the laws of the land, notwithstanding the Association entered into by the Continental Congress to the contrary." They further declared that "our Sovereign Lord King George the Third, is the only Sovereign to whom British Americans can or ought to owe and bear true and faithful allegiance," and that "our Representatives, in General Assembly convened are the only guardians of our Rights and Liberties; that without them no laws here can be made to bind us, and that they only are the channel through which our grievances can properly be represented for redress."

Ill-feeling ran high, and families were divided amongst themselves. To cite only one instance, Mr. Crannell, a worthy gentleman and esteemed citizen, was unswerving in his loyalty to the King, while his two daughters, Mrs. Livingston and Mrs. Tappen, became equally strong adherents of the popular side, and are said to have deeply offended their father very early in the dispute by wearing in his presence aprons embroidered with the legends "Liberty" and "No Tea."

Richard Everitt, the out-and-out Loyalist, was away from Poughkeepsie certainly for part of the time during the war. Clear Everitt seems also to have been away. Certain it is, however, that his house was used for various public purposes, one of the courts for a time sitting in one of the rooms, for in the minutes of the Supervisors, for the 1st. of June, 1784, we find the following: "To Clear Everitt for the use of his room for the use of the Court of Oyer and Terminer to set in June, 1778, £2." In addition to this use of the property, of which we have a definite record, there is a strong and persistent tradition associating the building with the Revolutionary leaders, and it seems not at all improbable that Governour Clinton may have occupied it at some time during his residence in Poughkeepsie. The following extract from the Loyalist *New York Gazette*, of the 4th. of July, 1781, apparently points to the Everitt house:

> "There is a set of mob legislators met at Poughkeepsie; a little time will shew whether they mean to expose themselves to all the vengeance of which the majority of the late Assembly and Senate live in constant dread, many of them changing their lodgings to elude the search of the avengers of the innocent blood they have shed. Mr. Clinton, the titular Governour, has fortified his hut against a sudden, surprise, and the rebel slaves of Poughkeepsie guard it every night."

In his *History of Dutchess County*, Philip Smith after the word "hut" interpolates "the fine stone mansion of Clear Everitt." Whether Governour Clinton took up his residence in the house at that time or whether he did not, if Clear Everitt was away from Poughkeepsie—and he seems to have been—we may be sure that his house was used by the Revolutionary leaders in some way, "for they had need of all the buildings they could obtain, as the little town was often crowded with distinguished visitors during the sessions of the Legislature. That Washington and la Fayette were entertained there is not improbable. The house has been called 'The old fort,' the 'Headquarters' and the 'prison house,' with probably some reason for all three." The Poughkeepsie gaol could not possibly have accommodated all the Loyalist prisoners who were sent for detention, nor was it usual to confine well-known and respectable persons in gaol if it could be avoided.

À *propos* of the confinement of Loyalists at Poughkeepsie, the following story is not only amusing but also illuminative of the methods of gaol keeping at the time and of the sentiment amongst the general population of the country districts.

. . . . "Of one youth, William Haff, who got into trouble during the Revolution, a romantic story is told. He lived a short distance east of Poughkeepsie and was doubtless a somewhat wild, roystering youth, but withal a great favourite amongst the people, and especially amongst the young women of his neighbourhood. He had incurred the animosity of a justice of the peace before whom he was brought for some prank and who made use of his authority by sentencing Haff to be publicly whipped. This was entirely too much for the proud spirit of the young man, and he forthwith pitched into the justice, gave him, so the story goes, a sound licking and then ran away to the southward, where he ultimately joined the British army. After a while, becoming homesick for the sight of his old friends, and especially for a certain young woman with whom he was acquainted, he ventured up into the vicinity of his old home, was captured, tried and convicted as a deserter, and sentenced to be hanged. While awaiting execution he was confined in the gaol at Poughkeepsie, which was guarded by soldiers. At certain times the prisoners were allowed the freedom of an hall, or corridor, which extended from the front of the Court House on Market Street, to the rear of the building, facing westward, for air and exercise. Haff did not lose his spirits because of his perilous situation, but, as among his other accomplishments, he was a fine singer, occasionally would stand at the front window and sing, his fine strong voice often attracting a crowd of people who stood in the street below to listen. Whether he had planned his subsequent action from the beginning, or whether it was suggested by the fact that he noticed the soldiers stopping their patrol to stand beneath the window with the crowd while he sang, is not known, but one day at noon Haff appeared at the front window and sang with unusual vigour and expression. There was a little pause, during which the sentries made the circuit of the building to see that all was safe, and Haff began singing again before they got back. A few minutes later there was another pause, and the soldiers remained on the Market street front waiting for him to resume, but this time he failed to reappear, and after waiting a few minutes they marched round the Court House, to find when they reached the west side that the window opening from the hall was open. Haff had jumped out and was already out of sight in the woods which then lay between the Court House and the river. An alarm was at once sounded and parties started to capture the daring prisoner, but they never saw him again till the war was over. Then amongst the conditions of peace there had been established a full amnesty for all military offenses, whereupon Mr. Haff returned to Poughkeepsie, sporting his red coat and full British uniform as he marched up and down the streets, to the chagrin of his former persecutors, but to the great admiration of some of the young people, including the young woman for whom he had risked his life, and whom tradition says appropriately he afterwards married."

XXX.

TEVIOTDALE

LINLITHGOW, LIVINGSTON MANOR
THE HOME OF ROBERT FULTON

I T IS hardly fair, in considering the historic homes of the Hudson Valley, to omit that of Robert Fulton, humbled and dilapidated as it now is, a sorry ghost of its former courtly self. Fulton may proudly and rightfully be claimed by his descendants as one of the foremost and finest Americans of his time, and as such all Americans should look up to him and honour his memory; for any man of Fulton's genius, kindness and personality should hold an high place in the esteem of his countrymen, whether they are so fortunate as to be able to claim relationship or not.

TEVIOTDALE (HOME OF ROBERT FULTON), NEAR LINLITHGOW

Robert Fulton was born in Little Britain, Lancaster County, Pennsylvania, on the 14th. of November, 1765. He was bom of an humble family, of Saxon origin. However, he never looked back on his meagre circumstances with any degree of shame but rather with pride, taking, in later years, a great delight in being considered the founder of his fortune, as he truly was. Upon the death of his father, Fulton inherited but a scanty patrimony, for the elder Fulton's estate, such as it was, had to be divided between his widow and four children. Such unattractive circumstances never hindered Robert Fulton nor marred his supreme optimism, and he immediately set about making a livelihood as best he could.

Fulton's early life was strongly influenced by his friendship with the West family. In fact, it was the knowledge of the success of his young contemporary, Benjamin West—who was later to become the President of the Royal Academy—that prompted Fulton to choose the profession of painting for his earliest activities. Few, indeed, know of Fulton as a painter, possibly because of the fact that his later achievements in another direction so overshadowed his more youthful efforts, and because so few of his portraits are preserved.

Although Fulton actually acquired a fairly good knowledge of the rudiments of education, he was an unwilling pupil and rather than apply himself diligently to his books, which were doubtless dull enough, he concerned himself with those much more fascinating problems that are invented by the imagination and are seldom to be found in dusty tomes. An anecdote characteristic of Fulton's temperament is told in connexion with his being. chastised by a Quaker schoolmaster who firmly believed in the efficiency of the rod. The schoolmaster had just finished beating Fulton across the knuckles and observed rather testily, "There, that will make you do something!" To which Fulton replied, with perfect candour and composure, "Sir, I came to have something beaten into my brains and not into my knuckles."

Fulton's diligence and perseverance gained for him at a still early age what must have been considered a comfortable income, at least it was large enough for him to buy a farm in Hopewell for his mother. After an attack of pulmonary trouble, Fulton took refuge in one of the fashionable resorts of Virginia, where he reached a decision to go to Europe in order to advance his knowledge of art. Consequently, we soon see him on his way, in 1786, bearing numerous letters of introduction that would enable him to enter the art circles of the Old World.

Although for several years Fulton supported himself entirely by the aid of his brush, it was not long before he became so engrossed in the problems of canal transportation and his inventions that he forsook his art almost entirely. Throughout this period of his life he was continually producing and perfecting small inventions, such as a new device for spinning flax and another for twisting hempen rope. But, at the same time, his interest was chiefly centred upon the problems of canal navigation. His report on this subject was translated into French and published in France in the seventh year of the Republic, and excited no little admiration. Until the summer of 1803, when the trial boat on the Seine was pronounced a success, Fulton's activities, although varied and interesting, were not valuable, except in that each one contributed to the success of his ultimate achievement. He invented a system of inclined planes for differences in the levels of canals, and he constructed the first submarine boat and offered it to the French Government, to the no small consternation of the British. But neither of these inventions seemed to be a great success.

Finally, in the spring of 1803, after months of work, drawing and careful figuring, he was ready to make his first trial of the Seine boat. At this point Fulton experienced the bitterest disappointment of his life. On the eve of his success, he was accosted by a messenger with the sad news, "Oh, Sir, the boat has broken in pieces and gone to the bottom." It was true, and although when rescued the machinery was found to be practically uninjured, the boat itself was so badly damaged that it had to be rebuilt, and consequently it was not until July, of the same year, that he was again ready to make the attempt. Although the experiment was disappointing in some of its details, it was in the main successful and, perhaps, the most accurate account available is the following, which originally appeared in the *Recueil Polytechnique des Ponts et Chaussées*:

"On the 21st. Thermidor [August 9th., 1803] a trial was made of a new invention of which the complete and brilliant success should have important consequences for the commerce and internal navigation of France. During the past two or three months there has been seen at the end of the Quay Chaillot a boat of curious appearance, equipped with two large wheels, mounted on an axle like a chariot, while behind these wheels was a large stove with a pipe, as if there were some kind of a fire engine intended to operate the wheels of the boat. Several weeks ago some evil-minded persons threw this structure down. The builder, having repaired this damage, received the day before yesterday a most flattering reward for his labour and talent.

"At six o'clock in the evening, aided by only three persons, he put the boat in motion with two other boats attached behind it, and for an hour and a half he produced the curious spectacle of a boat moved by wheels, like a chariot, these wheels being provided with paddles, or flat plates, and being moved by a fire engine.

"In following it along the quay, the speed against the current of the Seine appeared to us about that of a rapid pedestrian, that is about 2400 *toises* an hour [2.9 miles] while in going down stream it was more rapid. It ascended and descended four times from Les Bons Hommes as far as the pump of Chaillot; it was manœuvred with facility, turning to the right and left, came to anchor, started again, and passed by the swimming school.

" One of the boats took to the quay a number of savants and representatives of the Institute, amongst whom were Citizens Bossut, Carnot, Prong, Perrier, Volney, etc. Doubtless they will make a report which will give to the discovery all the éclat which it merits; for this mechanism, applied to our rivers, the Seine, the Loire, the Rhone, would have most advantageous consequences upon our internal navigation. The tows or barges which now require four months to come from Nantes to Paris, would arrive promptly in ten to fifteen days. The author of this brilliant invention is M. Fulton, an American and a celebrated mechanic."

Fulton was fully aware of the possibilities of his new invention, and although he was sensible of its shortcomings when it was still in an embryonic state, he at once set about improving his new toy and making it thoroughly practical from a commercial point of view. Consequently, the same summer that this trial boat appeared on the Seine, he wrote Messrs. Boulton and Watts, of Birmingham, and placed an order for an engine to be shipped to America, Unfortunately, owing to the existing trade laws, there were almost insurmountable difficulties to be overcome and it was not until nearly two years had elapsed, and Fulton had attended to the transaction in person, that he was able to see his engine on the way to America, whither he was shortly to return.

Upon his arrival in the States, Fulton, with the financial aid of Robert R. Livingston, immediately set to work constructing a boat to be equipped with his newly acquired engine, and to be suitable for use upon the Hudson between Albany and New York. But even now, his path was not entirely strewn with roses, for financial difficulties were soon to confront him. Only a few weeks before the completion of the project it was necessary for Fulton and Livingston to obtain a third party to the scheme who could provide financial assistance. Several fruitless attempts were made, but finally, after nearly a day had been spent trying to get the support of Mr. John Stevens, a brother-in-law of Chancellor Livingston, he was persuaded to give one hundred dollars of the required thousand, providing his name was withheld. Similarly, nine other men were given the opportunity of helping Fulton in a material way, and the 17th. of August, 1807, found the *Clermont* prepared for her first memorable voyage.

A most interesting description of the event may be found in one of Fulton's letters to a friend. He writes:

"My dear sir:

"The moment arrived in which the word was to be given for the boat to move. My friends were in groups on the deck. There was anxiety mixed with fear among them. They were silent, sad and weary. I read in their looks nothing but disaster, and almost repented of my efforts. The signal was given and the boat moved on a short distance and then stopped and became immovable. To the silence of the preceding moments now succeeded murmurs of discontent, and agitations, and whispers and shrugs. I could hear distinctly repeated, 'I told you it was so; it is a foolish scheme; I wish we were well out of it.'

"I elevated myself upon a platform and addressed the assembly. I stated that I knew not what was the matter, but if they would be quiet and indulge me for half an hour, I would either go on or abandon the voyage at that time. This short respite was conceded without objection. I went below and examined the machinery, and discovered that the cause was a slight maladjustment of some of the work. In a short time it was obviated. The boat was again put in motion. She continued to move on. All were still incredulous. None seemed willing to entrust the evidence of their own senses. We left the fair city of New York; we passed through the romantic and ever varying scenery of the Highlands; we descried the clustering houses of Albany, we reached the shores—and then, even then, when all seemed achieved, I was the victim of disappointment.

"Imagination superseded the influence of fact. It was then doubted if it could be done again, or if done, it was doubted if it could be made of any great value.

"Yours

R. FULTON."

Although Fulton's success was instantaneous, his preparations had been so quiet that few people knew of the affair and, in fact, the general public cared so little and was so ill-informed that only one newspaper made any mention of the achievement. That paper was the *American Citizen*, and it was contented to print the following modest paragraph:

"Mr. Fulton's ingenious Steam Boat, invented with a view to the navigation of the Mississippi from New Orleans upward, sails today from the North River, near State's Prison, to Albany. The velocity of the Steamboat is calculated at four miles an hour. It is said it will make a progress of two against the current of the Mississippi, and if so it will certainly be a very valuable acquisition to the commerce of Western States."

Fulton, extremely appreciative of the recognition accorded him by this paper, wrote a letter to the editor which was practically a log of the first trip of the *Clermont*.

The *Clermont* itself, or the *Experiment* as it was originally called, was an extraordinary looking affair, and if it should appear today it would probably excite as much derision as it did at its first appearance. It was a long, low vessel with two masts on each of which was to be spread a sail. There were low cabins on either side of the deck and, somewhat forward of the centre, two revolving paddle wheels, one on each side. These latter were placed so that the paddles dipped into the water, but they were not originally enclosed in a wheelhouse.

The financial success of the boat was immediate, but before placing her in regular service, she was overhauled in New York, wheelhouses were added, and other minor improvements made. On the 2nd. of September she was ready for regular duty and Fulton inserted in the *Albany Gazette*, and the *Evening Post*, of New York, the first advertisement of travel by steam. It read,

> "The North River Steam Boat
> will leave Paulus Hook Ferry on Friday, the 4th. of September, at 6 in the morning, and arrive at Albany on Saturday at 6 in the afternoon.
> Provisions, good berths and accommodations are provided.
> The charge to each Passenger is as follows:

To Newburgh	$3	Time	14 hrs.
Poughkeepsie	$3	"	17 "
Esopus	$4½	"	20 "
Hudson	$5	"	30 "
Albany	$5	"	36 "

> "For places, apply to Wm. Vandervoort, No. 98, Courtlandt St., on the corner of Greenwich St.
> "Way passengers to Tarry Town, etc., etc., will apply to the captain on board."

The notice goes on to state that the boat will leave Albany and New York at certain stated times, "Thus performing two voyages from Albany and one from New York within the week."

During the winter of 1807 the *Clermont* was enlarged and virtually rebuilt, and as the *North River* she made regular trips up and down the Hudson for several years. Fulton's entire time was now taken up with his boats; we have it, in fact, in his own words when he says in a letter to Joel Barlow, "My whole time is now occupied in building North River and steam ferry boats, . . ." His energies were not confined to his native country alone, for he was asked to establish steam navigation on the Ganges and in Russia. The latter he attempted to do, but owing to his untimely death he never witnessed the fulfillment of that enterprise.

Although it is hard not to consider Fulton's death, in 1815, untimely, he can scarcely be said to have had an empty life in any respect, particularly during his last few years, for from the first voyage of the *Clermont*, in 1807, until 1815, he is credited with no less than seventeen boats, including the first steam war frigate, the first torpedo boat, and the first steam ferries.

We live today in a world that is so beset with ingenious modern improvements that it is rather a step to return for a moment to the time when such things did not exist. We take for granted the conveniences of travelling when or where we will, just as we choose, and people living near and about our great cities think nothing of daily trips to and from town, a trip that formerly was perhaps a matter of days. Rapid transportation has developed so quickly that it is difficult to realise that only a little more than an hundred years ago the first application of steam as a propellant was scoffed at on the eve of its birth. After all, an hundred years is not a great length of time in the history of a nation, and perhaps another century will find steam supplanted by electricity, and a third century may find even electricity supplanted by some as yet undreamed-of powerful agency.

Each new link in the chain of inventions, which grows and advances with civilisation, has some one who may be called a foster parent, and that man is generally, and usually, of right, considered a great man and an international benefactor. His letters are cherished, his drawings, if any exist, are carefully placed in museums or rest in the hands of some ardent admirer or descendant, who cherishes them as his dearest possessions; his home, his birthplace, his grave, are all shrines that are continually being visited by people of a later generation.

A rather pleasing but romantic theory, and it is interesting to note how in at least one instance it does not hold true. How many Americans will go to Europe and pay their shilling or franc for the privilege of walking around the choir of a British Abbey or a French Cathedral whose beauties they are conscious of only through the eyes of Baedeker! What can be the associations with such a place unless, indeed, it has been hallowed by those little marks and scratches which at one time characterised the trail of the American tourist. How few Americans take the trouble to go up the Hudson a few miles above New York City and go to Teviotdale, the home of Robert Fulton. In fact, how few Americans have ever heard of Teviotdale or know of its existence or whereabouts. Yet, Teviotdale there is, and it is not particularly inaccessible. It is on the east bank of the Hudson and overlooking the river, two miles below Linlithgow, and when you go there what do you find? Alas! you do not find an house kept with the neatness of Ann Hathaway's cottage. You find a great, dilapidated stone house in a most disreputable condition. At the time of writing the house is so sorely in need of repairs that it is doubtful whether it can withstand the ravages of time for another ten years. Teviotdale is owned by a foreigner who is unfortunately a man of humble station. In fact, the present tenant-owner and his family seem quite content to occupy a portion of the cellar for dwelling quarters and use the balance of the house as an hay barn, and surely it can have little value as an hay barn in that it will keep only a small portion of the hay dry, due to the holes in the roof. The condition of the entire building is, if possible, more pitiful than the condition of Fort Crailo. It is a deplorable state of affairs to find one of the historic American mansions so sadly neglected, when annually Americans spend countless dollars supporting foreign shrines.

So stands the once handsome home of Robert Fulton (one of the finest Americans that ever lived), the home built by his father-in-law, Walter Livingston, and it is a disgrace to the American people to realise how little they cherish the memory of one of the greatest American inventors and humanitarians.

XXXI.

THE LUDLOW HOUSE

CLAVERACK

T HE Ludlow house in Claverack is one of the houses that has fortunately been preserved for us against the ravages of time, and the still more insidious and frightful ravages of Victorianism. And, due to the generous spirit of its owner, it is like to be preserved in its original condition for many years to come. This is a rather gratifying fact, and what pleasure it is occasionally to find an old home that has never passed out of the hands of the family who originally built it!

LUDLOW HOUSE, CLAVERACK, SOUTH FRONT

The house, set some little distance back from the highway on a rather extensive tract of ground, may, because of its extreme simplicity, arouse little or no curiosity in the casual passer-by, but anyone having a keen appreciation of architecture will pause and enter the grounds to scrutinise the building more thoroughly. The house itself is moderately large, beautifully proportioned, and in design is marked by several salient characteristics which make it of uncommon interest, The builder, evincing that same independence and contempt for the road as the builder of St. Paul's Church, on lower Broadway in New York City, has placed the back of the house on the street side and quite refused to consider the possibility of entering directly from the highway. This façade, an unbroken surface, is pierced on either floor by five windows, the central one in each case being a so-called Palladian window. The effect is not all unpleasing, having one Palladian window above another and it is a trick that Sir Christopher Wren was wont to employ.

In passing around the west end of the house, one encounters a small side entrance, a veritable gem. This doorway, refined to a

SIDE DOOR

DETAIL OF SOUTH FRONT

degree, has in the leadwork of the fanlight a carefully modelled angel, an innovation which, in addition to its æsthetic appeal, is all the more interesting because of its extreme rarity. The gambrel roof is of very unusual contour, with a very abbreviated lower slope.

The author may have said in his enthusiastic moments that the structure has been preserved for us in its entirety; true enough it has, but unluckily the porch which adorns the front, is a later addition. At least, it could not, from its aspect have been designed as part of the original composition. It is much more likely that a porch was never considered, but that the main floor, some two feet above the level of the ground, was reached by a large uncovered flight of stone steps. Although the house antedates the porch, the latter is an old piece of work and has a nice feeling.

The interior of the house has suffered no more than the exterior and still preserves its pristine dignity, the rooms are spacious and very simply planned, being symmetrically placed on either side of the central hallway. It is easy to imagine how, in the days of its prime, such a setting lent dignity and grace to distinguished and attractive throngs that frequented the Ludlow home.

XXXII.

LINDENWALD

KINDERHOOK

VAN NESS—VAN BUREN

T HE name Kinderhook (Kinder-hoeck) means Children's Corner. It was the original name given to the place and it appears on Adriaen Block's map, dated 1614-1616. This same name Kinderhook has remained unchanged since it was first bestowed, while nearly every place else along the shores of the Hudson has borne different names at different times.

LINDENWALD, NEAR KINDERHOOK, FRONT

Library of Congress, Prints and Photographs Division

The name is said to have been given by Hendrick Hudson or his crew because of the great number of Indian children gathered on the point to gaze in wonderment at the unwonted sight before their eyes, the *Halve Maan* riding at anchor in waters that had never before borne such strange craft. When the explorers reported this incident on getting home, down went the name of Kinderhook on the early charts. All this happened in September, 1609.

Kinderhook—the town is some distance inland from the river—early became a place of importance and it has always held its head high, conscious of its worth and assured position. Needless to say, therefore, the people of Kinderhook have always manifested a proper pride in their town and neighbourhood. In this connexion they tell an anecdote of Martin Van Buren which exemplifies the local sentiment on this point. It is said that when he was attending a royal reception in England, Queen Adelaide asked him how far back he could trace his ancestry. Bowing with all courtly grace, he replied, "As far back as Kinderhook, Your Majesty."

In a neighbourhood of old houses, many of which are rich in historic associations, Lindenwald is one of the best and most widely known through its intimate connexion with Martin Van Buren, Aaron Burr and Washington Irving.

In 1780 Peter Van Ness, one of the foremost and most esteemed men of the neighbourhood, founded there an earlier and much less pretentious abode than the present dwelling. This seems to have been demolished when the house we see today was built. The date 1797, on the door knocker, indicates the year when Peter Van Ness undertook the enlargement of his borders and built him an house more in keeping with his circumstances and the elegant fashion of the day.

When completed it must have been an admirable example of late Georgian domestic architecture. It was of brick with white woodwork, and the cornices and other exterior details displayed all the delicacy and elegance customary in the latter part of the eighteenth century. Through the main portion of the house runs a wide central hall, at the back of which, and at one side, the staircase is reached through an archway. The hall was thus unimpeded and afforded an excellent place for dances, receptions and other social gatherings, in addition to the spacious rooms on either side. All of the interior woodwork is elaborate and of exceptional beauty in its details, plainly reflecting the subtle influence of Henry Holland and his school in England.

Fortunately, the interior has not been spoiled and still bears eloquent witness to the good taste of the architect who designed it and the conscientious work of the artisans employed. One wishes sincerely that as much could be said for the outside, but, sad to relate, the exterior fell a victim to the Victorian mania for "improvement." The only comforting thing about it all is that the defacements *can* be removed and some day, perhaps, the exterior may be restored to its pristine beauty.

DOORWAY IN HALL

Library of Congress, Prints and Photographs Division

Indoors the proportions are so just, and the detail of the wood-work so beautiful, that one derives some consolation from that source, and the first shock caused by the appearance of the martyred exterior is somewhat mitigated. In the great hallway, too, there is another source of perennial interest and delight—the old landscape paper with which the walls are covered. It is one of the well-known polychrome papers made in France by Jean Zuber and is entitled the "Paysage à Chasse." The design is quaint and highly diverting and the colouring, even after all the years the paper has been on the walls, is still fresh and glowing though, of course, some what mel-lowed by time. The illusion of distance is whimsically heightened by the device of a low balustrade printed along the whole base of the paper and appearing to rest upon the baseboard.

Lindenwald is about two miles south of the town of Kinderhook itself and is near the Albany Post Road. The Honourable Peter Van Ness, who built the house, was a man of parts and at different times held many public posts, fulfilling their duties with credit and distinction. To quote from the epitaph on his tombstone, he was not only an "high-minded, honourable, sensible man, fearing none but God," but was also

> "a distinguished and influential patriot in the most trying times: having served his country with great credit in numerous public stations both civil and military: among which were the command of a company at the age of nineteen years by the unanimous choice of his men in the invasion and conquest of Canada by the British; the command of a regiment at the capture of Burgoyne in 1777; that of a member of the State Convention which adopted the Federal Constitution; and service as a State Senator, Member of the Council of Appointment, and chief judge of this county."

In due time the house became the home of Peter Van Ness's second son, the Honourable William P. Van Ness, usually known as "The Judge," although nearly all the members of this particu-lar family seem to have shone in the legal and judicial world. It was in the law offices of Judge William, in 1802, that Martin Van Buren completed his preparatory legal studies. William Van Ness was an intimate friend of Aaron Burr and enthusiastically sup-ported him in the presidential campaign of 1800, when his rival, Thomas Jefferson, was elected.

Van Ness's intimacy with Burr led him to act as Burr's second in that fatal duel with Alexander Hamilton in the early morning of the 11th. of July, 1804, and afterwards when Burr was under the cloud of obloquy following the rest of his career he was a frequent visitor at the home of his staunch friend. Indeed, Burr's ghost is said to haunt Lindenwald and one old negro man-servant, years afterward, gave a very circumstantial account of his meeting the apparition. The negro was going from the house to the barn when he saw, just ahead of him, a fastidiously arrayed gentleman in knee breeches whose appearance exactly tallied with that of Burr. This gentleman in knee breeches went skipping blithely along the path towards the barn, suddenly turned a series of amazing handsprings, and then grew rapidly smaller and smaller, finally disappearing from the negro's astonished gaze down a wood-chuck hole. When closely questioned about his encounter the darkey reluctantly owned up to having previously had numerous draughts of hard cyder.

Aaron Burr's place amongst the "damaged souls" of American history will always cast a shadow about his memory, but it seems only fair, when one can do so, to recount such incidents as may serve to lighten the gloom a little. One such incident is given in a back number of *Olde Ulster*, and tells how Burr once befriended a nameless lad at a country blacksmith shop. This lad, taking advantage of Burr's generously proffered patronage, turned out to be none other than John Vanderlyn, the painter, of whose record not only New York but all America may feel proud.

Washington Irving, too, was a frequent visitor at Lindenwald, and, for a time, he was employed there in the capacity of private tutor to the children. Portions of his works were written there and we know that he drew more than one of his characters from originals in the neighbourhood and incorporated incidents suggested to him by local happenings and current traditions.

In 1841, shortly after his defeat for re-election to the Presidency, Martin Van Buren bought Lindenwald—it was he who gave it the name—and made the place his home. The midnineteenth century description of the house, previously alluded to, is worth quoting in part because it conveys a slight picture of Van Buren's life there and explains some of the atrocities of transformation that befell the exterior, although the architectural terms and appreciations are grotesque and the notations about the wallpaper are wholly incorrect. Bearing these limitations in mind, it may be taken for what it is worth. It tells us that:

> "The house stands about four or five hundred feet back from the road, and on the lawn are many very old fir or pine trees, a nearly circular cluster of which masques the residence in part from passers-by. . . . Drives from the two widely separated gates meet at the house, which is of brick, painted yellow, and seven windows wide. The main building has two storeys and a large garret. Three chimneys rise above this main or front part of the house—two to the north, a wide one to the south. The middle of the front is pedimented, and a dormer slides forward on each side of this gable, which in the bedroom storey below has a large triple central window, with a curved pedimental top and two windows on each side."

This is a rare description of the so-called Palladian window above the house door; it is so ingenious and original in its naïveté that it demands a note of acknowledgement to the unknown author who devised it. The account then goes on to say that:

> "Before the centre of the main storey is a small covered portico, with an easy flight of steps and balusters. . . . The library Mr. Van Buren added in the rear of the south side and built next to it a tower, like a donjon keep, with an Italian summit, the openings few and slitted; the object, stateliness and the view. . . .
>
> . . . "Beyond the door appeared a fine straight hall which was paced as being about fifty-five by fifteen feet and appeared to be eleven or twelve feet high. Its four doors were in the early carpentry of this century with manipulation around their tops.
>
> "Here no doubt, sate old Martin many a warm afternoon, taking the breezes from the Berkshire hills to the Catskills. Here John Van Buren played the penitent. It was in the neighbouring town of Hudson that he and Ambrose Jordan clinched and fought in the court room like a pair of newly-introduced dogs, and the judge fined and sent them to gaol. Much did old Martin have to think about in the twenty-two years of retirement passed mainly here on his 200 acres; looking upon wayward, brilliant, or brain-wrought sons, hearing the wind moan and the locusts drone."

XXXIII.

THE ADAM VAN ALEN HOUSE

KINDERHOOK

A LITTLE way to the south of Kinderhook town, and on the road thence to Lindenwald, is the Adam Van Alen. house, made famous as the home of one of Washington Irving's characters, Katrina Van Tassell who was, in real life, Katrina Van Alen.

The house is of brick and, as the date figures wrought in black headers on the west wall tell us, was built in 1736. Although in a somewhat dilapidated condition, it has fortunately escaped the blighting hand of the Victorian "beautifier" who performed such terrible atrocities throughout the countryside, notably at Lindenwald, to seek no farther. Barring one small irrelevant gabled dormer and the addition of a short verandah, no further structural disfigurements have taken place. To all intents and purposes, the house is the same as it was when Katrina Van Alen served as the model for Irving's elaborations—the same, in fact, as it was in the middle of the eighteenth century.

It is oblong and of one storey with a dormered garret and a sharply pitched roof which spans a depth of one room, the rooms of the ground floor being strung out, one after another. The rooms are low and great pine beams support the joists and floor boards of the rooms above. Many of these boards are considerably more than fifteen inches wide. Downstairs there is some good panelling and the panelled doors are of unusual pattern and very engaging in their design. All the woodwork, including the great beams that traverse the rooms, has been allowed to take its colouring from time and the atmosphere and has assumed a wonderfully mellow deep brown, infinitely finer than any finish that could be gained from artificial means. In every way the house is a good example of the eighteenth century dwelling of the substantial Dutch farmers who prospered exceedingly on the rich lands of this part of

VAN ALEN HOUSE, NEAR
KINDERHOOK, SOUTH FRONT

Library of Congress, Prints and Photographs Division

NORTH FRONT

Library of Congress, Prints and Photographs Division

the country, increasing by their industrious tilth the fertility of a region which nature had already generously endowed.

Whether Sarah Van Alen, the wife of Johannes, actually lived in this house or in another Van Alen house not far away, is not certain. At any rate, the story told of her is worth repeating as it shews that the eighteenth century could boast women militant to good purpose, if not suffragettes of the modern type. "Sarah was renowned for her beauty, as of course were all Kinderhook women of those days. The overseer of roads was about to lay out a road through a piece of land the title to which was in dispute. Sarah was determined the road should not run as intended, and so, taking her spinning wheel, she sate herself down in the middle of the proposed roadway and began spinning, in defiance of the advancing workmen. The angry overseer shouted to his men to 'run right over her.' but they dared not disturb 'so much of beauty as could live.' . . . and the road remained unchanged, veracious tradition alleges." Perhaps this incident may account for some of the windings and crookednesses of the highway at this point.

It has been proved pretty conclusively, after much careful research, that Washington Irving drew the prototypes for several characters in *The Legend of Sleepy Hollow* from this neighbourhood. The originals of Ichabod Crane, Brom Bones and Dirk Schuyler were well known local celebrities. When Washington Irving was living at Lindenwald the nearby school was taught by a Mr. Merwin. "In the vicinity of his schoolhouse Irving laid the scene of one of the most inimitable tales in his *Sketch Book*, and our friend Merwin sate for the picture of Ichabod Crane." The beautiful Katrina Van Alen, of course, was the original of Katrina Van Tassell.

XXXIV.
THE PASTURES
ALBANY

"**A** HANDSOME house half-way up the bank, opposite the ferry seems to attract attention and to invite strangers to stop at General Schuyler's, who is the proprietor. . . . . I had recommendations to him from all quarters, but particularly from General Washington and Mrs. Carter (Church). I had besides given the rendezvous to Colonel Hamilton, who had just married another of his daughters, and who was preceded by the Vicomte de Noailles, and the Comte de Damas, who I knew were arrived the night before The sole difficulty, therefore, consisted in passing the river. Whilst the boat was making its way with difficulty through the flakes of ice, which we were obliged to break as we advanced, Mr. Lynch, who is not indifferent about a good dinner, contemplating General Schuyler's house, mournfully says to me: 'I am sure the Vicomte and Damas are now at table, where they have good cheer and good company, whilst we are here kicking our heels, in hopes of getting this evening to some wretched alehouse.' I partook a little of his anxiety, but diverted myself by assuring him that they saw us from the windows, that I even distinguished the Vicomte de Noailles who was looking at us through a telescope, and that he was going to send somebody to conduct us on our landing to that excellent house, where we should find dinner ready to come on table; I even pretended that the sledge I had seen descending towards the river was designed for us. As chance would have it, never was conjecture more just. The first person we saw on shore was the Chevalier de Mauduit who was waiting for us with the General's sledge, into which we quickly stepped, and were conveyed in an instant into a handsome salon near a good fire, with Mr. Schuyler, his wife and daughters. Whilst we were warming ourselves, dinner was served, to which every one did honour, as well as to the Madeira which was excellent, and made us completely forget the rigour of the season and

THE PASTURES, ALBANY, EAST
FRONT, FACING RIVER

New York Public Library Digital Collections

the fatigue of the journey. General Schuyler's family was composed of Mrs. Hamilton, his second daughter, who has a mild, agreeable countenance; and Miss Peggy Schuyler, whose features are animated and striking; of another charming girl, only eight years old; and of three boys, the eldest of whom is fifteen, and are the handsomest children you can see."

Such was the vivid impression of "The Pastures" made upon the Marquis de Chastellux when he first arrived there on a cold winter's evening. If the foregoing passage from his *Travels in North America* does not convey an adequate architectural description of the house of General Philip Schuyler, it does afford an illuminating sense of the homelike, hospitable atmosphere that surrounded the stately old Albany home. It faithfully sets forth the gracious, kindly charm that, after all, is just as much an essential part of such a dwelling as is the material fabric of bricks and mortar.

In February, 1761, Philip Schuyler, then twenty-eight years old, sailed for England, an important part of his errand being to adjust with the Government the accounts of General John Bradstreet, still unsettled after several years' standing. Despite twenty-one years' difference in their ages, the closest friendship existed between General Bradstreet and Philip Schuyler, and while Schuyler was securing a settlement of unpaid military accounts for the General, Bradstreet, with Schuyler's power of attorney for the management and disposal of his property, was acting as his representative while "The Pastures" was a-building. Work was begun shortly after Schuyler set sail, and when he came back in 1762, the new house was the first thing to greet his eyes as he neared Albany. Albeit only the names of Colonel Bradstreet and of Nicholas and William Bayard, her husband's friends and kinsmen, appear in the business transaction, we may be sure that Mrs. Schuyler, familiar as she was from youth with her father's and other large establishments and their needs, bore no small share in the planning and supervision of her new home.

The house, with massive brick walls and a double hip roof, pierced by generous square chimneys, is about sixty feet square and stands at the top of the first rise from the river. It faces east, and, from its elevated site, commands a wide view over the Hudson and the country roundabout. Though built in 1762, and an excellent example of the Georgian style, the details for the most part belong to that phase of the Georgian manner that obtained in England some years previously and do not betray any evidences of the newer form of expression then introduced by the Brothers Adam. This, however, is quite to be expected, for in the Colonies the changes in architectural mode were nearly always ten to fifteen years later than their first appearance in the Mother Country. All the work, both inside and out, is peculiarly pleasing, just in its proportions and consistent in decoration. It is not too much to say that "The Pastures" is one of the finest examples of American Georgian to be found anywhere in the country. The building has great dignity and breadth of scale, and its impressive aspect of amplitude is thoroughly satisfactory.

A white wooden balustrade surrounds the roof just above the eaves, and is carried across the front of the dormers. Across the east front of the house extends a range of seven broad windows, in which the glazing is of very unusual character. While the sashes have heavy muntins, in accordance with the usage of the time, the panes are exceptionally large, their dimensions being about nine inches by eleven. Of course, the windows are very broad and high, but the heroic-sized glazing tends very materially to accentuate the scale of the building. A curious thing about the house is that there are only three windows in the whole broad expanse of the western wall, and of these one lights the back of the lower hall while the other two light the staircase and western end of the great central gallery of the first floor. Notwithstanding its paucity of western windows, however, the house is exceptionally well lighted and cheerful.

The entrance, as it appears today, is not the same as when the house was built. About the end of the eighteenth century, or the beginning of the nineteenth, an hexagonal vestibule was added before the house door, and the flight of stone steps, with beautifully wrought iron balustrades, was pushed forward for an approach to the new entrance. This method of treatment is quite exceptional; at the same time it is highly pleasing. The details of this hexagonal vestibule are wholly in accord with the architectural tradition of the time it was erected, and yet the blending of modes has been so well done that everything is in harmony. Incidentally, this extra-mural appendage imparts a very distinctive aspect to the exterior.

On the ground floor, the front hall is thirty feet long by twenty feet wide and opens into the back hall, in which is the staircase, by a wide doorway with a leaded fanlight above it. The staircase, with its balustrade of spiral spindles, in a triple series of patterns, and its moulded mahogany handrail, commands universal admiration. In both the halls, and in all the spacious high-ceiled rooms opening from them, the panelling and the architectural details comport with the elegance and amplitude of the fabric. On the first floor a great gallery, twenty feet wide, runs the full depth of the house, and its walls, above the dado, are covered with an old French polychrome landscape paper. This gallery affords an admirable place for balls and other social functions—for this purpose it was doubtless planned—and from it open out the great bedrooms of similar dimensions to the rooms on the ground floor. Above these, and reached by a concealed staircase, is a lofty garret, extending over the whole house.

As might be expected, the house was furnished with elegant appointments in accordance with the distinguished setting and befitting the estate and quality of the owners. General Burgoyne, after his stay there, writes of it as "an elegant house"; John Trumbull, the painter, records, "I was much impressed by the elegant style of everything I saw"; the Marquis of Chastellux commented on "the handsome salon"; and, in writing to General Schuyler, Charles Carroll of Carrollton, notes "he lives in a very pretty style ". We may well believe that the house quite equalled the best houses of similar character in England in the taste and quality of its appointments, and such of the original household effects as are still preserved there, all go to confirm this opinion.

Round about the house were gardens and orchards, vineyards and well-kept borders full of flowers, with ample expanses of lawn. Back of the house, to the west, were the quarters of the negro slaves—comfortable brick structures where the faithful servitors were well housed. These quarters, unfortunately, were demolished many years ago.

Such was the ample courtly setting in which lived General Philip Schuyler and Catherine Van Rensselaer, his wife, dispensing lavish hospitality to all their friends and not forgetting the claims of the needy and distressed. No more appropriate background could be conceived for a couple who so notably fulfilled all the best traditions of eighteenth century domestic life, with diligence, affection and wisdom towards the immediate members of their own household, with gracious courtesy and kindly generosity towards their innumerable guests.

Philip Schuyler was the fourth in descent from Philip Pieterse Schuyler, who migrated to Albany from Holland prior to 1650. His great-uncle was that distinguished Peter Schuyler, "Quider," who was both feared by the Indians and beloved by them, because of his just dealing and integrity. His influence was felt throughout the colony in numberless ways. On one occasion, partly to impress the Six Nations with England's power and partly to arouse British interest in the provincial struggle with France,

Peter Schuyler took four Mohawk chiefs to London and had the Earl of Shrewsbury present them to Queen Anne as "Kings." After that they were driven through the streets in royal carriages.

When Philip Schuyler was only eight years old, the early death of his father, Johannes Schuyler, Jr., Mayor of Albany and Indian Commissioner, left him with an elder sister and two little brothers to the sole care of their mother, Cornelia Van Cortlandt Schuyler, a woman of remarkably fine character and much esteemed by all who knew her. Philip was educated at home, under a Huguenot tutor, until he was about fifteen years of age, when he was sent to a school in New Rochelle to be under the tutelage of Doctor Stouppe, the pastor of the French Protestant Church in that place. It was to this same school that John Jay went a few years later. Under Doctor Stouppe's care he became proficient in mathematics, and acquired a thorough command of French, which stood him in good stead in his after-years.

As a young man of eighteen or nineteen, we hear of him hunting and trading with the Indians along the upper Mohawk, as other young Albanians of his time were wont to do. He is described as being then "a tall youth with a florid complexion, a benevolent cast of features, a fine manly deportment, and distinguished for great kindness of manner." Needless to say, he was a great favourite with the Indians, for apart from any personal qualities, his very name meant to them kindness and fair dealing.

An interesting momentary sidelight upon Philip Schuyler's young manhood comes from a letter written at New York to his bosom friend "Brom" Ten Eyck, in Albany. He had reached New York from Albany by water on the 20th. of September, 1753, and landed at Ten Eyck's Wharf at one o'clock in the afternoon. The letter tells how he spent the rest of the day, and gives us an intimate glimpse of city life at that time:

"The same evening I went to the play with Phil (Livingston). You know I told you before I left home that if the players should be here I should see them, for a player is a new thing under the sun in our good province. Philip's sweetheart went with us. She is a handsome brunette from Barbadoes, has an eye like that of a Mohawk beauty and appears to possess a good understanding. Phil and I went to see the grand battery in the afternoon, and to pay my respects to the governour, whose lady spent a week with us last spring, and we bought our play tickets for eight shillings apiece, at Parker and Weyman's printing office in Beaver Street on our return. We had tea at five o'clock, and at sundown we were in the theatre, for the players commenced at six. The room was quite full already. Among the company was your cousin Tom and Kitty Livingston, and also Jack Watts, Sir Peter Warren's brother-in-law. I would like to tell you all about the play, but I can't now, for Billy must take this to the wharf for Captain Wynkoop in half an hour. He sails this afternoon. A large green curtain hung before the players until they were ready to begin, when, on the blast of a whistle, it was raised, and some of them appeared and commenced acting. The Play was called The Conscious Lovers, written you know by Sir Richard Steele, Addison's help in writing the Spectator. . . . But I said I could not tell you about the play, so I will forbear, only adding that I was not better pleased than I should have been at the club, where last year I went with cousin Stephen, and heard many wise sayings which I hope profited me something. . . . But I must say farewell, with love to Peggy, and sweet Kitty V. R., if you see her."

Many of the sedate heads of families in New York were much perturbed in mind by the advent of this company of players, and vowed that they would not lend countenance to the folly of play-going, whatever the Governour and his entourage of world-lings might do. The ladies of their families, however, seem to have been of another mind, and the annals of the day tell us that when the curtain went up there were but few of the notables missing from the audience.

When Philip Schuyler came of age, in the autumn of 1754, disregarding his rights of primogeniture, entitling him to all the real property previously belonging to his father, he made an equal division of the estate with his brothers and sister. The following year, upon the outbreak of the French and Indian War, he raised a company and was commissioned Captain by James DeLancey, then Governour of the Province. In the succeeding years, during his service under Bradstreet, began that intimacy to which allusion has already been made.

He was elected in 1768, along with Jacob Ten Eyck, to sit for the City and County of Albany in the Provincial Assembly, and from thence onward we find him, upon every occasion, stoutly espousing the side of the Colonies against the measures of the British Government. Some of the boldest resolutions introduced before the Assembly were draughted by him, and it is interesting to note that it was at his suggestion that Edmund Burke was appointed the agent for New York in England.

In 1775 he was a member of the Continental Congress; Major-General of the Northern Department under Washington from 1775 to 1777; a second time member of the Continental Congress in 1779; and, in company with Rufus King, one of the first two United States Senators from the State of New York, and he further rendered efficient public service to his country and State as Surveyor-General of the State, Chairman of the Board of Indian Commissioners, and one of the Commissioners appointed to settle the Massachusetts and Pennsylvania boundaries dispute.

He was no less useful and unselfish in his private capacity, and was always in the forefront of any undertaking that might be of benefit to the community or the State. As an individual he was conspicuous for his integrity, his kindliness of heart and manner, his generosity, his affability, his courtliness, as became a gentleman of the old school, and his unfailing hospitality, not only to the numerous distinguished friends who frequented his house, but also the many of lesser note who chanced to come thither. Such was the master of "The Pastures."

The mistress of "The Pastures" was the "Sweet Kitty V. R." of Philip Schuyler's letter of September, 1753, to his friend, "Brom" Ten Eyck. She was the daughter of John Van Rensselaer, of the Eastern Manor of Rensselaerwyck, who lived at Fort Crailo in Greenbush, just across the river, Her mother was Angelica Livingston. By all accounts she was a great lady, one of the most popular belles and "toasts" of her day. Lossing describes her as possessing delicately chiselled features, dark eyes and hair and an high colour. To the same source we are indebted for the information that she was "below the medium height but graceful in movement, with a sweet and winning manner and low, soft voice." She was the pride of her children, who regarded her with deep and devoted affection. As one little evidence of this filial pride, we may turn to the letter her daughter Angelica (Mrs. Church) wrote her mother long after the Revolutionary War, when Mrs. Schuyler was no longer young. Mrs. Church, whose husband was a member of Parliament, was then living in London.

> "I send you," she writes affectionately, "a tea caddy, and a card which will make you laugh. Embrace dear papa a thousand times. I pray to heaven that General Washington would send him ambassador here and that you would come with him. We would all live together, or in two adjoining houses, and you would make everybody love and respect you; besides, I should be so proud of my handsome mother. What pains I would take to do everything to please you, dear, dear mama—let it be so, pray do."

But besides rare beauty and distinction of person, Mrs. Schuyler possessed great determination and firmness of will, conspicuous executive ability and, as a grace to all her other qualities, spontaneous kindness of heart and action. Her manner was always "quiet, unobtrusive, kindly" and marked by that natural simplicity and lack of all assumption indicative of true dignity and gentle breeding. It is said that she was a somewhat silent person, and it is the liveliness and animation of her daughters that elicited allusions in accounts of the household by guests entertained at "The Pastures," yet it is evident that Mrs. Schuyler well knew the art of putting everybody at their ease and making them feel at home. Charles Carroll of Carrollton mentions "the ease and affability with which we were treated" making his visit at the Schuyler household a "most pleasing *séjour,*" while Tench Tilghman writes, "There is something in the behaviour of the General, his wife and daughters that makes one acquainted with them instantly. I feel as easy and free from restraint at his seat as I feel at Cliffden, where I am always at a second home."

Over and above the traits hitherto rehearsed, Mrs. Schuyler displayed calm self-possession and fortitude in the face of danger, and also remarkable good sense, with quick judgement and initiative when crises arose demanding these qualities, as they did more than once in the course of her life,

Perhaps the incident by which her daring and independence are best remembered was her hurried visit to Saratoga, as General

Burgoyne's army was approaching that place from the north. The panic-stricken refugees, fleeing towards Albany, were amazed at seeing a carriage with a single armed escort hastening north. Mrs. Schuyler sate composedly within. She was bound toward Saratoga to fetch away her household treasures from her summer home there, and when the fugitives protested against her continuing thither, she merely smiled and said, "The General's wife must not be afraid," and kept right on, undaunted. When she had rescued such valuables as she could carry away with her, she set fire with her own hands to the grain fields and then drove back to Albany.

After the battle of Saratoga and the surrender of General Burgoyne, occurred an incident indicative of the amenities of war in that day and also illustrative of the innate kindness, truly Christian generosity and magnanimous courtesy of General Schuyler. The Baroness Riedesel and her children, along with the wives of several other officers, had accompanied the army. For six days prior to the capitulation they had been obliged to seek shelter from the American cannonade in a cellar, and had endured great privation. Of what took place after the surrender, the Baroness writes:

"In the passage through the American camp I observed with great satisfaction that no one cast at us scornful glances. On the contrary they all greeted me, even shewing compassion on their countenances at seeing a mother with her children in such a situation.

"I confess that I feared to come into the American camp, as the thing was so entirely new to me. When I approached the tents, a noble-looking man came towards me, took the children out of the waggon, embraced and kissed them, and then, with tears in his eyes, helped me also to alight. 'You tremble,' said he to me, 'fear nothing.' 'No,' replied I, 'for you have been so kind and have been so tender toward my children that it has inspired me with courage.' He then led me to the tent of General Gates.

"All the generals remained to dine with General Gates. The man who had received me so kindly came up and said to me, 'It may be embarrassing to you to dine with all these gentlemen; come now with your children into my tent, where I will give you, it is true, a frugal meal, but one that will be accompanied by the best of wishes.' 'You are certainly,' answered I, 'a husband and a father, since you shew me so much kindness.' I then learned that he was the American General Schuyler."

After the battle General Schuyler found it necessary to stay on at Saratoga for some days, to look after his personal affairs; but he was deeply touched by the sufferings of the ladies and their children, and also by the plight of General Burgoyne and his officers. He therefore despatched Colonel Varick to Albany to advise Mrs. Schuyler of the coming of guests, and sent Baroness Riedesel with her children in his own coach, while General Burgoyne, Baron Riedesel and other officers were escorted thither on horseback.

Following the surrender, General Schuyler met General Burgoyne, and what took place is best described by Burgoyne's own words in a speech before the House of Commons:

> "I expressed to General Schuyler my regret at the event which had happened (the burning of Schuyler's Saratoga house), and the reasons which had occasioned it. He desired me to think no more of it, saying that the reason justified it, according to the rules of war. . . .
>
> "He did more: he sent his aide-de-camp to conduct me to Albany, in order, as he expressed it, to procure me better quarters than a stranger might be able to find. This gentleman conducted me to a very elegant house and, to my great surprise, presented me to Mrs. Schuyler and her family; and in General Schuyler's house I remained during my whole stay at Albany, with a table of more than twenty covers for me and my friends, and every other possible demonstration of hospitality."

Notwithstanding the ample roominess of "The Pastures," the house must have had some of the elastic qualities of a Virginia house on occasions like this. All the same, all comers were tucked in by hook or by crook and, by ingenious doubling up, everybody was made comfortable.

Of their reception, Baroness Riedesel writes:

> "They loaded us with kindness, and they behaved in the same manner toward General Burgoyne, though he had ordered their splendid establishment to be burned, and without any necessity it was said; but all their actions proved that, in the sight of the misfortunes of others, they quickly forgot their own."

As to Burgoyne's experiences, the Marquis de Chastellux recounts the following incident:

"The British Commander," he says, "was well received by Mrs. Schuyler and lodged in the best apartment in the house. An excellent supper was served him in the evening, the honours of which were done with so much grace that he was affected even to tears, and said with a deep sigh, 'Indeed, this is doing too much for a man who has ravaged their lands and burned their dwellings.' "

The great southeast parlour has very definite and unchallenged associations. It was in this room that the marriage of Elizabeth Schuyler with Alexander Hamilton took place in December, 1780. This wedding was, perhaps, the most brilliant and festive assemblage the house was ever to witness. "Betsy" Schuyler was the only one of the General's daughters to marry with his consent, and her wedding was as joyous and splendid an affair as parental affection, wealth, a wide family connexion and innumerable friends could make it. Upon this one ceremony was centred all the enthusiasm and effort that would have made three or four nuptial gatherings notable events, had the other daughters of the Schuyler household seen fit to pursue the same course as their sister. Betsy instead of leaping from the windows and eloping with the man of her choice, and seeking parental sanction and forgiveness after marriage was a *fait accompli*, was wed in the orthodox manner. When the opportunity came, therefore, to have a real, duly announced festivity to celebrate the occasion, the most was made of it. As we all know, the marriage was an happy one, and from then till the end of his life, Hamilton was a frequent sojourner beneath the roof tree of "The Pastures." He became in very truth a son of the family. His close association with the house is one of its most precious memories, and it is pleasant to think of him, after he had ceased to be a member of Washington's staff, returning to Albany to study law, and sitting in the great gallery on the upper floor, writing, with his wife beside him, and the while, with his foot, as he himself said, "rocking the cradle of his little boy."

During 1781, the "Cowboys"—those worthless scalawags who claimed to be Loyalists but were merely lawless hooligans bent upon violence and robbery, and a disgrace to the allegiance they professed—with Canadian and Indian confederates were making every effort to kidnap prominent citizens of Albany and carry them off to Canada to be held for ransom. General Schuyler, of course, was the chief quarry. Warned of their intentions and knowing that figures had been seen skulking in the shrubbery, the General "kept a guard of six men constantly on duty, three by day and three by night, and after these warnings he and his family were on the alert."

Towards evening of a sultry August day, in 1781, the family were sitting in the front hall, the slaves were scattered about the place, and the three guards were lying on the grass in the garden, when a servant came to say that a strange man wished to speak with the General at the back gate. General Schuyler knew at once what this meant. The doors were straightway shut and barred, the family hastened to an upper room, while the General ran to get his arms. From his bedroom window he saw armed men surrounding the house. As he fired a pistol from the window to arouse the sentinels and alarm the neighbourhood, the assailants burst open the door. It was only then that Mrs. Schuyler discovered that, in the confusion of flight, the baby, but a few months old, had been left in the cradle on the floor below. She was just going down again to rescue the child when the General interposed; but her third daughter, Margaret, like a flash rushed down stairs, snatched the sleeping infant and brought it up safely. As she sped up the stairs, one of the Indians hurled a tomahawk at her; but the missile, though passing within a few inches of the baby's head, did no hurt and stuck in the mahogany hand-rail. The savage dent it made is still to be seen. As she rushed up the stairs, the leader of the ruffians, taking her for a servant, called out, "Wench, wench, where is your master!" With ready presence of mind she answered, "Gone to alarm the town."

The cowboys and their confederates were in the diningroom packing up the plate and other valuables, as the leader called them together to consult. Just then the General threw up a window and, as though addressing a crowd of people, cried out in a loud voice, "Come on, my brave fellows, surround the house and secure the villains who are plundering." At that the ruffians beat a hasty retreat, taking with them the three sentinels that were in the house and a goodly quantity of silver plate. They made good their escape to Canada with their prisoners and booty. The three guards who had been asleep in the cellar, being awaked by the din, hastened to get their arms in the back hall, but when they got there they were gone, so that they fought with their brawny fists until they were overpowered. When they were exchanged as prisoners of war and found their way back to Albany, General Schuyler gave them each a farm in Saratoga County.

It is fascinating to look back over the long list of distinguished guests who have enjoyed the gracious hospitality of "The Pastures," and to call up before the mind's eye the many brilliant gatherings in which they were conspicuous figures. At the same time, we ought never to lose sight of the fact that hospitality at "The Pastures" was a chronic habit. To discharge well all the duties of hospitality, and to manage her household adroitly, were matters of both conscience and proper pride to such a woman as Mrs. Schuyler.

While Mrs. Schuyler was truly an "ornament to society," to use an expression of the time, a genuine hostess, and a wise and kindly dispenser of charity, she was also none the less an affectionate and prudent mother and a notable housewife. Providing for a large and also an elastic household at that time required a degree of foresight in laying in supplies, well nigh inconceivable to-day, besides the utmost care and thought in dispensing them. All this, be it remembered, was in addition to the oversight of a retinue of negro slaves, most of them constitutionally irresponsible, however faithful and well-intentioned they might be.

Just as in Virginia, every family of consequence prided itself on its own home-cured hams, prepared by jealously guarded recipes, "while spare-ribs and cheeks, head-cheese and souse, and all the other good things, came forth at 'killing-time.' " At Christmas time came rich plum puddings and plum cake, mince-meat pies, crullers and "oleykoecks," closely followed at New Year's by a profusion of cookies and tarts, and all the "buckwheat-cakes, waffles, and pastry of the winter months." The lavish use of ingredients called for is enough to appal the modern housekeeper. "Take an hundred and twenty-five oysters, take twenty-five pigeons, take dozens of eggs, quarts of cream, pounds of butter, say the old cook books! Take fifteen pounds of beef and spice it for three days; throw in a bottle of claret before serving, says the old recipe. The good things are shared with the married daughters when they have households of their own. Indeed, the ladies of that day interchanged gifts from their storerooms much as the gentlemen did from their wine cellars."

It would be ungracious to omit mention of Prince, a faithful old slave, genuinely beloved not only by every member of the family but by all their friends as well He was invaluable in the capable and ready service he rendered, and in the carrying out of her exacting arrangements Mrs. Schuyler must have depended to a great extent on his intelligent assistance. In writing to her mother from London, Mrs. Church enquires, "How is old Prince! When I don't see the old man's name I think he is dead." He was not bom in the colony but had been brought from Africa in his youth. "It was reported soon after he became a member of the household that he refused to eat with the other negroes on the ground that he was their superior in rank in Africa. His meals were then served to him apart from the others. Soon he was promoted, and he became a trusted and most faithful upper servant. So well was Prince known to the guests of the Schuyler house that John Jay, writing from Spain to Schuyler, says that he has chosen as the key to his cypher despatches the name of that faithful servant who, for thirty years has never failed to stand at the dinner table behind his mistress's chair."

It matters not whether we regard the household at "The Pastures" with reference to the master, the mistress or the children, we cannot fail to be impressed with the dignity, genuineness and kindness of the lives they lived, and the sincerity with which they instinctively and unconsciously observed the principle that *noblesse oblige.*

XXXV.
KINGSTON-ON-HUDSON
ULSTER COUNTY

KINGSTON began life in 1653 when the first permanent settlers in the neighbourhood, following the lead of Thomas Chambers, established themselves on the fertile lands along the banks of the Esopus. At first there was no attempt to found a town or any centre of population. The settlers, more intent on husbandry than anything else, built their farmhouses on their lands wherever it pleased them best, and let the world wag as it would. This easy-going method of letting town organisation take care of itself, and come when it would, might have worked very well had it not been for the Indians. The red men, having tasted the white man's "fire-water," and fallen into disagreement with certain of the farmers, from time to time, became a menace and it was clearly necessary for the Dutch to take some measures for self-protection.

SENATE HOUSE, KINGSTON-ON-HUDSON

Library of Congress, Prints and Photographs Division

Their scattered manner of residence, their own individual indiscretions in dealing with the natives, and the Indians' uncertain temper all contributed to bring about a state of affairs in which the settlers were time and again placed in a most ignominious position to say the least. This we may readily gather from the character of the petition for assistance they sent to Governour Stuyvesant. "The savages," they say, "compel the whites to plough their maize land, and when they hesitate threaten, with firebrands in their hands, to burn their houses. . . . That the chiefs have no control of their men. We are locked up in our houses and dare not move a limb."

This was in May, 1658, and the extent of their settlement at that time may be surmised from the statement in their petition that "they had 990 schepels of grain in the ground, and had 60 or 70 people, who support a reader at their own expense."

In response to their call for aid, Governour Stuyvesant came with a force of sixty or seventy men under arms. He arrived on the Wednesday before Ascension Day and gave notice that the people were to meet him the next day in the afternoon after service. When they were all come together, he told them plainly that "the killing of one man and the burning of two buildings was not enough to make war. They must concentrate and form a village with a stockade, so as to be able to protect themselves." To this they objected on the ground of their poverty and their inability to house their crops so near harvest. They prayed that the troops might remain and that they might be allowed to postpone building the village until after the harvest. The Governour replied that there was no security for them as they were then living; they must either concentrate, with their dwellings close together in a village, or else they must remove to Fort Orange or Manhattan. If they would agree to concentrate, then he would stay until the work was finished.

The next day Stuyvesant had a conference with the Indian warriors, and upbraided them with their insolence to the whites, their murders and their burnings. Still, he assured them, he had not come to make war, but to punish the guilty and to find out why they were acting thus and constantly threatening the settlers. After a little, one of the chiefs said, "The Shawanakins sold our children drink, and they were thus the cause of the Indians being made crazy, which was the cause of all the mischief. The sachems could not always control the young men, who would often fight and wound. The murder was committed not by one of our tribe, but by a Minnisink, who had skulked away among the Haverstraws. The one who fired the two small dwelling-houses had run away, and dared not cultivate his own soil. We are innocent, not actuated by malice, do not want to fight, but cannot control the young men."

The result of all these conferences and explanations was that Stuyvesant told the Indians plainly, "You must repair all damages, seize the murderer if he comes amongst you, and do no further mischief. The Dutch are now going to live together in one spot. It is desirable that you should sell us the whole of the Esopus land and remove farther into the interior; for it is not good for you to be so near the Shawanakins, whose cattle might eat your maize, and thus cause frequent disturbances." To all of this the Indians acquiesced, while the Dutch settlers came to Stuyvesant and entered into a written agreement with him, as follows:

"We, the subscribers, assembled inhabitants of the Esopus, having found from time to time, through a very sorrowful experience, and to the damage of us all, the faithless and unbearable boldness of the Indians' barbarous nature—how uncertain it is to depend on their words—how careless and perilous it is to live separate and wide apart among such a faithless and insolent nation, have (on the proposition and promise of the Director-General, the lord Petrus Stuyvesant, to furnish with a night-guard, and in case of necessity with further help) resolved among one another, that in order better to protect ourselves, our wives and children, it is necessary to leave our separate dwellings immediately after the signing of this, in the most speedy manner possible, and to concentrate in such place as the Lord Director shall choose, and surround it with palisades of proper length; and in order that through these means, if it please the all-good God to lend his blessing, we may be better prepared to preserve ourselves and ours from a sudden onslaught of the Indians, we bind ourselves one to another, after prayer to the Lord, to take the means named in hand without any objection, and to complete them as speedily as possible, under a fine of one thousand guilders, to be paid for the benefit of the place, by any one who may oppose the same by words or deeds.

In further witness whereof we have hereto set our hands, in presence of the Lord-Director-General and Gouvert Loockermans, old Shepens of the City of Amsterdam in New Netherland. Done the last of May, 1658."

The most suitable site for the town duly chosen, the settlers set to work with a will to build the stockade as the Lord-Director ordered, and in three weeks' time "the palisade was substantially completed, the buildings removed, a bridge thrown over the brook beyond the gate near the northwest corner of the stockade, and a guard-house and temporary barracks built. The location of the stockade was such that on the north, east and west sides it ran along the brow of a steep declivity, with small streams of water, through wet marshy ground at the foot and an extensive prairie flat beyond on the north and east sides; and on the west was a valley, with a brook running through the centre, bordered by considerable marshy ground." This site was eminently suitable for defense. The palisades ran along what is now North Front Street on the North, Main Street on the south, Green Street on the west, and East Front Street (now Clinton Avenue) on the east; "thus being protected by very steep banks on three sides, and exposed on a level only at the south."

The people now felt more secure, but there were always distant rumblings of trouble with the natives and the Dutch were not always either considerate or prudent in their relations with the red men. Their own actions, indeed, often fomented mutual distrust and, in the autumn of 1659, some of them were themselves responsible for a dastardly outrage which, "entirely unprovoked and uncalled for, and without excuse, set the warwhoop resounding throughout the country, accompanied with all the horrors of savage warfare." Thomas Chambers had not removed into the village, but continued to live on his farm. Amongst his other retainers were eight Indians whom he had employed to husk his corn. At this task they were busy until late in the evening and, during the course of the evening, they asked for brandy. A large jug of this he gave them when their work was finished. Thereupon they repaired to a brook nearby and had their frolic, becoming not only merry but noisy. Hearing the yells from this drunken orgy, the commandant of the guard directed a squad of his men to march out of one gate and into the other, "so as to see what the turmoil was, but not to commit any violence." The report that a few Indians were enjoying a drunken spree was enough to set some of the hotheads in the town agoing, and against the orders of Ensign Smit, eight or nine of them set out and attacked the Indians, who were now lying in a stupour, "firing a volley of musketry amongst them, killing some and wounding others. . . . The Dutch thereupon returned to the fort with great speed, after that *most valiant* exploit, murdering Indians stupidly drunk." War to the knife followed this outrage, as was to be expected, and peace was only restored, after much sorrow and bloodshed on both sides, by the treaty entered into "under the blue sky of heaven," on the 15th. of July, 1660.

In May, 1661, the town was given a charter conferring municipal powers and the name "Wiltwyck" was bestowed upon it, "in commemoration of the fact that the soil was a free gift from the Indians." The official birth of the town is thus set forth in the Wiltwyck records:

"May 16, 1661. Director-General Petrus Stuyvesant, delegated and authorised in all matters of government relating to the public welfare of all the country of New Netherland, by power and commission from the noble Lords Directors of the privileged West India Company, observing the situation and condition of a place called the Esopus, which has now been inhabited and settled six or seven years; hath, in consideration of the situation and population thereof, erected the locality into a village and given it the name of Wiltwyck, whereby it shall he called now and henceforward."

The government of the town was to be administered by a schout and three schepens, who were to pay "due attention to the conduct, conversation, and abilities of honest and decent persons, inhabitants of their village."

The schout and schepens were obliged to hold their court every fortnight, harvest time excepted, unless necessity might otherwise require. "All criminals and delinquents guilty of wounding, bloodshed, fornication, adultery, public and notorious thefts, robberies, smuggling or contraband, blasphemy, violating God's holy name and religion, injuring or slandering the supreme magistrates or their representatives," were required with informations, affidavits and witnesses, to be referred to the Director-General and Council of New Netherland. Lesser crimes and misdemeanours, including "quarrels, injuries, scolding, kicking, beating, threatening," and the like were left to the adjudication of the local magistrates.

Notwithstanding all the paternalistic supervision enjoined upon the schout and schepens as a part of their duty, whereby the little town might be ordered in all godliness and quietness, the "old Adam" was rampant in the breasts of some of the villagers and would out, now and again, to the public scandal resulting in such unseemly actions as kicking, quarrelling and calling of names. Witness the following court record, dated the 17th. of January, 1671, less than ten years after Wiltwyck had been chartered as an exemplary place of residence:

"The hon. Heer Beecqman, Compt.

vs.

Edward Wittekar, Deft.

The hon. Heer Beecqman *nomine Ex Officio* says he and Michiel De Modt fought outside the gate, and demands the fine therefor in accordance with the laws.

Michiel De Modt says that Edward Wittekar challenged him upon the sword and came with a sword, and Michiel Modt also took a sword and went against him, and while they were engaged the hilt of his sword became detached, and the three persons came separated them.

Claes Claesen says that Wittekar said to the wife of Van der Coelen that he would kick her in her own house, whereupon Casper Cuyper said that he would do the same to Edward Wittekar, and in this manner the Pole took part in the quarrel and said, "What is this fighting here about?" and that Michiel Modt said he was an old soldier and not afraid. Thereupon Edward Wittekar fetched his sword and challenged Michiel the Pole and went together before the door and began to fight. Then the button fell off the hilt, and they were immediately separated; which has been affirmed under oath by Claes Claesen, Casper Meeuwesen and Cornelis Woutersen.

Edward Wittekar says he had called him a tail.

Dirck Keyser says that he was standing at Jan de Backer's door and saw Edward Wittekar go with a sword; whereupon the aforesaid Dirck said, *Ick moedt strucken raepen!* and went to Van der Coelen's house, and says not to know what had passed before that time. Then Edward Wittekar challenged the Pole and they engaged in a duel with the sword.

They were all questioned whether any one heard that Wittekar was called 'a tail' or anything else. Answer, 'No.'

The hon. court orders Edward Wittekar to pay for his offence a fine of 60 gldrs. in behalf of the officer and Michiel Modt 24 gldrs."

Such village rumpuses must have served as a welcome, and doubtless an wholesome, relief to the tedium of humdrum bucolic existence that prevailed most of the time. They must have been doubly welcome because every precaution was taken that a strongly paternalistic administration could take to render life innocuous. In addition to the fatherly supervision of manners and morals enjoined upon the schout and schepens, the Director-General promulgated a set of by-laws for the observance of the villages when the charter was granted. No person was to work on Sunday; no

**VAN STEENBURGH HOUSE,
KINGSTON-ON-HUDSON**

one should give an entertainment, sell spirituous liquors, or be intoxicated on that day, under penalty of fine and imprisonment; for the prevention of fires, the construction of wooden chimneys was prohibitted—also the building of roofs covered with cane or straw, unless the garret floor was laid tight with boards; the schout and schepens were to appoint fire wardens, who were to visit every house at least once in every month to see that they were properly built and cleaned, fining delinquents one florin for the first offence, two for the second, and four for the third; all persons were to keep good fences and gates; every one was to enclose his lot within four months and build an house on the same in one year or forfeit it; the stockade was to be kept in good order, and the gates closed every night under a penalty of three guilders; no one was to propose a religious dispute under a penalty of three days in gaol, on bread and water; every one must respect and assist in family worship.

This very naïve combination of injunctions for the governance of temporalities and spiritualities, of moral behaviour and the performance of civic duties, affords an illuminating commentary on the conceptions of the time. It is distinctly diverting to learn on what days one might or might not get drunk with impunity and without outraging the neighbours' sense of propriety. It is also quite as diverting to have the obligations of Sunday sobriety placed in the same category of sanctions with the prohibition of wooden chimneys, while the iniquity of proposing a religious dispute stands shoulder to shoulder with the duty to maintain fences and gates in good order. When we look back at provincial village history of this sort it becomes perfectly transparent where many of our modern law-makers look for inspiration. Verily, history repeats itself.

Before the town of Wiltwyck received its charter, the old Dutch church had its beginnings, and a very important part it played in the lives of Wiltwyckians and Kingstonians thence onward. A little while before the outbreak of the Indian war that was terminated by the treaty "under the blue sky of heaven," the classis of the Dutch Church at Amsterdam, heeding the spiritual wants of their brethren at the Esopus, encouraged Harmanus Blom, then preparing for the ministry in Holland, to visit New Netherland.

Arriving at Esopus in August, 1659, he preached two sermons on Sunday and had a conference with the Indians outside the stockade. Thereupon the people organised a church, gave Mr. Blom a call to become their pastor, and he returned to Holland for examination and ordination. Being ordained, he was charged to preach in New Netherland "both on water and on the land, and in all the neighbourhood, but principally in Esopus." Dominie Blom ministered faithfully to his flock until his resignation in 1667, after which the church was without a regular pastor for eleven years. In the autumn of 1678 came Dominie Van Gaasbeek, and the following year the congregation built a new and substantial stone church, forty-five by sixty feet in size, which is said to have been highly finished and to have had windows of stained glass with armorial bearings blasoned in them.

The dominie was a person of great importance and weight in the community and his influence was felt in many a sphere where to-day it would seem strange. As arbiter of disputes and adviser in matters of moment, he wielded a power by no means vague or imaginary. Notwithstanding the awe-inspiring atmosphere that surrounded the persons of the dominies, they really were human, as you would be convinced by scanning the bills for rum and tobacco consumed at clerical meetings.

Sunday observance and universal church-going were rigidly insisted upon as obligations of the first importance, but human frailties nevertheless came in for a share of consideration. At prayer meetings, commonly held from house to house, both spiritual and spirituous comfort were often dispensed alike, and one instance is recorded in which a certain member of the congregation asked the dominie to excuse him from having the meeting in his turn because he could not afford to pay for the drinks! All this, doubtless, is distasteful to folk of a certain stripe to-day, but they must remember that such were the customs of the vigorous, whole-hearted and highly coloured days when the foundations of the country were firmly laid.

One bibulous affair connected with the church is so delicious in all its thoroughly human spontaneity that it would be a great oversight not to chronicle it. At the burning of Kingston the old church bell was destroyed and the people had nothing to summon them to prayers. Some years later, Colonel Henry Rutgers presented the congregation with a ship's bell to hang in the steeple. But it did not sound right. It had a profane tone and reminded the town fathers of the ships' bells they had heard on the British men-of-war in New York Harbour or, what was even worse, of the ships' bells they had heard right in their own part of the river when Sir James Wallace brought General Sir John Vaughan to burn Kingston. It was plain that another bell must be obtained. But where should they get one? They imported their dominies from Holland, so why not import a bell thence, too? This, after proper deliberation, they decided to do. In due time, in the year 1794, the bell, a "genuine Holland Amsterdam bell," arrived accompanied by a very pious letter, all in dignified Dutch, from the bell founder, one Paulus Kuk, who prays "that when on the day of rest she [the bell] lets her voice be heard, the congregation may diligently come up to the House of the Lord to hear His word and to make needful use of it."

Alack, and alas! The good people were doomed to bitter disappointment. The bell was hung, but when they went to ring it, it would give out only a weak and dish-panny note. They had been buncoed. The "genuine Holland Amsterdam bell," after all was no better than an old cow bell, and Paulus Kuk, despite all his pious protestations, was a fraud. In righteous wrath they were about to pack their troublesome purchase back to Holland, when Colonel Rutgers again came to the rescue with some timely suggestions about hanging. They followed his advice, and lo! the bell gave forth a beautifully strong, clear tone. Wrath gave place to joy and so exuberant was their delight that they brewed gallons of punch, good old Dutch punch, and drank it—that's what it was for, to be sure—drank every bit of it and, so tradition has it, dominie and people reeled on the sidewalk and rolled in the gutter, and some of the flock even got locked in the church over night by accident. They all had a royal good time while the punch lasted and were none the worse for it afterward. If anyone with an overdeveloped sense of decorum is disposed to censure this merry little outburst of spirits, it is just as well that they should remember that some punches that look quite harmless have a direfully insidious way about them that sets heads and heels topsy-turvy.

These punch-drinking old worthies could be straight-laced enough, too, upon occasion. A dominie's bride, newly arrived from Holland, with a trousseau of the latest fashion, raised a dreadful clack by her indiscreet behaviour at a ball. Rejoicing in the possession of a wondrous brand-new red satin petticoat, and anxious to display it to advantage, she raised her skirts a trifle too high, as she danced, to suit the notions of her husband's flock. The ensuing hubbub was not quieted until an indignation meeting was held and the bride requested not to wear the objectionable garment again. Only a trifling incident this, but straws shew the set of the current. The Kingstonians, it is plain to be seen, had certain pronounced notions of decorum.

Irregularity in attendance at church services was severely frowned upon and brought with it a social stigma just as surely as did riding, racing or engaging in other profane pursuits on the first day of the week, while punctuality at service could scarcely be avoided after the pains taken to remind every head of a family by personal visitation that the hour of prayer had arrived. "It was the custom . . . immediately before ringing the last bell for church service, to be notified by a rap at each door from the ivory-headed cane of the grey-headed sexton, who sang out aloud, 'church-time'; and for this circuit was paid by each family two shillings per annum." The church bell was used not only on Sundays and to announce week-day services, but, in early times was rung "three times a day by way of notice to tidy housekeepers, of their breakfast, dinner and supper hours."

Another duty of the sexton, beside making his rounds of a Sunday morning to announce the service by word of mouth, was to carry to the clerk all written requests for the prayers of the congregation. The clerk had a long rod, slit at the end, into which he stuck the notices, and handed them to the minister, who in those days occupied a very high pulpit in the shape of an half globe mounted on the top of a column and surmounted with a sounding-board. The minister wore a black silk mantle, a cocked hat, and a neck-band with a linen cambric 'beffy' on his breast. Cravats were then uncanonical. The first psalm used to be set with movable figures, suspended on three sides of the pulpit. The deacons, when service was ended, rose in their places, the pastor distilling on them the dew of charity in a short address; they bowed, each took a bag fixed to a long black pole, with a small alarm-bell fastened to the end, and went their rounds collecting the contributions.

As the Kingston church was not furnished with any heating appliances until a very late date, it was the custom in winter for elderly matrons to be accompanied by a younger member of the family, or by a negro boy or girl, carrying a foot-stove and a test full of live coals to keep her feet warm during service. "Her body and hands were protected by a short red cloak and the marten-skin muff and tippet." The older generation were very averse to making any change in the heating arrangements and when, at last, in deference to the wishes of the younger people, stoves were installed, they always fanned themselves vigorously during service, even during the coldest winter weather, and declared they were perishing from the heat. Their conviction was so strong in this respect that one Sunday, when, by some mischance, there were no coals and the sexton had placed lighted candles inside the stoves to assist people to keep warm by the help of their imagination, these opponents of stove heat fanned as vigorously as ever and declared that the atmosphere of the church had been especially oppressive that morning.

Kingston abounds in houses of the old Dutch type, substantially built of the native limestone. To one not accustomed to them, these old Dutch houses are an unfailing source of wonder. Their appearance is thoroughly deceptive. As you first look at them, they seem modest-sized, low-roofed, oblong structures of sturdy masonry, with little sloping dormers peeking out over the beetling eaves like the eyes of a frog. To outward seeming most of these houses were built of one storey and an half, to escape the tax levied on more pretentious dwellings. But cross the threshold and a surprise awaits you. Room after room opens out from somewhere, you can't imagine quite where. You dodge around a corner and unexpectedly find yourself in a room whose existence you could not have guessed. You open a door, thinking to find a cupboard, and behold, there is yet another room staring you in the face. Apparently the law in physics about two things occupying the same space at the same time does not hold good here. Then, equally surprising, there is really a good-sized upstairs, roomy enough to hold endless more things. Now you are ready to believe that it has been said that a Dutchman's house is like his breeches—capable of holding anything he can cram into them.

Such thrift of space is amazing. Every nook and cubbyhole is made use of, and everything is tucked away as snugly as on shipboard. Did not the old Dutch housewives learn a great deal about economy of space from the ships and canal-boats of Patria?

Before the doors of the houses there were often *stoeps* with settles at each side. "There, in warm, pleasant weather, the family with perhaps some neighbours, congregated, after the day's work was over, spending an hour or two in social chat," before going early to bed. Sometimes, too, the matron of the house might be seen leaning over the lower half of the door and joining in or listening to the chat.

After the reduction of Forts Montgomery and Clinton in the Highlands, General Sir John Vaughan proceeded up the river to Kingston. In writing afterwards of the burning of the town, General Vaughan says: "Esopus [Kingston was still very commonly called Esopus] being a Nursery for almost every Villain in the Country, I judged it necessary to proceed to that town." Having arrived there, he judged it necessary also to burn it, which he did on the 16th. of October, 1777. Only one house in Kingston escaped the touch of fire, and this "fireproof" building, as a local historian has jocosely dubbed it, was the Van Steenburgh home. A tablet on the front of the dwelling commemorates the burning of the town and this single instance of immunity from the flames, but it does not tell the whole story of how the little blind god played the rôle of fireman and took a hand in the preservation of the Van Steenburgh roof tree.

A widow of engaging manners and charming presence, then living in the house, so the story goes, had met a number of British officers while on a visit to New York some months previously. As luck would have it, the officer commanding the detachment detailed for the firing of that part of Kingston where the Van Steenburgh house stood, had been deeply smitten by the widow's charms. At her entreaties he promised to spare her home, but added that, by way of precaution, it would be well to display the British flag prominently. Thereupon, according to tradition, when the work of destruction began, the fair widow climbed to the roof and from this lofty perch waved the Union Jack, or her red flannel petticoat, as some aver, over her safe abode while the houses of her neighbours crackled and burned.

Fortunately for the Kingstonians of that day, and for those of us nowadays who have a genuine regard for ancient buildings, the old Dutch houses were so stoutly put together that the fire wrought but comparatively small damage. This was soon repaired and, in consequence, the town preserves, even now, much of its primitive Colonial appearance.

The people of Kingston had been apprised of the approach of General Vaughan and of their own danger, but they had no means of defense. Nearly all the able-bodied men had been draughted into the two New York regiments with General Gates or else were with the army of General George Clinton in the Highlands. The panic was complete. The one course of action that seemed open to them was to flee as fast as they could. Accordingly the women and children, and all the old and infirm men who had been left, packed up their valuables and betook themselves to Old Hurley.

Having rallied his forces at New Windsor, Governour Clinton was hastening as fast as he could to the defense of Kingston, but even with forced marches he was unable to get his men farther than Marbletown on the night of the 15th. of October. However, he pressed on to Kingston himself and was evidently watching the movements of the British for he wrote to General Gates as follows:—

"Kingston, Oct'r 16th, 1777 one o'clock

Sir,

I am to inform you that the Enemy's Fleet of upwards of thirty Sail anchored last night about six miles below the Landing Place of this Town, which they now lie directly opposite to and appear to be making dispositions for Landing. I have so few men with me that I cannot say I have the best Prospect of having so good a Defense as might be wished. A Reinforcement is on the way to me which I left last night and which I believe will not come up in Season and at any Rate must be exceedingly fatigued. I am just informed that the Enemy are coming to the Land. I think it necessary to give you this Information that you may take such Steps as may to you appear necessary to render their Acquisition of this town of as little Importance as possible.

I have the Honour to be your most obedient & humble Servant

George Clinton

P.S. I most sincerely congratulate you on your Success to the northward.

To Major Gen'l Gates."

TAPPEN OR SLEGHT HOUSE, KINGSTON-ON-HUDSON

Library of Congress, Prints and Photographs Division

HOFFMAN HOUSE, KINGSTON-ON-HUDSON

Library of Congress, Prints and Photographs Division

The *New York Gazette*, published under British auspices gives this account:—

"There were destroyed Three Hundred and twenty-six houses, with a Barn to almost every one of them, filled with Flour, besides Grain of all kinds, much valuable Furniture, and affects, which the Royal Army disdained to take with them. Twelve Thousand barrels of Flour were burnt, and they took at the town four pieces of Cannon, with ten more upon the River, with 1150 stand of Arms with a large quantity of Powder were blown up. The whole Service was affected and the Troops re-embarked in three hours."

As the landing, firing and re-embarking were all accomplished in three hours, the time left for setting fire to three hundred and twenty-six houses, with barns besides, must have been less than one hour, for it would have taken all the rest of the time to march up from the river and back again.

While contemplating the panic of flight and the burning of the town, it is interesting to compare another item from the *New York Gazette* of the 16th. of February, 1761:—

"Kingston, (Ulster County) January 28, 1761

This Day our gracious and illustrious Sovereign King George the III[d], was proclaimed here: In the afternoon *Abraham* Low, Esq; High Sheriff of this County, attended by all the Officers of the Horse and Foot Militia, the Justices, and Trustees of this Town-Corporate, and several of the principal Freeholders and Inhabitants of the County, marched in a regular Procession to the Court-House, where His most Royal and Sacred Majesty was proclaimed, in the Presence of a numerous Audience of People, with all the Solemnity and Joyous Acclamations due upon such an Occasion—The Procession returned in Order to the House from whence they came, where the following Toasts were commemorated, His Majesty King GEORGE the Third; after which a Royal Salute followed from our Cannon;—The Princess Dowager of Wales, and all the Royal Family,—when a Round followed from our Cannon;—The King of Prussia,—another Round;—Mr. Pitt;—Success to the Expedition Fleet;—Success to His Majesty's Arms by Sea and Land;—Our worthy President;—General Amherst,—General Murray,—General Gage,—The Land we live in;—With many others, unnecessary to mention.—After which followed several Rounds from our Cannon:—And the Evening concluded with all the Demonstrations and Marks of Loyalty and Joy—usual upon such an Occasion.—

N.B. This might have been inserted in our last Week's Paper, if the Kingston Mail had met with no delay. (*And we know no Reason, why our Customers that Way should not be obliged with having their Loyalty express'd in print, as well as others.*) "

From the steps of this court-house, in front of which the accession of George III. was proclaimed amidst such professions of joy and loyalty, in 1761, sixteen years later was promulgated the Constitution of the State of New York. It was the work of a committee of the Convention of the State, and that committee consisted of the following members:—John Jay, John Sloss Hobart, William Smith, William Duer, Abraham Yates, Robert Yates, Gouverneur Morris, Robert R. Livingston, John Morrin Scott, Henry Wisner, Samuel Townsend, Colonel Charles De Witt, and Colonel John Broome. The draught of the report is in the handwriting of John Jay, by whom it was chiefly drawn. The amendments and alterations were mostly introduced and sustained by John Jay, James Duane, Gouverneur Morris, Robert R. Livingston and Charles De Witt. The first session of the Convention in Kingston was holden on the 19th. of February, 1777, but not until the 6th. of March was the committee ready to report, and on the 20th. of April the Constitution was finally adopted.

It has always been held that the Constitution was draughted in the old Senate House for it was there that John Jay had rooms and did most of his writing. It was in this house also that the Senate of New York held its sessions until the operations of the Legislature were suspended because of the critical condition of affairs and the approach of the British forces. The Senate House, which was built about 1678, was used by the State Senate because there was no room for them in the Court House, all the available space being required by the courts when in session. The Senate House was really the Ten Brook house, hut has been called by its present name for years because the Senate occupied it in the period of emergency. Major John Armstrong—of Newburgh Letters fame—in later life lived in this house for some time when he was resident in Kingston in order that his children might enjoy the educational facilities the place afforded. Aaron Burr, likewise, is said to have lived or visited here on one or more occasions, and those who delight in such eerie things profess to have heard his ghost on summer evenings playing the violin softly in one of the upper rooms. The house is a long, low one and an half storey structure, with an extension at the rear, built of the native bluish limestone and in all its details and peculiarities of design and structure is thoroughly representative of the early Dutch manner.

Another house, said to be even older than the Senate House, is the Hoffman House, on North Front Street, near one of the old town gates. Tradition says that it was built, or that a part of it was built, in 1658. It is believed to have done duty as a fort on more than one occasion, and, according to local report, was once the scene of a massacre. Much more agreeable is the recollection of a later incident. It is said that when the Hoffman family were living there, during and after the Revolutionary War, a daughter of the family was sitting on the stoop at the house-door. It was one of the occasions when Washington was in Kingston. The Commander-in-Chief, with his staff, was riding past the house; the glances of the young officers were too much for the maiden who precipitately fled indoors disclosing, as she went, a well-turned ancle. "My God, what an ancle!" ejaculated Washington, always quick to perceive and appreciate feminine charms.

The house is massively built of the native stone, with walls of unusual thickness—quite thick enough to have answered the requirements of a fort in the early days—and flooring boards or rather planks, often more than fifteen inches wide. There seems to be no particular plan to the house and the rooms are at all sorts of different levels so that it is difficult to know at any particular point whether you are upstairs or downstairs. The place is now the local Salvation Army Headquarters and the exterior walls are covered with a brownish red wash.

The generous-sized rooms, the wide fireplaces, the ample cellars and kitchens and pantries all accord well with the stories of the hospitality and good living that used to prevail there. Opening into the room on the right, as you enter, is a doorway of unusual proportions, low, but so broad that it would take the "full of a door of a man" to half fill it. For more than two hundred and fifty years this venerable building, besides serving as a dwelling and when necessary, a fort—at which times a lookout tower rose from the roof, wherein a watch was kept to apprise the townspeople of the approach of the redskins and warn the men at work in the fields to get speedily within the stockade—has been used also as an hospital and, again, as a storehouse for military supplies.

The Sleght house, at the point where Crown and Green Streets come together, is now the local headquarters of the Daughters of the Revolution and is preserved in the most admirable condition. The building is really much older than it looks and dates from long before the Revolutionary War. Its associations, however, are largely with the Revolutionary period and the names of General Washington, Governour Clinton, the Tappens, the Sleghts and the Wynkoops are closely connected with it. In the early nineteenth century a book and stationery shop was maintained here and the *Ulster Plebeian* was published within these walls. The porch before the door, and the doorway and door likewise, are quite modern and date from only a few years back when the house was taken over by the Daughters of the Revolution. They are not, therefore, to be regarded as in any way indicating architectural usage peculiar to the neighbourhood.

In order to form a well balanced mental picture of Kingston— especially Kingston of the early days, or Kingston at the end of the eighteenth century and in the early years of the nineteenth—it is necessary to take some account of the social usages that obtained. Dutch customs were then almost wholly prevalent. For one thing, ladies were in the habit of exchanging afternoon visits,

> "one, two, or three, as might be convenient, sending a message to a neighbour, that, if agreeable, they would spend the afternoon with her. If convenient, the answer was in the affirmative, if not, another early time would be named. Upon the day fixed, the visiting matrons appeared about two o'clock in the afternoon, work in hand—usually knitting. The entire afternoon was spent in a neighbourly chat, and about five o'clock the gentlemen of the families made their appearance. That was a signal for tea. No elaborate preparations were made for entertainment at the tea-table, nor expected. The table, of course, was decorated with the old-fashioned silver, and short cake, plain cake, and preserves were the principal accompaniments of the old Hyson. Soon after ten the guests took their departure. In due time the visit was

returned in like manner. Of course morning and afternoon calls were made between acquaintances and friends, and particularly upon strangers."

"For tea-parties, verbal invitations were usually given the previous day. On such occasions the lady guests were expected about five o'clock in the afternoon, and the gentlemen about six, or a little after. About seven tea and its accompaniments were served by passing them to the guests seated about the room. After tea the evening was spent by the young people in games of different kinds, to suit their fancy. Sometimes a contra-dance or two might be indulged in to the music of the jewsharp played by one of the slaves."

XXXVI.

OLD HURLEY BY KINGSTON

OLD HURLEY is just as Dutch as Dutch can be—Dutch in its people, Dutch in its houses, Dutch in its looks, Dutch in everything but name, and that was Dutch for the first few years of its history when it was known as Nieuw Dorp, that is, New Village.

It is essentially Dutch in its very habits and disposition—villages, mark you, have habits and disposition as well as people and the wonted ways of a place create its atmosphere of individuality. With characteristically Dutch conservatism, Hurley has slumbered on through its more than two and an half centuries of existence, little changed in outward appearance with the lapse of time, and tucked away, as it were, in a backwater past which the swirling eddies of feverish American progress have raced heedless of its presence, it has preserved for us a refreshing bit of the days and ways of the New Netherlands of Peter Stuyvesant and his sturdy colleagues.

VAN SICKEL TAVERN, OLD HURLEY (REAR VIEW)

How little the flight of the years has affected the aspect of Hurley Town, and how true to the spirit of its Old World proto-types it has remained, may be gathered from the impression it produced on the mind of the Dutch Minister who was taken to see it not many years since. After carefully surveying the village from end to end, he expressed the opinion that it was more truly Dutch, old Dutch, than almost any place now left in Holland.

Hurley cheeses and Kingston refugees have given Hurley most of its renown in the outside world. So plentiful and so famous at one time were the former, that Hurley was popularly credited with having "cheese-mines." The "pot cheeses" of Hurley were much esteemed by Kingston folk and there grew up a brisk trade in this toothsome commodity. As time went by, Pot Cheese became syn-onymous with Hurley, and with gentle derision not a few of the citizens of Kingston were wont to allude to the Hurleyites as "pot cheesers," or, perhaps, greet them with a jingle that ran:—

> "Some come from Hurley, some from the Rhine;
> Some pop fresh from a Pot Cheese Mine."

Needless to say, this Kingstonian pleasantry was not keenly relished by the dwellers at Hurley.

**VAN DEUSEN HOUSE, STREET
FRONT, OLD HURLEY**

The following old Dutch verses, done into English by a local antiquary, tell of plenty at Hurley, not only of pot cheese but of many other kinds of foodstuffs as well:—

"What shall we with the wheat bread do?
Eat it with the cheese from Hurley.
What shall we with the pancakes do?
Dip them in the syrup of Hurley.
What shall we with the cornmeal do?
That comes from round about Hurley?
Johnny cake bake, both sweet and brown,
With green cream cheese from Hurley."

Does not this reflect the reign of peace, plenty and contentment! The old Dutch, indeed, is truly realistic as the question comes "Wat zullen wij met die pannekoeken doen?", and at the answer, "Doop het met die stroop van Horley," one involuntarily licks his chops over the dripping sweetness of "die stroop."

The very mention of cheese and cheese-making brings to the mind idyllic visions of fat farming country with sleek kine feeding, knee-deep in pastures of heavy-matted clover, from whose blossoms the bees are distilling their next winter's store of honeyed treasure. Such a mental picture for Hurley town is not far amiss. Lying in comfortable contentment in the bottoms along the banks of the Esopus, its horizons both near and far bounded by the Catskills and their foothills, it approaches the ideal of bucolic felicity, and one freely admits that "Nieuw Dorp exists a pastoral, or else Nieuw Dorp is not."

Comfort, solid comfort, is the keynote of Hurley indoors and out. Its houses, built along the one village street, their farm-lands stretching back beyond them, have a convincing aspect of substantial prosperity and cheer. Long, low buildings they are, with thick stone walls and their upper gable ends weather-boarded. Their roofs, jutting just above the windows of the ground floor, begin their climb to the ridge-pole, enclosing within their shingled slopes great, roomy garrets that seem like very Noah's Arks, with everything under the sun stowed away in their cavernous recesses.

Such portion of this upper storey as the old Dutchman saw fit to spare from storage purposes, they made into chambers for their increasing families, and pierced the roof slope with tiny dormers. Oftentimes, however, the only light came in at the gable ends through windows on each side of the massive chimneys. It was not at all unusual to give the whole upper storey to the storage of grain and other farm products, while the family lived together below on the ground floor, their sleeping rooms opening off in unexpected places from the rooms of general use. Not seldom did one gable end have a broad door in the upper storey, and a projecting beam and pulley above it, for the hoisting of bulky articles from outside. Curiously enough, the grain was very commonly stored in casks and hogsheads.

The cellars were not one whit behind the garrets in their capacity for holding supplies. The people of New Netherland were valiant trenchermen before whose eyes the pleasures of the table loomed large, and they used up an amazing lot of victuals. Such overflowing store of potatoes and carrots, turnips, pumpkins and apples as went into those capacious bins! Rolliches and head cheeses were there a-many, with sausages, scrapple, pickles, preserves and jams, to say nothing of barrels of cyder. These all contributed their share to that elusively complex odour of plenty that rose up through the chinks of the floor and prevaded the rooms above. Only those who have met them face to face, in all their substantial corporeality, can realise the indescribable cellar smells of old Dutch farmhouses.

Everywhere economy of space was practised, and things were tucked away in all sorts of odd corners. Some of the bedchambers were scarcely as large as a steamer stateroom, and these ofttimes had little pantry cupboards beside the bed—a truly convenient arrangement for those disposed to midnight pantry raids. Tradition says that the good people of Hurley even took their cheeses to bed with them that the heat from their bodies might help the ripening process.

In plan, these houses seemed to be truly fortuitous. Apart from two or three large rooms opening off from a central hall or from whatever room the house-door was in, the other rooms cropped up in the most baffling manner, placed wherever whim or individual convenience dictated.

Hurley's gardens were and are a source of genuine delight. They are charmingly inconsequent and unconventional. There is not a jot of plan or pretense about them. Hurley vegetables grow side by side with gentle flowers in the most democratic promiscuity. Cabbages and cucumbers rub elbows with roses and lilies. Plebeian sunflowers and four o'clocks stand unabashed beside patrician boxwood and blooms of high degree, while onions and lavender in sweet accord, send their roots into common ground within a foot of one another. The Dutch gardens if not grand, at least are comfortable and useful, and have an air of sociability about them that puts one immediately at ease.

But let us look backward for a moment and scan the page of Hurley's early history. Before 1660 the settlers at Esopus—the beginnings of Kingston—had fallen foul of the Indians and suffered severely at their hands. Doubtless the Dutch themselves were partly to blame for, notwithstanding strict prohibitions, firewater, guns and ammunition found their way to the wigwams and produced the usual results.

Matters had come to such a pass that Peter Stuyvesant was obliged to adopt drastic measures and summoned the Indians to meet him at the present site of Kingston. Though reluctant and sullen they appeared, pledged their good behaviour in future and, by way of indemnity for past injuries, ceded their lands along the Esopus where Hurley now stands. This treaty was solemnly ratified on the 15th. of July, 1660, "under the blue sky of heaven," as the old record quaintly has it.

In May, 1662, on a portion of the Esopus lands, a settlement was started under the auspices of a company from Beverwyck, near Fort Orange. This was the beginning of Nieuw Dorp. By the following spring the new settlers and agents of the Beverwyck syndicate were so prospering, and so busy in tilling the soil, that they disregarded the warnings of danger from the Indians. Heedless of the order that a guard should be set when the men were working in the fields, each man was intent on cultivating his own land with a will.

On the 7th. of June, 1663, the savages, inflamed by contra-band rum, burst suddenly upon the settlement with fire and tom-ahawk. Everyone was taken completely unawares and there was no opportunity for resistance. It was all over in a few minutes. The village was left in ashes, three men had been killed, and one man, eight women and twenty-six children carried away captive. Amongst the latter were the wife and three children of Louis du Bois and this circumstance, as we shall see by-and-by, ultimately led to the establishment of a new settlement in the Walkill Valley. Fortunately, the captives were not harshly treated and were all eventually recovered.

The Indians were soon brought to terms and it was not long before the village was rebuilt and the settlers again tilling their lands. It was not, however, until several years later when New Netherland had become the Province of New York, that the village got a really good second start in life. The lands were re-surveyed more accurately, conflicting claims were adjusted, and Governour Lovelace renamed the place Hurley, after Hurley on Thames, in Berkshire, the seat of his family.

Thenceforth, despite wars and rumours of wars, Hurley lived peacefully on in its retired nook, and prospered. The French and Indian War of the mid-eighteenth century stirred only an occa-sional ripple on the surface of its placid existence. What the people were in Holland, that they were in New Netherland—for New Netherland substantially it still was, albeit the land had come Tinder British rule—and what they were elsewhere in New Netherland, that they were in Hurley only, perhaps, somewhat more conservative and tenacious of old customs and ideas, as is apt to be the case in places remote from the active scene of events. But the Dutch of the Hudson, notwithstanding their intense con-servatism, were not the slow, stupid, fatwitted louts pourtrayed by Washington Irving and his copiers, although, to us of English blood and traditions, many of their ways seem strange, and some amusing. They were broad-minded, alert, wholesome, human people who took life pleasantly and got whole-souled enjoyment from their frequent festivals.

Hurley's days of excitement all came close together at the time of the Revolutionary War—the arrival of Cadwallader Colden, junior, to live at the house of Captain Jan Van Deusen, the descent of the Kingston refugees, the encampment of General Clinton's troops and the execution of Lieutenant Daniel Taylor, whom they hanged as a spy, the sitting of the Council of Safety until the cold weather drove them away, and, towards the end of the war, the visit of General Washington when he stopped at the village, on one of his progresses, long enough to receive an address of welcome.

Cadwallader Colden, junior, the son of a former Lieutenant-Governour of the Province, was, as might be expected, a Loyalist, and though he took no active sides in the political troubles of the day, the excited Whigs of New Windsor and Newburgh adjudged him a dangerous person and procured him to be confined in the Fleet Prison at Kingston. In September, 1777, he was released on parole from this place of detention and sent to live at Hurley. The oath he was required to take sheds an interesting sidelight on the events of the times. It reads:

"I, Cadwallader Colden Esq., Do Solemnly Promise unto Charles DeWitt & Gouverneur Morris, a Committee of the Councill of Safety of the State of New York by the Councill afors'd appointed to mark out and Settle the Limits & Restrictions by which I Shall be Confin'd, upon my Enlargement from the fleet Prison, That I will forthwith Repair to the House of Cap'n Van Deusen, at Hurley, and will not go more than two miles from said House without the Permission of his Excellency George Clinton, Esq. the gov'r of the said state, That so Long as I shall Continue Confined as aforesaid, I will not by writing, word or Deed Do or be Privy to any acct, matter or thing whatsoever to Promote the Interest. Jurisdiction, Claim or Authority of the King or Parliament of Great Britain in or over all or any Part of North America, And I Pray God to help me as I shall keep this my Solemn Oath & Engagement.

"Cadwallader Colden

"Sworn at Kingston in the County of Ulster
   this 3rd. day of Sep'b, 1777
"Gouv'r Morris
"Ch : D. Witt"

Before General, the Honourable Sir John Vaughan set fire to Kingston, on the 16th. of October, 1777, the townspeople had seen the British fleet in the river and well knew that they might expect an attack. They also knew that Governour Clinton's troops could not get to Kingston in time to oppose any resistance. Prompt departure was the only course left open to them. Along the road to the west streamed a scurrying, motley procession of people, cattle, pigs, pack animals and waggons laden with poultry and farm implements, and such household effects and valuables as the haste of flight permitted them to collect.

To plentiful, prosperous, cheese-making Hurley they went, and were received with open arms and fed and sheltered, though the coming of so many refugees sorely taxed the resources of the village. Governour Clinton's forces, about a thousand strong, arrived on the 17th.—the day after Kingston was burned—and they, too, were welcomed and fed, and lay there encamped, for some time.

While in Hurley, Governour Clinton made his headquarters at Van Sickel's tavern. This hostelry, from the day it was built, early in the eighteenth century, till its destruction by fire a few years ago, was always an inn and is said to have enjoyed the distinction of having the longest continuous licence of any public house in the country. From the bough of an apple tree back of the inn they hanged Lieutenant Taylor, the full story of whose capture and trial is told in connexion with the Falls house at New Windsor, where these incidents took place.

The precipitate haste of departure from New Windsor and the rapid march, first to Marbletown, and then on to Hurley, had prevented an earlier execution of the sentence, although the Governour had approved the finding of the court-martial and signed the death order. On the way from New Windsor, the prisoner "had a long, thin rope around his neck, which was coiled and carried after him by a soldier. On halting at Marbletown he was led into the church, then used as a depôt, and being seated near the pulpit the poor wretch bent himself forward to hide his face, and the rope was then coiled upon his back."

On the morning of the 18th. of October the troops were paraded back of the tavern, Taylor was stood on top of an hogshead, the rope was made fast to the apple-tree bough, and then a soldier kicked the hogshead from under. As reward for his grisly job, the executioner got the dead officer's boots. In a manuscript journal kept by a person in Clinton's force, apparently a chaplain, is this entry:

> "October 18th., Saturday. Mr. Taylor, a spy taken in Little Britain, was hung here. Mr. Romain and myself attended him yesterday, and I have spent the morning in discoursing to him, and attended him at the gallows. He did not appear to be either a political or a gospel penitent."

Small wonder that emetics, coiled ropes, lengthy exhortations and the sundry gentle attentions of an hostile soldiery should have failed to produce conversion to a political creed which he honestly believed to be rebellion! They buried him under a flagstone before the door of the inn. All this edifying spectacle, we may be sure, the townspeople and the refugees from Kingston did not miss; it was ever after one of the outstanding events in the history of Hurley.

Hurley now became the capital of the State for a season. On the 18th. of November the Council of Safety, which had fled from Kingston to Marbletown and sate there in the interval, moved to Hurley and held their sessions in Captain Van Deusen's house. The weather soon got so cold that the members of the Council suffered greatly. They paid "Cornelius Duboys" twenty shillings "for collecting the parts of a stove, belonging to, or used by the late Convention of this State, from the ruins of the courthouse and gaol at Kingston, and transporting the same to Hurley," but "the experience of that stove had so warped its judgement and nature that it was no longer the genial giver of warmth," and the Councillors, with blue noses and chattering teeth, were literally frozen out and forced to vacate the premises. After ordering Captain Van Deusen to be paid "the sum of thirty dollars in full for the use of his room and firewood, and other services for this Council," the refrigerated lawgivers adjourned to Poughkeepsie and the old house dropped back into the somnolence of village humdrum.

HALLWAY

DOOR DETAIL

The annals of Hurley supply several illuminating glimpses of negro slavery as it obtained amongst the Dutch. For example, the following document occurs in the town records:

> "Whereas, by the Last will and Testament of Cornelius Newkerk Late of the Town of Hurley Deceased it appears that his Negro man named Charles was to Continue the sole property of his Wife Diana During her Life Time and after her Decease to Descend to his heirs, the Underwritten Subscribers Heirs to the Said Cornelius Newkerk, And Whereas we the Said Dianah and Underwritten Subscribers Heirs to the Said Cornelius Newkerk do hereby mutually agree to and with the Said Negro man Charles, that he Shall have his freedom from the Date of these presents, Provided that he the said Charles Do Maintain and Support his mother Gin an Aged Negro Wench in Such a manner that we the Subscribers may Not hereafter become Chargeable Nor Accountable in Supporting or maintaining Gin Negro Wench, upon the above Conditions we Do hereby Manumit the above Said Negro Charles and Order the Same to be Entered in the Clerk's Office of the Said Town of Hurley this 15 Day of August, 1800."

A few years prior to this, a negro man from Hurley was permitted to go about the neighbourhood examining prospective new masters and offering himself for sale, the lawfulness of his errand and the consent of his owner testified by this note:

> "The bearer Sym, his wife, a young healthy wench, and a negro boy of about two years old, are for sale. The negro has Permission to look a master for himself and his wife and child.
> The Terms of the Payment will be made easy to the Purchaser. Whoever is inclined to purchase is desired to apply to
> "Coenradt Elmendorph
>
> "Hurley, March 12, 1785."

Sym, it appears from later memoranda, either did not find a new master to his liking or else did not commend himself by his presence and qualities, for he and his wife and child remained in the possession of Elmendorph.

A careful examination of the lists of families shews that every Hurley "family of any considerable standing" held one or more slaves. The slaves seem to have been well treated, and were not only contented and comfortable, but in many instances were deeply attached to their masters and their masters' families. They were not customarily torn away from their wives and children; if they were to be sold they were often allowed to choose their own masters, or, if they proved incorrigible, they were sold into Jamaica.

DINING ROOM

When we remember the almost universal belief in witchcraft and demonology entertained well into the eighteenth century, we should expect to find some occurrence of that nature connected with an old town like Hurley. Nor shall we be disappointed. In the Elmendorf House, once a tavern, there was kept for a long time the "visible evidence that witches did exist at Hurley. It seems that a witch once got into the churn and the butter would not come. Now the cure for this is a red-hot horseshoe dropped into the refractory cream, and this method was adopted with entire success, the horseshoe being so thoroughly heated that the cream had not entirely cooled its ardour by the time it reached the bottom of the churn, where was left its faint imprint. The churn was so well exorcised that never again did the witch venture within."

The last immediate thrill of excitement Hurley experienced in the Revolutionary War was when General Washington, on his way to Kingston, after a visit to the northern out-posts, passed through the town on the 16th. of November, 1782. It was a cold, rainy day and, as the cavalcade reached the comer where the Kingston road leaves the village street, his Excellency was halted in front of the Houghtaling house, then an inn, to hearken to Matthew Ten Eyck, the chief burgess, read "The Humble Address of the Trustees of the Freeholders and Inhabitants of the Town of Hurley, To His Excellency George Washington, General and Commander-in-Chief of the American Army." While the magistrate read this welcome from a dry shelter, the distinguished visitor sate on his horse, hat in hand, listening, with his usual *savoir faire*, the raindrops trickling down his face, outwardly serene, but inwardly swearing, we may be sure, for Washington could swear upon occasion and did. It is pleasant to note that a glass of wine was brought out from the house and offered his Excellency, so that not all the dampness was without. According to another local tradition, several small boys, advantageously posted on a fence opposite, blew a salute on pumpkin-vine trombones, and the General was so amused and pleased at their efforts that he called them into the tavern and gave them each a taste of wine from his own glass. Whether the ambitious juvenile performance of pumpkin music really brought a vinous reward it is impossible to say, but, at any rate, it seems reasonably certain that the General got some spirituous comfort to sustain him on his way to Kingston.

XXXVII.

NEW PALTZ

T HE story of New Paltz might fittingly be entitled "The Annals of a Quiet Village." Although its people have now and again been startled by the alarums of war, the immediate village has led a singularly peaceful existence; and since its settlement in the latter part of the seventeenth century the years have passed, punctuated only by Sundays with the usual village gathering and the usual courtings and matchmakings, from which, in due course of time, the village Dominie reaped his profits.

In many ways New Paltz resembles Old Hurley, only, if anything, it is more perfect in its seventeenth century aspect, although surrounded by modernism on all sides. Old Hurley has stood still, and such changes as have been wrought have taken place in the village itself. New Paltz, on the other hand, has grown, but the growth has gone on round about and outside of the old Huguenot settlement and left it almost untouched, so that the one original village street presents today much the same appearance that it did more than two hundred years ago.

The settlement of New Paltz seems to have come about through the early misfortune that befell Old Hurley, for when, in 1663, the Indians fell upon Old Hurley, burned the houses and carried away captive a number of the inhabitants, the wife and children of Colonel Louis Dubois were amongst those taken prisoner. In the rescuing party that immediately set out on the trail of the marauders was Colonel Dubois, and as he passed through the country he noted the fertile lands and plentiful streams of the valley of the Walkill, where New Paltz now stands. As we know, he was fortunate enough to take back his wife and children, and all the Huguenot captives were in due time restored to their homes. But Colonel Dubois had remembered the fair grounds he had traversed, and it was not long before he, Abram Hasbrouck and several others of that number of Huguenots who had taken refuge under the Dutch flag, sought permission to purchase land of the Indians and make settlements. The Indian deeds of sale are dated the 28th. of April and the 26th. of May, 1677, while the letters patent, bearing the confirmation of the grant and signed by Governour Andros, bear date the 29th. September, 1677.

HASBROUCK HOUSE, NEW PALTZ

Library of Congress, Prints and Photographs Division

**ELTING HOUSE, SOUTHWEST
CORNER, NEW PALTZ**

Colonel Dubois was virtually the leader of the settlement. The eleven heads of families who came thither from the neighbourhood of Old Hurley were nearly all related one to another. From Kingston the little party came in three carts to New Paltz, and the place where they encamped, about a mile south of the village and on the west side of the Walkill still bears the name of "Tri Cor," which means, in English, "Three Carts." Tradition has it that when they alighted from the carts one of the party read for them the thirty-seventh Psalm.

About thirty years after the first settlement the log huts of the pioneers yielded place to more substantial dwellings of stone, and these are they that have come down to us today with their mellow, pristine charm. The little street, appropriately enough, is called Huguenot Street. At the south end of the street, on the west side, is the Jean Hasbrouck house, built in 1712. Next it is the Dubois house, built in 1705. This house has undergone some alterations, with the addition of verandahs, but it is still possible to see the old loopholes on the street front, contrived for defense in case of Indian violence. Over against it is the Bevier-Elting house, once upon a time a store, between which and the other mercantile establishments at the foot of the street, kept by the Hasbroucks, there was a sharp rivalry.

Although the people led quiet and orderly lives, for the most part undisturbed by the doings of the world round about them, they were far from dwelling in rustic crudeness, for as early as 1699 the people of New Paltz were sufficiently advanced in social refinements to have regularly-taught dressmakers. The articles of apprenticeship for Sara Frere are still in existence, according to which, upon the advice of her brother Hugues, she was bound to M. David Bonrepos and Blanche Dubois, his daughter-in-law, dressmaker. By the terms of this agreement, M. David Bonrepos, the schoolmaster and his daughter-in-law, engaged to instruct the said Sara in the art of dressmaking, "to feed her, lodge her, and educate her in the fear of the Lord, and to furnish her with whatever shall be necessary, having regard to her habits and manner of bringing up."

While surrounded by the Dutch and on most friendly terms with them it seems that none of the original Patentees, and not many of the immediate children, intermarried with their Batavian neighbours. For fifty years all the church records were kept in French; for the next seventy years, by which time the Dutch leaven had penetrated the Huguenot settlement, the church records were kept in Dutch, until supplanted by English.

The people of New Paltz had their own schoolmaster, their own customs and, what was much more remarkable, their own system of land tenure and legal administration, so that they were, to all intents and purposes, an independent, self-governing body, actually an *imperium in imperio*, recognised and respected so long as the Colonies remained under the British Crown, and permitted for some years after the Revolutionary War until, in 1785, the town was incorporated in the State Government, and, by special act of the legislature, the grants and partitions of the ancient local government were confirmed.

This little democracy was known as the Government of the Dusine, or Twelve Men. It was really government by a Parish Council, consisting of the twelve heads of families. These twelve men were chosen annually, and had power to act and "set in order and unity all common affairs." By common consent these twelve men were entrusted with the power to divide the lands by lot within the New Paltz Patent and they gave title thereto by word of mouth without written deeds. They also made rules with reference to the building of fences, and imposed fines for the violation of these rules. Such exercise of judicial power as there was, was likewise vested in their hands, and it does not appear that any appeal from the acts of the Dusine was ever carried to the Colonial Government.

Besides the Dusine, there were regularly chosen town officers with varied duties. The members of the Dusine were chosen annually at a town meeting, and were descendants in either the male or the female line from the original Patentees whom they represented. In a way their status or position would seem to be almost analogous to that of the Venetian noblemen whose names at birth were written in the Libro d'Oro. At the town election meetings the Dusine were chosen by *viva voce* vote. This curious little government of the Dusine has no parallel in the colonial history of America.

BEVIER HOUSE, NEW PALTZ

Library of Congress, Prints and Photographs Division

DU BOIS HOUSE, NEW PALTZ (STREET FRONT)

Albeit the people of New Paltz spent uneventful lives and kept much to themselves, they took their own wholesome share in the sports of the day. Foot racing, cock fighting, horse racing and, in winter, skating furnished amusement and excitement for the young and sometimes for the old as well.

They tell the story of one young wag who got even with Dominie Bogardus—a son of that more famous Dominie Bogardus of New Amsterdam—for a reproof that the Dominie had administered, but a reproof that was not relished by the recipient. One day the Dominie was invited by the young blade to ride, and was given a horse that was accustomed to race at a certain place. As the Dominie approached this spot a confederate flicked the horse with a whip, and the other horses in company all started down their wonted course at the top of their speed, the Dominie utterly unable to hold in his mount. By common consent his horse was allowed to get ahead, and when it reached the goal, where others in the secret were already waiting, a wildly jubilant shout went up—"Hurrah for the Dominie!"

FREER HOUSE, SOUTHWEST VIEW, NEW PALTZ

Still another evidence that the people of New Paltz and its neighbourhood were far from being slow-witted dolts and of lumpish, inert disposition, was the fact that it was commonly said in the early days that when a young man went wooing, the young lady to whom he was paying his attentions never thought of enquiring whether he would get drunk, but simply whether he was *ugly* when drunk.

XXXVIII.

MAPLE GROVE

MARLBOROUGH

T HE descendants of Louis du Bois, one of the "Dusine," that little band of Huguenots whom we have already seen settling New Paltz in 1670, founding there what was tantamount to a little state of their own, multiplied and prospered. They also spread beyond the bounds of their first centre of colonisation.

MAPLE GROVE, MARLBOROUGH

In 1757, Colonel Lewis du Bois, the son of Lewis du Bois of Newburgh, having acquired from his father a tract of three thousand acres at Marlborough, built himself a commodious house on the second rise from the river, not far from the King's Highway. It was stoutly framed of heavy timbers and encased with clapboards, the first clapboarded house to be erected in Ulster County.

The pitch roof was truncated at the ends, jerkin-head wise, a fashion of roof that seems to have found favour amongst the colonists of this part of the Hudson. We see much the same sort of thing at the Hasbrouck house in Newburgh, the house now known as Washington's headquarters. The old shingles have been replaced by a modern patent roofing material, but fortunately the original lines have not been changed nor tampered with. Barring the addition of a small nineteenth century verandah on the south front, and the substitution of large-paned sashes for the old multiple glazing of the lower floor, Maple Grove presents substantially the same appearance as it did when the doughty Colonel inhabited it, surrounded by his family and a retinue of black slaves.

Within, the woodwork is simple, but of great dignity. The chimney-piece in the west parlour presents a rather unusual bit of design—attributable doubtless, to the local joiner and carpenter—with its oblong panel enclosed by a decorated fret border and flanked by two short fluted pilasters rising from the mantel shelf. The very buxom dentils and modillions of the wooden cornice accord with the heavy manner of Palladian interpretation that obtained in the Colonies about the middle of the eighteenth century.

The mode of life maintained by Colonel du Bois was not only patriarchally ample and comfortable, but elegant as well, according to the standards of the time, for Maple Grove enjoyed the distinction of being the first house in the neighbourhood where a china dinner service was used, and curious housewives from the country round about came journeying thither to gaze with interest on this unwonted piece of luxury.

When the War for Independence came, Colonel Lewis du Bois had already won his spurs. He had served with distinction in the French and Indian war. When the Revolutionary conflict broke out he was entrusted with various matters of importance in organising the local resources.

Colonel du Bois being a personage of prominence in the vicinity, and his anti-British sentiments and activities being well known, when the British forces ascended the river in October, 1777, on their way to burn Kingston, under General Vaughan, Maple Grove, which could be plainly seen from the river, became the object of marked attention from the gunners on the men-of-war who fired red hot cannon balls at it in hopes of setting it a-fire. They failed of their purpose, but the cannon balls were preserved and, for years afterward, the children of the household, when they went into the attic to play on rainy days, used to roll them back and forth along the floor to simulate thunder. It was not until the present generation that a member of the family took the balls into custody and put them in the museum of the Historical Society in Newburgh. In this house was held the meeting of the Masonic lodge when Benedict Arnold's name was deleted from the rolls.

After the alarums of war had passed and the country had once more settled down to the pursuits of peace, Colonel du Bois took up again the accustomed tenour of his life at Maple Grove, busying himself with the management and improving of his estate. It was a fair and fruitful land, yielding a kindly return for the labours of cultivation.

In Colonel du Bois's day vine growing and fruit culture did not loom so large in importance as they do now, although vineyards and fruit orchards have always been matters of concern on the Hudson's west shore ever since the seventeenth century, for in the Van Rensselaer correspondence may be found frequent allusions that shew the first Patroon's solicitude about sending out and cultivating the best kinds of shoots and stocks.

Most of the cultivation of Colonel du Bois's acres was performed by negro slaves, of whom he had a considerable number. They found life, in the main, comfortable and happy, certainly far more protected and care-free than they did after they had been emancipated. Slavery was abolished by law in New York in 1825, but before that date not a few masters had manumitted their negroes. Colonel du Bois was one of them. His old friend, Colonel Leveritch, who lived just across the river and also owned many blacks, came often to Maple Grove to spend a day or two, and they tell the story that on one of these visits, when the two cronies were comparing notes, Colonel du Bois expressed his opinion that slave labour was unprofitable and that they would find themselves in pocket if they freed their slaves and hired the necessary farm labourers.

"How is that?" said Colonel Leveritch.

Said Colonel du Bois, "We plough our lands in the spring, we raise our crops and fatten our hogs, and then in the autumn, when all the crops are in, we kill the hogs, smoke the hams and bacon, and salt down a lot of pork. Then comes the winter, and the blacks have to be kept and looked after. The blacks did the work, it is true, but during the winter and spring they eat up all the results of their work, and we are no better off than we were before. And the same thing goes on in a circle, year after year."

"That's so," said Colonel Leveritch, "I never thought of it in that way before."

"I'm going to free my slaves," said Colonel du Bois.

And he did. He had evidently come to the same conclusion as had old Isaac de Peyster Teller about the appetites of his "damned niggers."

Freeing the slaves, however, was easier talked about than put into effect. When the slaves were told, six months beforehand, that they were going to be freed, there was much rejoicing and picknicking. They were kept over the winter and then they all trooped off in high glee over their newly-acquired liberty. In the autumn, though, they all came straggling back, one by one. When Colonel du Bois asked them what it meant, and reminded them that now they were free, they answered that they didn't know where to go, or they couldn't get work, or they hadn't anything to eat, or nowhere to sleep. In short, they couldn't take care of themselves. The long and short of it was that Colonel du Bois had to take care of them all another winter, willy-nilly.

Even after the second general exodus, the following spring, a certain number stayed on in their new capacity as hirelings with some responsibility for their own welfare, and faithful servants they were, devoted to the interests of the family who had so long owned them and deeply attached to the individual members of the household. It was exactly the same as it was in the South. Nor was there less regard, on the part of the family for their faithful black servitors. When they were away from home, they always thought of some little gift to bring back that they well knew would be esteemed for itself, but still more on account of the giver.

XXXIX.
THE MILL HOUSE
MARLBOROUGH
1714

WHEN the *"Half Moon,"* in its ascent of the Hudson, in that memorable year 1609, lay to one night off the little point that juts into the river not far above Newburgh Bay, Hendrick Hudson and his men were diverted, if not awed, by the dancing of the Indians on the beach, their dusky forms with towering feather war bonnets silhouetted in the glare of the fire that formed the centre of their circle. The Indians were *kintecaying*, that is to say, they were performing one of their periodic ceremonial dances connected with the rites of their religion.

To Hudson and his men, steeped in the superstitious credulity of their age, the savages seemed so many devils performing unholy incantations and forthwith they named the place "De Duyvil's Danz Kammer," that is, "The Devil's Dance Chamber," and Danz Kammer it is often called to this day. The point was one of the Indians' favourite spots for *kintecaying* and for tribal meetings, and a well-worn trail led thither from the high ground to the west, crossing, as it came, a rushing, boulder-strewn beck in the glen behind the point.

There, where the trail crossed the stream, hidden from the river by the hill in front, Gomez the Jew built his house, in 1714, with unerring Israelitish instinct for establishing himself on a natural trade route near where he might intercept the current of whatever profit flowed past his door. He knew that the red men frequented this trail and that they usually had furs to barter. Bent upon the traffic in peltries, he wished to be where he could get the first pick of whatever the Indians had, when they came down from the hill country to the north and west, before other traders could enter into competition

Gomez built his house of stone with walls near three feet thick. Like many of the other early dwellings of the region, it was of one storey, with a huge stone fireplace at each end, and a capacious garret overhead. Inside the house he had one large trading room and two smaller rooms, in one of which he stored his furs, while in the other he kept his beads. Some of these beads have been found in recent years in the garden.

MILL HOUSE, MARLBOROUGH, SOUTH FRONT

Gomez prospered exceedingly in the traffic with the red men, and as his means increased, he sent his store of peltries in his own ships to Spain and Portugal. At the time of his death he was one of the wealthiest merchants in New York City and was much respected by his fellow citizens. The memory of his presence in the neighbourhood is still perpetuated in the name of the little stream running past his door, which is often called the "Jew's Creek."

In 1772 Wolfert Acker, a sturdy Dutch American, bought the place. He was a great grandson of Jan Acker, one of the early Dutch settlers in New Netherland, and a grandson of the elder Wolfert Acker, whom Washington Irving immortalised in "Wolfert's Roost." This same Wolfert Acker, of Mill House, organised and operated the first line of packets on the Hudson,

DETAIL OF NORTH SIDE

and also one of the first ferries north of New York City. At the time of the Revolutionary War, Acker was an active Whig, and his house was frequently the meeting place for the Whig leaders in that part of the country.

It was early in the period of Acker's ownership of Mill House that the upper storey of brick was built on top of the lower storey of stone. For this addition the bricks and tile were made on the spot by Acker's negro slaves, who used home-made moulds and fetched the clay from the banks of the Hudson. The brickwork of the upper walls, laid in Liverpool bond, is of particularly pleasing quality. Acker lived until 1830 to enjoy his home by the banks of the Jew's Creek.

After Acker, the next owner of Mill House was Henry Armstrong, who came thither with his bride to pass their honeymoon and stayed sixty years! Here he wrote his Civil War novel, "Rutledge," laying many of the scenes in this very house.

XL.

WASHINGTON'S HEADQUARTERS

NEWBURGH

1709-1727-1750-1770

WEIGAND–MEYNDERS–HASBROUCK

WHEN the State of New York, in 1849, purchased the house at Newburgh used by General Washington for his headquarters and made the land about it a public park, it was the first State park in New York and the first State park in the whole country. The preservation of this historic site as a park, in full view of all who pass up and down the river by boat, gives the people of to-day an opportunity to judge whether Hendrick Hudson was right or wrong when, on sailing into Newburgh Bay, he commented on the pleasantness of the spot. The park on its high bank, surrounding the Headquarters, has preserved something of the former aspect of the land, before its ancient beauty was sullied by the accumulation of sordid ugliness with which a commercial age is wont to deface its river banks wherever there is a centre of population.

The Palatines who settled at Newburgh at the beginning of the eighteenth century evidently agreed with Hudson about the comeliness of this haven whither good Queen Anne had helped them escape from the distractions of their own land. The Quassaick Creek, flowing into the Hudson just below this point, was further inducement to the colonists.

One of the early settlers, Martin Weigand by name, in 1709, built a log house on or very near the spot where the house occupied by Washington now stands. In 1727, the first part of the present house was built—what is now the southeastern portion—supplanting the log house of 1709. In 1747, Colonel Jonathan Hasbrouck bought the house and land from Burger Meynders, who had acquired it a number of years before from Martin Weigand. In 1750 Colonel Hasbrouck greatly enlarged the house, adding what are now the western and large central portions. Just before the Revolutionary War, in 1770, to be exact, he added the northern part.

HASBROUCK HOUSE, WASHINGTON'S HEADQUARTERS, SOUTHWEST VIEW, NEWBURGH

Library of Congress, Prints and Photographs Division

The house of 1727 was rectangular; in the final addition of 1770, also, the rectangular plan was preserved, merely extending the body of the house, through its whole depth, to the north by the width of one room. All the walls are massively built of native stone and are an enduring witness to the honesty of workmanship that went into their construction. The roof is a prodigious affair, but of a form both unusual and agreeable. As the house is only one storey in height with an attic, the eaves project just above the ground floor windows. Notwithstanding the customary Dutch outward flare at the eaves, which generally tends somewhat to modify the impression of height, the house has become so deep as a result of the repeated additions that the span is exceptionally wide and the ridge, perforce, correspondingly high. This circumstance, along with the comparatively low walls, front and back, gives the roof, with its well-nigh unbroken expanse of shingles, an almost beetle-browed aspect. At the north and south ends the gables are truncated to form jerkin-heads.

There is a great deal of space inside the house—six large rooms and a broad, commodious hall on the ground floor, to say nothing of the rooms abovestairs and a lofty garret—far more space than one would suspect from looking at the outside, but then this is such a usual characteristic of Dutch houses that it causes no surprise.

One of the most remarkable features about the building is to be found in the three fireplaces of the two older portions. A sufficient wall space is blackened and equipped with cranes and other appropriate paraphernalia; a section of the floor is paved with flagging to serve for an hearth; a broad opening is cut in the ceiling, with the beams framed around it, and that is all there is to it! There is no chimney-breast, no fireplace opening enclosed by masonry, no flue; the fire is built on the stone flooring against the wall, and the smoke goes up through the oblong aperture in the ceiling. In fact, one might almost say that the fireplaces are not fireplaces at all. Massive brick chimneys are supported partly by the walls, but most of their weight rests on the tremendously heavy beams that traverse the rooms and do much more than serve as joists for the garret floor.

These chimneys, with all their peculiarities of construction, can be fully seen in the garret. There, also, in the framing of the roof, anyone who has eyes to see may read the whole record of the successive enlargements that have taken place. The original roof framing has been retained inside the larger framing required by the additions. A few years ago, when some repairs became necessary, the house was most accurately and conscientiously restored, is now in perfect condition, and is maintained under adequate guardianship.

Colonel Jonathan Hasbrouck, the owner and occupant of the house at the time the Revolutionary War broke out, a grandson of Abraham Hasbrouck—one of the original Hugeunot Patentees of New Paltz, whom we have already met—was born in Guilford in 1722. Prior to the war he had held various positions of trust in the community, and during the war he was colonel of a regiment that saw much active service, although ill health kept him away from the actual command for a great part of the time.

Before the arrival of Washington to make his headquarters there, however, the house had come in for a share of military—or shall we say naval?—notice. When the British fleet sailed up the river in October, 1777, just before the burning of Kingston, Colonel Hasbrouck's family took refuge in the cellar expecting the frigates would cannonade the house, which they did. But the cannon were aimed too low and the shots merely ploughed into the bank some distance below the building.

It was upon the same occasion of the approach of the British forces, after the fall of Forts Clinton and Montgomery, that the family were apprehensive for the safety of their valuables. "Whatever else the red-coats might spare if they stopped at Newburgh, it was a plain case that the family plate of so noted a rebel as Colonel Jonathan Hasbrouck would not be left at its owner's home." Rachel Hasbrouck, the eighteen-year-old daughter of Colonel Jonathan, mounted her mare Firefly, with the silver packed in a pair of saddlebags, and set out alone for her grandfather's house at Guilford. At the foot of the mountain, on the lonely road thither, she was stopped by a band of Loyalists. The leader, succumbing to the charm of her bearing, declared she was "too pretty to be molested." Whilst the men were discussing whether or not to take her into custody, the young lady settled the question herself by striking Firefly with her whip and dashing on. Some of the men fired after her, but the shots went astray and Mistress Rachel arrived safely at her destination.

Colonel Hasbrouck died in 1780, but his married son Isaac with the rest of the family continued to occupy the house and when General Washington made his headquarters here, from April 4th., 1782 to August 18th., 1783, he and Mrs. Washington boarded with them, according to family tradition, the Hasbroucks doubling up to make room for their distinguished guests. It is elsewhere stated, however, that the Hasbroucks moved out, leaving the Washingtons in complete possession. The Washingtons evidently brought with them some of their own household belongings for, upon their finally quitting the headquarters, we know that Mrs. Washington gave one chair to Rachel Hasbrouck and another chair to one of the other daughters. Besides there are to be found allusions to other articles they had with them.

DETAIL OF HOUSE DOOR

Library of Congress, Prints and Photographs Division

To the left of the door as you enter on the land front, in the 1770 addition, is a parlour, which the General and Mrs. Washington used as their private sitting room. Back of this, and opening into the "room with seven doors and one window" was the General's private office. Next to this, at the northeast corner, was their bedroom. The "room with seven doors and one window" was used by Washington as a general place of meeting with his officers and for the transaction of official business, besides frequently doing duty as a dining hall, although there was another room adjoining where meals were often eaten.

EAST OR RIVER FRONT

Library of Congress, Prints and Photographs Division

The period from April 4th., 1782, to August 18th., 1783, during which Washington occupied the Newburgh house, was a longer time than he spent at any other headquarters. To the Commander-in-Chief it must have been, in after years, a period of varied recollections, some of them bitter, others highly gratifying. Here he endured harrowing anxieties and suspense, here he experienced also deep satisfaction and happincss, so that when he went forth from the door for the last time he must have done so with mingled feelings of relief and regret, the latter, however, very much lightened, for the lodestone of Mount Vernon was drawing him to the shores of the Potomac.

When Washington established his quarters at Newburgh, there was general confidence throughout the land that Yorktown had virtually put an end to the war and that the coming of a full and final peace was only a matter of time. Nevertheless, no definite steps had been taken in that direction and, as Commander-in-Chief of the American Army, it was Washington's duty to be watchful in every particular and maintain his organisation in constant preparedness. There were internal difficulties, too, to be overcome—the tardiness and apparent indifference of Congress, the growing discontent of officers and men at the way in which they felt they were being treated by the Government, the contentions and jealousies between the States, and an host of minor vexations and perplexities—so that Washington's position at this period was not one of care-free idleness, however much social gaiety there may have been as the time of the Newburgh and New Windsor encampment drew to a close.

On Friday, the 10th. of May, 1782, just a little over a month after he had entered into quarters at Colonel Hasbrouck's, Washington received a letter from Sir Guy Carleton apprising him of the proceedings in the House of Commons on March 4th., the address to the King in favour of peace, and the bill reported in consequence, enabling his Majesty to conclude a peace. The letter is worth quoting for the light it throws on Sir Guy's personality and the evidence of kindly feeling. He writes:—

"Having been appointed by his Majesty to the command of the forces on the Atlantic Ocean, and joined with Admiral Digby in the commission of peace, I find it proper in this manner to apprise your Excellency of my arrival at New York.

The occasion, Sir, seems to render this communication proper, but the circumstances of the present time render it also indispensable; as I find it just to transmit herewith to your Excellency certain papers, from the perusal of which your Excellency will perceive what dispositions prevail in the government and people of England towards those of America, and what further effects are likely to follow. If the like pacific dispositions should prevail in this country, both my inclination and duty will lead me to meet it with the most zealous concurrence.

In all events, Sir, it is with me to declare that, if war must prevail, I shall endeavour to render its miseries as light to the people of this continent as the circumstances of such a condition will possibly permit."

Only twelve days later, the pleasure of prospective peace was dimmed by the profound annoyance following the receipt of Colonel Lewis Nicola's letter, written on behalf of a seemingly considerable element, suggesting the possibility and propriety of Washington, aided by the army, seizing supreme power and placing a crown upon his own head. It was in the Newburgh house that Washington penned an indignant rejection of any such proposal. He wrote:—

"With a mixture of great surprise and astonishment, I have read with attention the sentiments you have submitted to my perusal. Be assured, Sir, no occurrence in the course of the war has given me more painful sensations than your information of there being such ideas existing in the army, as you have expressed, and I must view with abhorrence and reprehend with severity. . . . . . . I am much at a loss to conceive what part of my conduct could have given encouragement to an address, which to me seems big with the greatest mischiefs, that can befall my country. If I am not deceived in the knowledge of myself, you could not have found a person to whom your schemes are more disagreeable."

But the clouds lifted somewhat, a few days later, when, on Tuesday, the 28th. of May, the orders for the day announced that:

"The Commander-in-Chief is happy in the opportunity of announcing to the army the birth of a Dauphin of France; and, desirous of giving a general occasion for testifying the satisfaction which, he is convinced, will pervade the breast of every American officer and soldier on the communication of an event so highly interesting to a Monarch and Nation who have given such distinguishing proofs of their attachment, is pleased to order a *feu de joie* on Thursday next."

The celebration, however, was postponed until Friday when, so we learn from *Heath's Memoirs,* at West Point,

"an elegant dinner was provided, by order of the Commander-in-Chief; of which the officers of the army, and a great number of ladies and gentlemen, invited from the adjacent country, partook. Thirteen toasts were drank [*sic*] announced by the discharge of cannon. At evening there was a grand feu-de-joy, opened by the discharge of 13 cannon, three times repeated. The feu-de-joy, being fired in the dark, had a pleasing appearance to the eye, as well as the ear; and was so ordered for that purpose."

"At half-past eleven o'clock," *Thatcher's Military Journal* informs us, "the celebration was concluded by the exhibition of fireworks very ingeniously constructed of various figures. His Excellency, General Washington, was unusually cheerful. He attended the ball in the evening, and with a dignified and graceful air, having Mrs. Knox for his partner, carried down a dance of twenty couple in the arbour on the green grass."

On Saturday, the 10th. of August, came a letter from Sir Guy Carleton and Admiral Digby acquainting the Commander-in-Chief that:

> "the negotiations for a general peace have already commenced at Paris, and that Mr. Grenville is invested with full powers to treat with all parties at war, and is now at Paris in the execution of his commission. And we are likewise, Sir, further made acquainted that his Majesty, in order to remove all obstacles to that peace, which he so ardently wishes to restore, has commanded his ministers to direct Mr. Grenville that the independency of the thirteen Provinces should be proposed by him in the first instance, instead of making it a condition of a general treaty."

The letter also contained proposals relative to the indemnification of the American Loyalists for their loss of property.

During all this time of anxious uncertainty, life at headquarters was somewhat varied and relieved by the coming and going of distinguished visitors who came thither to pay their respects to the General and Mrs. Washington. Besides all the officers of prominence in the army and many of the notable personages in the affairs of the day, there were the French officers, and nearly everyone of distinction who happened then to be in the neighbourhood. The list would be too long to give in detail, but some of the contemporary comments and occurrences are so illuminating that any account of the Newburgh period would be incomplete without them.

On the 5th. of December, came the Marquis de Chastellux to spend a day or two before bidding Washington a final farewell. The entry in his diary gives so faithful and intimate a picture of the official life in the Newburgh headquarters that it is worth quoting in full.

> "We passed the North river," he writes, "as night came on, and arrived at six o'clock at *Newburgh*, where I found Mr. and Mrs. Washington, Colonel *Tilgham* [Tilghman] Colonel *Humphreys*, and Major *Walker*. The headquarters of Newburgh consist of a single house, neither vast nor commodious, which is built in the

Dutch fashion. The largest room in it (which was the proprietor's parlour for his family, and which General Washington has converted into his dining room) is in truth tolerably spacious, but it has seven doors and only one window. The chimney, or rather the chimney back, is against the wall; so that there is in fact but one vent for the smoke, and the fire is in the room itself.

I found the company assembled in a small room which served by way of parlour. At nine supper was served, and when the hour of bed-time came, I found that the chamber, to which the General conducted me, was the very parlour I speak of, wherein he made them place a camp bed. . . . .

The day I remained at headquarters was passed either at table or in conversation. General *Hand*, Adjutant-General, Colonel *Reed* of New Hampshire, and Major *Graham* dined with us. On the 7th. I took leave of General Washington, nor is it difficult to imagine the pain this separation gave me; but I have too much pleasure in recollecting the real tenderness with which it affected him, not to take a pride in mentioning it."

The Count de Rochambeau arrived the same morning that the Marquis de Chastellux left and remained for his farewell visit till the 14th.

The room with seven doors and one window seems to have made a lasting impression on many of those who visited Washington at headquarters, as we may judge from the following anecdote, published in the New York *Mirror*, in 1834, for which Colonel Nicholas Fish was said to be responsible:

"Just before La Fayette's death, himself and the American Minister, with several of his countrymen, were invited to dine at the house of that distinguished Frenchman, Marbois, who was the French Secretary of Legation here during the Revolution. At the supper hour the company were shewn into a room which contrasted quite oddly with the Parisian elegance of the other apartments where they had spent the evening. A low boarded, painted ceiling, with large beams, a single small, uncurtained window, with numerous small doors, as well as the general style of the whole, gave, at first, the idea of the kitchen or largest room of a Dutch or Belgian farmhouse. On a long, rough table was a repast, just as little in keeping with the refined kitchens of Paris as the room was with its architecture. It consisted of a large dish of meat, uncouth-looking pastry, and wine in decanters and bottles, accompanied by glasses and silver mugs, such as indicated other habits and tastes than those of modern Paris. 'Do you know where we now are?' said the host to La Fayette and his companions. They paused for a few minutes in surprise. They had seen something like this before, but when and where? 'Ah! The seven doors and one window, ' said La Fayette, 'and the silver camp-goblets, such as the marshals of France used in my youth! We are at Washington's headquarters on the Hudson, *fifty years ago.*' "

La Fayette had ample opportunity for noting the peculiar construction of this roof for he and his wife had often been guests at headquarters. One memory of their visits preserved in the Hasbrouck family traditions is that the Marquis was so large and heavy a man that his wife was obliged to use five needles in knitting his stockings, and that when he went out in the saddle his valet was accustomed to take along an extra horse for his use.

Early in January, 1783, Washington received tidings that the preliminary treaty of peace had been signed in Paris on the 30th. of November preceding. As may be imagined, he experienced great relief of mind. Relief on this score, however, was soon to be counterbalanced by grave anxiety on another account. In December the officers had drawn up a memorial to Congress, setting forth their grievances and asking redress. A committee had carried this memorial to Philadelphia, but as they were unsuccessful in eliciting anything but vague promises, the general discontent and resentment amongst the officers rapidly increased. Of all this smouldering unrest Washington was well aware, for on Tuesday, the 4th. of March, he wrote Alexander Hamilton:

> "The predicament, in which I stand as a citizen and soldier, is as critical and delicate as can well be conceived. It has been the subject of many contemplative hours. The sufferings of a complaining army on one hand, and the inability of Congress and tardiness of the States on the other, are the forebodings of evil, and may be productive of events, which are more to be deprecated than prevented. . . . The just claims of the army ought, and it is to be hoped will have their weight with every sensible legislature in the United States, if Congress point to their demands and shew, if the case is so, the reasonableness of them, and the impracticability of complying with them without their aid."

The fears expressed in this letter were by no means groundless, for only six days later the celebrated "Armstrong Letters"—also called the "Newburgh Letters"—were circulated in the camp, in effect advising the army to take matters into their own hands and make demonstrations that should arouse the fears of the people and of Congress, and "therefore obtain justice for themselves." At the same time anonymous notices were circulated through the army, calling for a meeting of the general and field officers at the "New Building" on Tuesday the 11th.

As soon as Washington found this out, as he did at once, he expressed his disapprobation of the whole proceeding as disorderly, and requested the general and field officers, with one officer from each company and a proper representation from the staff of the army, to meet at the "New Building" at noon on Saturday, March 15th. At this meeting Washington read an address, pointing out the mischievous effects that would inevitably follow should the army adopt the counsels advocated in the letters, and then retired from the meeting, leaving the officers to discuss the subject unrestrained by his presence.

Tidings of the signing of a general Treaty of Peace at Paris, on the 20th. of January, 1783, were brought by the *Triumph*, a French armed vessel sent by the Marquis de la Fayette, which arrived at Philadelphia on the afternoon of the 23rd. of March. The intelligence was immediately communicated to Washington.

Not long after, came the desired authorisation from Congress and it may be imagined with what deep thankfulness and satisfaction Washington issued the following general orders, on Friday, the 18th. of April:

> "The Commander-in-Chief orders the cessation of hostilities, between the United States and the King of Great Britain; to be publicly proclaimed tomorrow at twelve at the New Building; and that the Proclamation, which will be communicated herewith, be read tomorrow evening at the head of every regiment and corps of the army; after which the Chaplains with the several brigades will render thanks to Almighty God for all His mercies, particularly for His overruling the wrath of man to His glory, and causing the rage of war to cease amongst the nations."

Even before this happy culmination to what must have been a period of extreme anxiety, the discipline of the camp was inevitably somewhat lightened, and "the increased facilities for social intercourse were improved to the fullest extent. Entertainments were given by all the principal officers; while at headquarters Mrs. Washington was surrounded by all the court of the camp." From this period of the encampment many anecdotes have come down to us that agreeably illuminate the lighter side of contemporary history.

Baron von Steuben was always a welcome guest to the ladies and the officers. On one occasion Mrs. Washington asked him how he now amused himself since the certainty of peace had greatly lightened his labours. "I read," said the Baron, "and write, my lady, and chess, and yesterday, for the first time, I went a-fishing. My gentlemen told me it was a very fine business to catch fish, and I did not know but this new trade might by-and-by be useful to me. But I fear I never can succeed—I sate in the boat three hours, it was exceedingly warm, and I caught only two fish; they told me it was very fine sport."

"What kind of fish did you take, Baron?"

"I am not sure, my lady, but I believe one of them was a whale."

"A whale, Baron, in the North River?"

"Yes, I assure you, a very fine whale, my lady—it was a whale, was it not?" appealing to one of his aides.

"An *eel*, Baron," suggested the aide.

"I beg your pardon, my lady," said von Steuben, turning again to Mrs. Washington, "but that gentleman certainly told me it was a whale!" At this, Washington joined as heartily in the laugh as did the rest of the party.

At another time, when he was dining at headquarters along with Robert Morris, and Morris was complaining bitterly of the miserable state of the treasury, the Baron turned to him and said, "Why, are you not a financier? Why do you not continue to create funds? "

"I have done all I can," said Morris, "it is impossible for me to do more."

"But you remain financier, though without finances?"

"Yes."

"Well, then, I do not think you are so honest a man as my cook. He came to me one day at Valley Forge and said, 'Baron, I am your cook, and you have nothing to cook but a piece of lean beef, which is hung up by a string before the fire. Your negro waggoner can turn the string and do as well as I can. You have promised me ten dollars a month; but, as you have nothing to cook, I wish to be discharged, and not longer to be chargeable to you.' That is an honest fellow, Morris."

The dinners and suppers at headquarters were marked by characteristics that those who attended them long remembered. Dinner came at two or three o'clock, and both dinners and suppers were "as plentiful as the country could supply, and as good as they could be made by Continental cooks. The repasts ended, French wines for our French allies and those who affected their tastes, and more substantial Madeira for Americans of the old school, circulated freely, and were served in little silver mugs or goblets made in France for Washington's camp equipage. In the summer time, the guests soon withdrew from the table to the open grounds; but in the autumn the long evenings were frequently passed around the table, beside the blazing fire. On such occasions apples and hickory nuts mingled with the wine; and the amazing consumption of the former, by Washington and his staff, was a theme of boundless wonder to the French officers."

During the time when his headquarters were at Newburgh, Washington was occasionally obliged to resort to ingenious expedients to supply his table. Continental bills were often worthless and coin could not always be obtained to exchange. Once when the specie ran out, so did the supply of eggs at the same time. In his *History of Orange County*, Eager tells us that if there was one eatable Washington preferred to all others it was eggs, and the army had consumed all the eggs produced and found in the neighbourhood of the village. When John Phillips of Newburgh, one of Washington's Life Guards, part of whose duty it was to provide for the General's table, told him the desperate state of affairs in the provision department, Washington straightway wrote out an order on the Quartermaster-General for a butt of salt. The General very well knew that just then salt was even scarcer than money. At the Quartermaster's office they were sorely puzzled to know what the Commander-in-Chief wanted so much salt for. Nevertheless, it was conveyed to its proper destination by two yoke of oxen, and Phillips was then instructed to give out notice to the country people that salt would be exchanged for eggs at headquarters. This produced the desired effect and, in a few days, eggs were as plenty at headquarters as blackberries in June. When the army left Newburgh, there were still several casks of salt in the house unconsumed.

XLI.

GENERAL KNOX'S HEADQUARTERS

NEW WINDSOR

ELLISON—MORTON 1734-1754

THE house known as the Knox Headquarters of New Windsor, and now preserved as an historic landmark through the generous instrumentality of a few interested persons who have presented it to the State of New York, was occupied on several occasions by Major General Henry Knox as his official residence while the American army was encamped in the neighbourhood. It was also, at sundry times, the abiding place of divers other distinguished officers. The record of General Knox's terms of occupancy is very explicit and consists of a certificate signed by him, dated at West Point the 9th. of September, 1783, stating that he, General Greene, and Colonels Biddle and Wadsworth "occupied three rooms,

**JOHN ELLISON HOUSE, KNOX'S
HEADQUARTERS, SOUTH
FRONT, NEW WINDSOR**

New York Public Library Digital Collections

as military,quarters, in Mr. John Ellison's house, five weeks in the months of June and July, 1779," and that "I, the subscriber, occupied three rooms as military quarters ten weeks in the fall of the year; also, from the 20th. of November, 1780, to the 4th. of July, 1781, I occupied two rooms as military quarters; and from May, 1782, to September, I occupied one room, for the same purpose, making fourteen weeks."

General Knox's residence there extended in all over a period of more than a year, and during a portion of this time Mrs. Knox was with him to grace the establishment and act as hostess, for wherever the Knoxes were there was sure to be hospitality and entertainment. Even during the darkest days of the American fortunes they managed to buoy up the spirits of those around them, and Mrs. Knox's energies in this direction were not confined to the official circle for she was indefatigable in her ministrations to the cheer and welfare of the soldiers. It seems probable that Mrs. Knox was at the New Windsor headquarters from November 1780, to July, 1781; judging from allusions to certain incidents, it is not impossible she may have been there at other times, too.

This same house also served for a time as headquarters for Major-General Gates when he was in command of the New Windsor cantonment. Its occupancy by General Gates is attested by a statement in the travels of the Marquis de Chastellux, written in December, 1782. He says, "After viewing the barracks, I regained the highroad; but passing before General Gates's house, the same that General Knox occupied in 1780, I stopped some time to make a visit of politeness." The Comte de Rochambeau also is said to have stayed there during a brief visit to Washington.

The old weather-boarded, wooden part of the house, which appears at the right-hand side of the picture of the southeast front, was built in 1734. Twenty years later, in 1754, Thomas Ellison, who was living in the house that Washington subsequently used as his New Windsor headquarters, built the stone addition for his son John. The stone structure thenceforth became the main portion of the house, the earlier weather-boarded part being given over altogether to the kitchens and slave quarters.

Tradition in the Ellison family has it that the original wooden part of the house was built by Thomas Ellison for the slaves who took care of his hunting dogs and looked after the extensive tract of land on which the dwelling stood. If this tradition be correct, it was a very unusual habitation for slaves in that day or at any time, for slaves were commonly housed in log cabins of the rudest construction, with only one or two rooms. This house, on the contrary, is quite as commodious and comfortable as the home of the average well-to-do farmer of the period. There are two large and expensively built chimneys, and the boxing of the ceiling beams and sundry other niceties of detail indicate a degree of attention to comfort and appearance hardly to be looked for in a negro cabin. It seems more probable, therefore, that it was intended for a tenant farmer who made some provision for the slaves and hunting dogs as a part of his duties.

The wide central hall, running through the older house from front to rear, made a convenient and pleasant sitting room and may have served as a dining-room also before the stone enlargement was built. Even after that, the farm labourers and domestic servants doubtless used it for the purposes just mentioned. Curiously enough, it has eight doors and only one window, but, nevertheless, is well lighted. There is also a wide fireplace, quite characteristic of the houses of that time, so arranged that the enormous backlog could be hauled in by an horse and rolled into place, the horse being led out by the door opposite to that by which he had entered. This was a customary practice in the early days, and even after more elegant enlargements were made, the great logs for the kitchen fireplaces continued to be brought in in this manner. The mention of backlogs of such size recalls the fact that in some families it was the custom to allow the slaves a Christmas holiday so long as the great hickory yule log, brought in on Christmas Eve, continued to burn. With an eye to prolonging this period of grace as long as possible, the slaves are said to have picked out very knotty logs and to have soaked them for weeks beforehand in the nearest creek.

FIREPLACE IN PARLOUR

In its architecture, the stone structure of 1754 exhibits a curious mixture of derivations. It was just at the time that the Classic influence was beginning to make itself felt along the upper reaches of the river, but without supplanting the traditional Dutch methods of building. The southeast front foreshadows the coming Georgian mode and the panelling within is unmistakably of Early-Georgian provenance, while the sides and back of the structure are altogether Dutch as well as the roof, which might be said to change from English to Dutch at the ridge-pole.

In the back part of the hall is a curious device contrived for use in case of armed attack. Just above the landing of the stair is a square opening or embrasure through which the defenders could project their muskets and command the stairway in case the front door was battered down and the assailants succeeded in forcing an entrance. Its presence shews what possibilities were in men's minds prior to the French and Indian War and the state of preparedness they found it expedient to maintain.

Another curious feature is the so-called "witch's stair," leading from the upper floor to the lofty attic above it. The pitch is very steep and almost ladder-like. In order to make the ascent within the limited space available, the narrow treads, of acute triangular shape, are set with the apex successively alternating from side to side, so that each step, at its broadest part, affords just room enough for the sole of the foot of anyone ascending, or the heel of anyone descending. It is an ingenious device and solves the difficulties of space and pitch, but it is not the most comfortable stair in the world either to go up or down, as may readily be imagined. In going either way, unless you step with the proper foot first, you are sure to come to grief.

In the older part of the house there is a bedroom opening from the kitchen and in this room there is a trapdoor opening into a vault where was, doubtless, the strong-box of the owner. The existence of this place of concealment for valuables may have helped, at least, to give rise to the ghost story connected with the house. Tradition has it that one mistress of the house, while endeavouring to pass from one room to another, through a closet which opened into both rooms, fell through an open trap-door into the cellar and broke her neck. Since then she has been seen, from time to time, to pass through these same rooms wringing her hands.

But we do not have to rely upon ghost stories of more or less vague character for our interest in this house. There are plenty of memories resting upon well-authenticated facts to engage our attention. No violence will be done to the truth of history by assuming that most, if not all, of the distinguished officers of the American army, as well as equally distinguished officers of the allies, often passed in and out of the door of this old house during all the time that the portly General Knox and his scarcely less portly spouse—they were both distinctly "substantial" persons—were in residence there, stopping to chat and to drink the health of their host and hostess in a glass of wine or a "thimblefull" of something more potent.

In addition to being fond of entertaining, the Knoxes were exceptionally good conversationalists and wherever they were there was no dullness or lack of talk that was well worth while. Their quarters, we are told, "seemed like an home in the midst of the camp and the officers were glad, no doubt, to spend as much time there as possible. Time hung heavy on their hands; they had

plenty of leisure to be social, and doubtless they availed themselves of every opportunity to relieve the monotony of their life
in camp."

While General and Mrs. Knox were occupying the Ellison
house, Mrs. Knox from time to time "gave her choice soirees,
graced by the presence of Mrs. Washington and other ladies of
taste and refinement, with whom the region abounded." It was
in this house, too, if a generally received local tradition be correct, that Washington, on one occasion, opened a ball with Maria
Colden for his partner. She was a relative of the Ellisons and, at
that time, one of the most admired belles of Orange County. As
a memento of this festivity, three of the young ladies scratched
their names on a window pane with a diamond. The three names
are perfectly legible—Sally Jansen, Gitty Winkoop, and Maria
Colden. This window pane is still preserved in the house.

When the army was encamped at New Windsor, during that
tedious period of waiting for the generally expected declaration of peace, the officers were not wholly dependent upon the
active genius of Mrs. Knox for providing interesting diversion,
as we may judge from the following notice published in the
neighbourhood:—

"The Gentlemen of the Army, with a number of the most
respected inhabitants of Ulster and Orange, purpose a Fox Hunt
on the twenty-third day of this instant, when all gentlemen are
invited with their hounds and horses. The game is plenty, and it
is hoped the sport will be pleasant. The place of rendezvous will
be at Mr. Samuel Wood's in New Windsor Precinct, where good
usage will be given, and an elegant entertainment provided.

Camp near New Windsor, Dec. 3, 1782."

There are other memories of Washington connected with the
Ellison house than those of balls and soirees. There were morning
calls with Mrs. Washington, and there were also visits on far more
serious occasions. From a passage in the *Travels* of the Marquis de
Chastellux we get an intimate little sidelight that brings the life of
the day very close to us. Just before Christmas, in 1780, he writes
that after spending the night at a public house, he continued his
journey, starting as early as possible, as he had still twelve miles

to go to reach New Windsor. Since he intended to spend only one night there, he was anxious to pass at least the greater part of the day with General Washington, who then had his headquarters at Thomas Ellison's house. "I met him," he writes,

> "two miles from New Windsor; he was in his carriage with Mrs. Washington going on a visit to Mrs. Knox whose quarters were a mile farther on near the artillery barracks. They wished to return with me but I begged them to continue their way. The General gave me one of his aides-de-camp (Colonel Humphreys) to conduct me to his house assured me that he should not be long in joining me; and he returned accordingly in half an hour."

There is also good reason to believe the tradition that Washington stopped at the Ellison house and, after taking some refreshment, rode on in company with several generals of his *staff* to the "New Building" or "The Temple" on that memorable morning of the meeting of officers he had convened there because of the anonymous address circulated in the camp counselling drastic measures to bring Congress to terms, the addresses penned by Major John Armstrong and known as the "Newburgh Letters." "General Gates," we are told, "presided. Washington took his station in the desk, drew from his coat a written address and, lifting his spectacles to his eyes, remarked:— 'Gentlemen, you will permit me to put on my spectacles, for I have not only grown grey, but almost blind in the service of my country.' Eyes were everywhere suffused with tears and the meeting was at the sway of its commander." How the meeting ended and how every vestige of disaffection was crushed are matters of well known history which it is unnecessary to recount again.

There are those who stoutly maintain that the Ellison house was really the birthplace of the Society of Cincinnati. In a certain sense, this may be true. The first *written* suggestion for the forming of such an organisation came from General Knox after he had left New Windsor, in the summer of 1782, and is dated at West Point. It is more than likely, however, that the subject had been talked over informally with his friends by General Knox while he was still quartered here, and up to that point there is no impropriety in connecting John Ellison's panelled parlour with the conception of the Society.

During the greater part of the Revolutionary War the Ellison house was virtually the centre of an encampment. "It would be as difficult to fix the periods at which some part of New Windsor was not occupied by either militia or regular troops during the Revolution, as to specify the times when it was so occupied or by what particular bodies of men . . . . In 1779-80 nine brigades of the Continental Army were encamped here, and other brigades and regiments in 1780, 1781, 1782 and 1783. The precise grounds on which these encampments were located, with the exception of those in 1782 and 1783, are equally buried in oblivion. In regard to the last, however, the record is clear. . . . The right and left wings of the army, with the exception of the Connecticut regiments, were cantoned on both sides of the Silver Stream, in the vicinity of the John Ellison house, which became the headquarters of General Gates in command, in October, 1782, and remained there until June, 1783." Substantial huts and barracks were constructed for the soldiers, and also that building known variously as "The New Building" and "The Temple," a structure designed for general army purposes and as a place for public worship. "In this cantonment," writes General Heath, "the army spent the winter very comfortably, and it proved to be their last winter quarters."

Upon the occasion of his visit in December, 1782, the Marquis de Chastellux writes of the character and appearance of these barracks:

"On the 7th. I took leave of General Washington. Colonel Tilghman accompanied me on horseback to shew me the road, and the barracks that serve as winter quarters for the American army, which were not quite finished, though the season was far advanced and the cold very severe. They are spacious, healthy and well built, and consist of a row of *log houses* containing two chambers, each inhabited by eight soldiers when complete, which makes five to six effectives, a second range of barracks is destined for the non-commissioned officers. These barracks are placed in the middle of the woods on the slope of the hill, and within reach of the water. As the great object is an healthy and convenient situation, *the army are on several hills not exactly with each other.* But it will appear singular in Europe that these barracks should be built *without a bit of iron, not even nails,* which would render the work very tedious and difficult were not the Americans very expert in putting wood together."

Mention is so often made of "The Temple" or the "New Building" in connexion with the New Windsor and Newburgh cantonments, and allusions to it are so frequent in association with the John Ellison house, that it requires some further notice in this place. It stood upon a rise that is now called Temple Hill. General Heath, in his military diary, tells us that:

> "Upon an eminence the troops erected a building handsomely finished with a spacious hall, sufficient to contain a brigade of troops on Lord's Day, for public worship, with an orchestra at one end; the vault of the ceiling was arched, at each end of the hall were two sitting rooms conveniently situated for the issuing of general orders, for the sitting of Boards of Officers, Court Martials, etc., and an office and store for the Quartermaster's and Commissary's departments. On the top was a cupola and flag staff."

A contemporary drawing by William Tarbell represents the structure as a large, substantial building, "resting upon a stone foundation rising four or five feet above grade to the window cills. The windows were perhaps eight feet high and the whole height, from the ground to the eaves, from fifteen to twenty feet. The windows shewn are nine in number (one side only represented), five of which are on the south and four on the north, with a doorway near the centre, on either side of which are two Corinthian columns, surmounted by a cupola and flagstaff." From the plain testimony of the drawing, it was a framed structure, with a steep, shingled roof.

This short-lived building was singularly invested with important Revolutionary associations and memories. What is said to be the only celebration that Washington ever ordered was held here on the 19th. of April, 1783, to mark the signing of a general treaty of peace and the issuing of military commands for the cessation of all hostilities, although, as a matter of actual fact, hostilities had ceased long before and the order now issued was merely *pro forma*. On this occasion, we are told, the assembled army, "with voices and instruments, rolled Billing's anthem, 'No King but God!' bold and strong against the sky." It was here, in that meeting holden at noon, on the 15th. of March, preceding, that

Washington turned back the rising tide of discontent and disaffection amongst the officers, voiced by the Newburgh letters. How the magnetism of his presence carried the day, we have previously seen. It was here, too, pursuant to the formation of the Society of the Cincinnati more than a month before at Mount Gulian, that the meeting was held at which General Washington was elected President of the Society, a post he continued to hold until his death.

The Temple was struck by lightning on the 11th. of June, 1783, and was afterwards wrecked by order of the Quartermaster-General and the material sold at auction on the 13th. of September following, so that no vestiges of this building are now to be seen.

XLII.

THE FALLS HOUSE

I T IS sad to relate that an house, about which centred not a few historical associations, was in recent years demolished, partly through the obstinacy of an owner, partly through a disposition to gratify the sensationalism of cinema producers. The Falls House was deliberately and intentionally burned down, and by prearranged understanding the cinema photographers set up their cameras and made a film record of the incident! Truly, the age of barbarism seems not yet past.

Long before the War for Independence, near the hamlet of Little Britain in the Town of New Windsor, a saw mill was built on the banks of Silver Stream with a dwelling house conveniently nearby. For some years prior to the outbreak of hostilities between the Colonies and the Mother Country, the mill was run by Edward Falls who, with his family, tenanted the house—whence the name by which it is commonly known. Early in 1777 Edward Falls met his death by accident in the mill and left his widow in sole occupancy of the house.

Thither for refuge, to the house of the Widow Falls, came the wife and children of Governour Clinton—they had been living near the river in New Windsor—when Forts Clinton and Montgomery fell on the 6th. of October, 1777, and thither came Governour Clinton himself, making the house his headquarters during those few strenuous days when, as Commander-in-Chief of the forces of the State, he was rallying the troops before hastening on to the defence of Kingston where, it was expected, the British would strike the next blow.

Apprehensive lest Sir Henry Clinton's forces might essay some land raids on their way to Kingston, Governour Clinton sent his wife and children across the river and commissioned his brother-in-law, Doctor Peter Tappen, to conduct them to a place of safety far enough east of the Hudson to remove all cause of anxiety. Doctor Tappen took his charges to the house of Mrs. Barnes in Pleasant Valley.

At noon, on the 10th. of October, while Governour Clinton was still at the Falls House, an horseman rode up to the camp guard and, when challenged, replied, "I am a friend and wish to see General Clinton." He was forthwith conducted to General Clinton but, to his dismay, on being ushered in found the gentleman for whom he had asked was not *his* General Clinton. The stranger was Lieutenant Daniel Taylor, of Captain Stewart's Company, in the Ninth Regiment of the British troops, and the General Clinton whom he expected to find was *Sir Henry* Clinton. He was an express messenger sent by Sir Henry with a despatch to General Burgoyne. When he had passed the Highlands, encountering troops in British uniform he imagined that Sir Henry's forces had moved forward and drew near the camp. The men were wearing captured British uniforms that had not yet been redyed blue and this deceived him.

Discovering the fatal mistake he had made, Taylor was seen to put his hand to his mouth and swallow something. The action at once excited suspicion and Governour Clinton immediately sent for Doctor Moses Higby of Newburgh, who was then living nearby at the Corley house. At the Governour's orders, Doctor Higby administered a powerful emetic. What ensued Clinton told in his letter to the Council of Safety:

> "The letter from Clinton to Burgoyne, taken from Daniel Taylor, was enclosed in a small silver ball of an oval form, about the size of a fusee bullet, and shut with a screw in the middle. When he was taken and brought before me he swallowed it. I mistrusted this to be the case from information I received, and administered to him a very strong emetic calculated to act either way. This had the desired effect; it brought it from him; but, though closely watched, he had the art to conceal it a second time. I made him believe I had taken one Campbell, another messenger, who was out on the same business; that I learned from him all I wanted to know, and demanded the ball on pain of being hung up instantly and being cut open to search for it. This brought it forth."

The letter contained in the silver bullet, written on tissue paper, read as follows:

"Fort Montgomery, Oct. 8th., 1777.

"Nous y voici and nothing between us but Gates. I sincerely hope this little success of ours may facilitate your operations. In answer to your letter of the 28th. Sept., by C. C., I shall only say, I cannot presume to order, or even advise, for reasons obvious. I heartily wish you success.

Faithfully yours,
H. CLINTON.

Gen. Burgoyne."

The taking of Forts Clinton and Montgomery came too late to be of use to General Burgoyne, and Sir Henry had not yet heard of Burgoyne's surrender.

At a general court-martial held at New Windsor, the 14th. of October, and presided over by Colonel Lewis du Bois, this verdict was found:

"Daniel Taylor, charged with lurking about the camp as a spy from the enemy, confined by order of General Clinton, was brought before said court, and to the above crime the prisoner plead not guilty. But confessed his being an Express from General Sir Henry Clinton to Burgoyne when taken and that he had been employed as an Express also from General Burgoyne to General Clinton, and was taken in the camp of the army of the United States, near New Windsor, by Lieut. Howe. Taylor likewise confessed his being a first Lieutenant in Captain Stewart's Company in the Ninth Regiment of the British troops, and but one man in company when taken. The prisoner pleaded that he was not employed as a spy, but on the contrary was charged both by General Clinton and Burgoyne not to come near our camp; but meeting accidentally with some of our troops in British uniform, he was thereby deceived and discovered himself to them.

"The court, after considering the case, were of opinion that the prisoner is guilty of the charge brought against him, and adjudged to suffer death, to be hanged at such time and place as the General shall direct.

"A true copy of the proceedings;

Test.

LEWIS DU BOIS,
President."

The rest of Lieutenant Taylor's story has already been told in the account of Old Hurley. His execution as a *spy* seems hardly justified by the facts connected with his arrest; a local historian states that letters found in Taylor's possession indicated that he was a resident of Kinderhook who had enlisted in the service of the King, a circumstance that may well have infused some hostile animus in the decision of the court.

While the army was encamped at Newburgh and New Windsor in 1782 and 1783, the house was no longer occupied by the Widow Falls but by one Woods and is said to have been filled to its capacity by officers of the army. One of them is believed to have been Major John Armstrong, he of the facile pen who composed the "Newburgh Letters" that produced such a tempest. In all likelihood, therefore, these letters were written in this house.

Armstrong unquestionably expressed the sentiments of a great body of army officers, and expressed them very well. The grievances he set forth were keenly felt and demanded remedy, but the means he suggested for obtaining the remedy were, to say the least, injudicious. Armstrong's loyalty has never been seriously impugned; it was his judgement in this case that was greatly at fault. His subsequent record and the posts of trust and responsibility he occupied in later life prove the esteem in which he was held by his contemporaries.

XLIII.
THE CLINTON HOUSE
LITTLE BRITAIN, NEW WINDSOR

U NFORTUNATELY, the Clinton house at Little Britain, in the town of New Windsor, must be included in the list of historic places that a former generation was too indifferent to save from destruction. Most of it was demolished many years ago to accord with the "improvement" scheme by which the then owner was obsessed. Nevertheless, some early pictures of the place remain, and, as the family seat of distinguished makers of Colonial and Revolutionary history, it deserves description.

Charles Clinton, the Immigrant, arrived in the Province in 1729 and about 1731 built the earliest portion of the house at Little Britain. The walls were of stone while the gable ends, above the ground floor, were filled with siding or clapboards. This nucleus of what the house later became, as the family increased and conditions of existence became easier, was a very unpretentious dwelling, though staunchly built. On the ground floor was one large room, about twenty feet square, with two windows and a door in front and one window and a door at the rear. A capacious fireplace and massive stone chimney breast occupied most of the north end of the room, while the upper storey consisted of one large chamber, unceiled and open to the rafters.

Some years later an addition was built at the right side of the original structure, the extension having one door and three windows on the front. To this enlargement subsequently a new kitchen was attached. The next enlargement came to the left of the old first portion. It was erected about 1761 and was reckoned a very superior piece of domestic architecture at the time, being graced with carefully finished interior details reflecting the prevailing manner of the period and having a verandah on three sides of the exterior. Thus the final form of the house shewed a long, rambling composition with a roof line of varied height—obviously a continuous growth of different periods, and marked by a certain unconsciously acquired picturesque quality as well as an intimate domestic character. When the greater part of the house was demolished, the small portion left standing was converted into an ice house!

Two branches of the Clinton family have figured conspicuously in the history of the Province and State of New York. One was the elder branch and was represented, first by the Honourable George Clinton, the youngest son of Francis, sixth Earl of Lincoln, who was Governour of the Province from 1743 to 1753, after which he returned to England. The second member of this branch of the Clinton family to appear in the pages of New York history was the son of the Provincial Governour, George Clinton—General Sir Henry Clinton, who commanded the British forces in America during a part of the Revolutionary War.

The other branch of the family was far more intimately and permanently connected with the fortunes of the Province and State. It was a cadet branch and was descended from William Clinton, grandson of Henry, second Earl of Lincoln, a staunch adherent of the Stuarts in the Civil War and an officer in the army of King Charles I. Clinton served with devotion until the King was martyred and the Royalist forces scattered, and then fled to the Continent to escape the malice and fury of the roundheads. There he remained for several years in France and Spain. Returning to Scotland, he married a lady of the family of Kennedy. Soon after he was obliged to seek personal safety in Ireland where he died a few years later. His grandson, Charles Clinton, having decided to go out to the American Colonies, leased his estate to Lord Granard, enlisted a company of friends and neighbours to accompany him, and sailed from Dublin in the spring of 1729, intending to land at Philadelphia. Provisions of all kinds ran short and a peculiarly fatal type of measles broke out with the result that ninety of the company died. Clinton and the survivors prevailed upon the captain to change his course and make for the nearest land, which happened to be Cape Cod. This they made on the 4th. of October, after a miserable voyage of five months.

Part of the company remained on Cape Cod till the spring of 1730, when they all removed to Ulster County and settled in the district now known as Little Britain. This part of Ulster County, it will be recalled, afterwards became a part of Orange County when the division of counties took place and boundaries were readjusted. Here in Little Britain Charles Clinton was an acknowledged leader amongst his neighbours as he had been in County Longford, whence they had all migrated. He was a capable mathematician and surveyor and well qualified by disposition and training for any of those pioneer duties demanding guidance or resolute action that might be required of him. He soon became an agent for the sale of patented lands in his neighbourhood and was appointed a Justice of the Peace not long after his arrival.

In 1756 he was commissioned Lieutenant-Colonel of the Second Regiment of Militia of Ulster County and, Governour Sir Charles Hardy commissioned him Lieutenant Colonel of the Battalion under the command of Colonel Bradstreet. In this capacity he served in the French and Indian War, being stationed at Fort Herkimer, in the Mohawk Valley, in 1758, and in the summer of that same year was present at the taking of Fort Frontenac. At the close of the war he returned to Little Britain and, in 1769, was appointed Judge of the Court of Common Pleas of Ulster County.

The remainder of his days, apart from the time devoted to the discharge of his judicial functions, he spent in the cultivation of literature and the management of his estate. In writing of him at this period, Doctor Joseph Young says:—

> "Colonel Charles Clinton possessed an acute genius, a penetrating, solid judgement, and an extensive fund of useful as well as of ornamental knowledge, with the affability and polished manners of a polite gentleman. He was a tall, straight, graceful person, of a majestic appearance."

It is also recorded of him that in both his private and public relations he sustained a pure and elevated character, exerting a broad and wholesome influence throughout the whole district where he lived.

He was born on the estate of his father, James Clinton—an officer in the British Army—in County Longford, in 1680, and died in his eighty-third year, at his home in Little Britain, the 19th. of November, 1773. He was a confirmed Whig in his political convictions and dying, as he did, just on the eve of the Revolution, he enjoined his sons to "stand by the liberties of America."

These sons, James and George, were both born in the house at Little Britain. The former was General James Clinton, of Revolutionary renown and the father of DeWitt Clinton; the latter was General George Clinton, Revolutionary Governour of the State of New York and subsequently Vice-President of the United States. General James Clinton served with distinction throughout the Revolutionary War, but was absent from his home, the rambling old house at Little Britain, so much of the time in the discharge of his military duties that there is little or nothing of special interest to relate in connexion with the homestead in the way of historic incident.

General George Clinton, the second distinguished son born in the Little Britain home of the family, "was to the State of New York what Washington was to the nation." In early manhood he gave substantial promise of the activity and courage that were such conspicuous characteristics throughout his subsequent career. At the time of the French and Indian War, when he was less than twenty years old, he left home and sailed in a privateer. Returning from this adventure, he demanded and received a place in the expedition under his father and his elder brother James against Fort Frontenac. After the close of the war he applied himself to the study of the law under the tutelage of Chief-Justice William Smith.

In 1759 he was appointed Clerk of Ulster County, while the following year he was elected to a seat in the Provincial Assembly. Thence onward he was immersed in Colonial politics and his voice was heard in every discussion of importance. In the events immediately preceding the outbreak of the Revolutionary War he played a prominent rôle, while from the commencement of hostilities till the end of his life, his personal history and the history of New York State are so closely interwoven that it is impossible to separate one from the other. He appears at every turn, and in every event of importance he is either on the spot himself or else so intimately concerned with it, that a biographical recapitulation of his activities would involve a complete synopsis of Provincial and State history from 1760, when he entered the Provincial Assembly, till the date of his death, 1808.

Since the aim of this volume is primarily to deal with the history of *houses* rather than individuals, introducing only the persons and events that have some direct connexion with the particular place under survey, and since Governour Clinton, after his early youth, spent most of his time away from Little Britain, there is no occasion to enter here into a detailed biographical account of an historical character so well known and so much written about elsewhere. It will be sufficient to call attention to one or two incidents that are generally overlooked, incidents that shed a pleasing and somewhat intimate light of their own on the traits of a personage commonly subjected to the matter-of-fact analyses of public history that all too often are coldly impersonal and belittle or obscure minor items that subtly but none the less surely reveal living, human personality. In this case, too, these incidents have a certain connexion with the neighbourhood of New Windsor. Notwithstanding Governour Clinton's vigorous and unswerving opposition to the Crown, and his passionate allegiance to the American cause into which he had thrown himself with fiery ardour, he did not forget the past services and kindness of old friends, and when those friends were Loyalists he did not waver in giving them such protection as he consistently could, provided they remained passive in the struggle and refrained from actions prejudicial to the American interests. And this he did in the face of bitter and sometimes venomous opposition from the many intemperate hotheads of his own side. His old legal preceptor was a "King's man"; to him he assured liberty, under restraint, but to the letter of assurance added, "Don't write to me again while the war lasts." Cadwallader Colden and Vincent Matthews, of his own immediate neighbourhood, met the like treatment at his hands, while it seems not improbable that Colonel Thomas Ellison, who had in time past assisted the Clintons, may have had some special consideration accorded him whereby his property both in New York City, under British control, and in New Windsor, within the American lines, was safe from confiscation proceedings. In whatever circumstances arose, whether in public or in private life, he did fearlessly and promptly whatever he conceived his duty. When, after the close of the war, in New York City he saw a British officer in the hands of a mob bent on tarring and feathering him, Clinton rushed single-handed to the rescue and saved him from this ignominy.

There has been not a little dispute in the past over the exact place of DeWitt Clinton's birth. Some contend that he was born at Deerpark when his mother was there on a visit; others insist just as stoutly that he was born in the family homestead at Little Britain. This was the house always occupied by his father, General James Clinton, after the death of Colonel Charles Clinton, the Immigrant, and apparently before that time also the General had made his home there. All things considered, the assumption that DeWitt Clinton first saw the light in the Little Britain house seems not only perfectly reasonable but also capable of substantiation. In that case, the Clinton homestead was the birthplace of three remarkable men, all of whom played a conspicuous part in the making of American history. This is sufficient distinction to entitle the house to be included amongst the Hudson Valley's historic homes, even though it lack the array of dramatic events connected with some of the other dwellings of noted personages or the quarters occupied by them for a season. DeWitt Clinton's early boyhood was passed in the Little Britain house, but as he spent part of his youth at school elsewhere and entered public life as a very young man, comparatively little of his career is locally identified with the house of his birth and childhood. Since he, too, has received full biographical attention, as well as his uncle the Governour, it would be idle to reiterate in this place what has been ably treated in other works that are readily accessible, wherein it has been possible to give all the illuminating minutiæ of circumstances not germane to the purpose of this volume.

XLIV.

THE "TREASON HOUSE"

HAVERSTRAW

JOSHUA HETT SMITH

BETWEEN Stony Point and Haverstraw, and somewhat nearer the latter, still stands a dwelling known as the "Treason House." At the time of the Revolutionary War it was the home of Joshua Hett Smith and was the scene of one act of that tragedy in which an amiable and blameless British officer lost his life and a trusted American General lost his honour.

It was from the door of this house that Benedict Arnold issued to keep his rendezvous with Major André at the foot of Long Clove Mountain, on the night of the 21st. of September, 1780. Thither, just before daybreak, Arnold led the ill-fated André, and within these walls, in a room on the upper floor, during the morning of the 22nd. of September, were consummated the plans for the betrayal of West Point and the undoing of the American hopes.

Joshua Hett Smith, the master of the house, was a barrister and a brother of Chief Justice William Smith, of New York City. The family were exceedingly well-connected, widely known and respected, and of influential associations. It was obviously to Arnold's advantage, for many reasons, to have the apparent help and countenance of Smith in his dealings as a shield against any suspicions that might be aroused by his communications with the British authorities. Chief Justice Smith had remained in New York City after the British occupation, and the Smith family had considerable interests there, so that it was natural that certain restricted communications should be permitted and maintained between the members of the family relative to their own private affairs.

Whether Joshua Hett Smith was a knave or a fool has never been really determined. The general feeling seems to have been that he was the dupe and cats-paw of Arnold and did not know the nature of the negotiations he was assisting. One would imagine that ordinary common-sense would have told him that something was agley. At any rate, his rôle was pusillanimous, and his behaviour at the time and subsequently indicated that he knew it was.

Previous to this, Arnold had made arrangements to have his meeting with André take place at Smith's house, in case the conference took any great length of time. Although André had definitely declined to come within the American lines to carry on the negotiations, Arnold had apparently resolved that he should be brought ashore from the *Vulture*. Smith had complaisantly taken his family to Fishkill to visit friends, and then returned to Beverly House to conclude the necessary plans with Arnold. Arnold gave him the customary pass for a flag of truce along with an order to Major Kierse, at Stony Point, to supply him with a boat whenever he should ask for it, and directed Smith to go out to the *Vulture* by night and bring ashore an important personage who was expected to be there and have communications of importance to make from the British military authorities. Smith failed to visit the *Vulture* at the time he was directed to go, owing to the flat refusal of the boatman to make the trip, and he was obliged to send word of this to Arnold. It was then that Arnold himself came down the river and, fortunately for the course of his plans, received from the hands of Colonel Livingston at Verplanck's Point a letter that had just been sent ashore from Captain Sutherland of the *Vulture*. The missive was apparently a remonstrance against firing upon a flag of truce, and was addressed to Colonel Livingston; it was in the handwriting of André though signed by Sutherland, and was in reality a covert message to Arnold that Major André was on board the *Vulture*.

Arnold fully understood the need of haste if his plans were not to miscarry. The boatman whom Smith had endeavoured to use the night before again refused to row out to the *Vulture*, but in the end yielded to Arnold's threats of punishment. At midnight they silently pushed off from shore and brought the skiff alongside the man-of-war. After some explanations, Smith was permitted to go aboard and found Captain Sutherland and Beverly Robinson in the cabin who, besides Major André, were the only persons on the ship privy to the transaction under way. Smith bore a sealed letter from Arnold to

Beverly Robinson, couched in terms to avoid incrimination should it chance to fall into the wrong hands. It read:—

"This will be delivered to you by Mr. Smith, who will conduct you to a place of safety. Neither Mr. Smith nor any other person shall be acquainted with your proposals. If they (which I doubt not) are of such a nature that I can officially take notice of them, I shall do it with pleasure. I take it for granted that Colonel Robinson will not propose anything that is not for the interest of the United States as well as himself."

Besides this letter, Smith also carried two passes, signed by Arnold, which Robinson fully understood to mean that Arnold expected André to come on shore. They were also meant to secure the boat from detention by the water-guard. The first of these read:—

"Permission is given to Joshua Smith, Esquire, a gentleman, Mr. John Anderson [Major André], who is with him, and his two servants, to pass and repass the guards near King's Ferry at all times.

B. Arnold, M. Gen'l.

The second read:—

"Permission is granted to Joshua Smith, Esq., to go to Dobb's Ferry with three Men and a Boy with a Flag to carry some Letters of a private Nature for Gentlemen in New York, and to return immediately.

B. Arnold, M. Gen'l.

N.B.—He has permission to go at such hours and times as the tide and his business suits.

B. A.

After Major André was introduced to Smith, both entered a small boat and landed on the western shore of the Hudson, at the foot of Long Clove Mountain, where Arnold was waiting in the thick bushes. "They were left alone, and for the first time . . . . Arnold's lips uttered audibly the words of treason. There, in the gloom of night, concealed from all human cognisance," they discussed the details of the plan . . . . "The hour of dawn approached, and the conference was yet in progress. Smith came and warned of the necessity of haste. There was yet much to do, and André reluctantly consented to mount the horse rode by Arnold's servant, and accompany the general to Smith's house, nearly four miles distant. It was yet dark, and the voice of the sentinel, near the village of Haverstraw, gave André the first intimation that he was within the American lines. He felt his danger, but it was too late to recede. His uniform was effectually concealed by a long blue surtout, yet the real danger that environed him, he being within the enemy's lines without a flag or pass, made him exceedingly uneasy. They arrived at Smith's house at dawn, and at that moment they heard a cannonade in the direction of the *Vulture*. Colonel Livingston had been informed that the vessel lay so near the shore as to be within cannon shot. Accordingly, during the night, he sent a party with cannon from Verplanck's Point, and at dawn, from Teller's Point, they opened a fire upon the *Vulture*, of such severity that the vessel hoisted her anchor and dropped further down the river." With what anxious forebodings André beheld this movement, we may well imagine. He had been deceived by Arnold and brought within the American lines unwittingly and against his express stipulation. When the firing stopped, he was greatly relieved, but the departure of the *Vulture* greatly increased his danger and the difficulty of his position which he already felt keenly enough. However, there was nothing now to do but to go through with it.

When all the details had been fully discussed and definite plans adopted, Arnold got into his own barge and was rowed up the river to his headquarters at Beverly House. André passed the rest of the day alone, remaining indoors, and when evening came he requested Smith to take him back again to the *Vulture*. This Smith positively refused to do and, as an excuse, pleaded an attack of ague. "If he quaked," says Lossing, "it was probably not from ague, but from fear, wrought by the firing upon the *Vulture*; for he offered to ride half the night with André, on horseback, if he would take a land route. Having no other means of reaching the vessel, André was obliged to yield to the force of circumstances."

He agreed to cross the river at King's Ferry to Verplanck's Point and then make his way to New York by land. The possibility of having to do this had been discussed with Arnold and the latter had strongly urged him, in this emergency, to take off his uniform and wear civilian's clothes. "This act, and the receiving of papers from Arnold, were contrary to the express orders of Sir Henry Clinton, but André was obliged to be governed by the unforeseen circumstances in which he was placed." He took off his military coat and put on a coat that Smith lent him. Poor André's abandoned red coat turns up again in the letter that Joshua Smith wrote a few days later, while he was detained under arrest at Beverly House, to his brother Thomas:—

"Dear Brother,—I am here a prisoner, and am therefore unable to attend in person. I would be obliged to you if you would deliver to Captain Cairns, of Lee's Dragoons, a British uniform Coat, which you will find in one of the drawers in the room above stairs. I would be happy to see you. Remember me to your family.

I am affectionately yours
Joshua H. Smith."

Smith agreed to accompany André on his way as far as the lower outposts of the American army. Just a little before sunset, therefore, on the evening of the 22nd. of September, accompanied by a negro servant, they crossed King's Ferry and, passing through the works at Verplanck's Point, took their way towards White Plains. How André was captured near Tarrytown has been told again and again and the story needs no repeating here. It is not generally known, however, that he took this road against the advice he had been given, because it was said to be more or less infested by the "Cow-boys" from whom, since they professed loyalty to the Crown, he considered that he had nothing to fear.

During the Revolutionary War the Neutral Ground in Westchester County became a political and social hell for the inhabitants, thanks to the activities of the Cow-boys and Skinners, both of whom made the place so intolerable that not a few of the dwellers in that region moved away and "allowed their lands to become a waste, rather than remain in the midst of perpetual torments." The Cow-boys were professedly Loyalists, while the Skinners were Whigs. The Cow-boys got their name from their habit of making raids and driving off the cattle of the farmers, taking them into New York to sell them to the British forces and to the citizens. Political allegiance sate lightly upon the consciences of Cowboys and Skinners alike and merely furnished an excuse to lend some slight degree of justification for their existence. In reality they were ruffians and marauders, and their chief object was plunder. They were treacherous, rapacious and brutal, and though commonly opposed and ready to do battle under their respective banners, they were time and again in league and shared the fruits of their forays. While they were especially active in Westchester County, their theatre was not confined to the east bank of the river, and they carried on their depredations on the opposite west shore with almost as much energy, sending their bands far back into the hill country beyond.

One of the most notorious of these West Shore Cow-boys was Claudius Smith whose visitations fell heavily upon Blooming Grove, Cornwall and Monroe, in Orange County, and upon all the neighbourhood round about. He is said to have early evinced a disposition for dishonesty, thievery and plunder, a course of ill-doing in which he was encouraged by his father. When pursued by armed forces, the band of marauders led by Claudius Smith sought refuge in caves and well-nigh inaccessible fastnesses of the hills. Now and again Smith would distribute a portion of his booty to some of the poor, thus emulating Robin Hood in slight measure.

Once, when taken prisoner and detained in the gaol at Goshen, a band of his followers attacked the building and threatened mischief to the sheriff. The result of the bold action was that Smith and a companion were freed and the entire crew left Goshen after making a rich haul of money, livestock and general provisions.

In 1778 Smith led a plundering expedition against the house of Major Strong and, when that gentleman was laying down his arms under the assurance of safety, brutally shot him in cold blood, killing him instantly. The gang then pillaged the house, after which they fled to the mountains. This atrocity so aroused Governour Clinton that he offered a reward of $1250.00 for Smith's arrest, and $250.00 for the arrest of each of his sons.

Not long afterward it was learned that Smith was in Smithtown on Long Island, whither he had fled under British protection, and was lodged in the house of a widow. One dark night a small party of Americans crossed the Sound in a whaleboat, determined to capture the outlaw. They entered the house where he lay, without knocking, and were directed to his room. Although he was taken by surprise, it required the combined strength of four men to bind and gag him. He was then taken back to Goshen Gaol by an armed guard who had been instructed to shoot him dead if his followers made any attempt at a rescue. He was hanged on the 22nd. of January, 1779, and as the noose was being put around his neck, he stooped down, unbuckled his shoes and kicked them off, saying:—"My Mother said I should die like a trooper's horse, with my shoes on; I want to make her a false prophet and liar."

Thus ended the career of one of the most notorious ringleaders of those lawless spirits who made the war an excuse to indulge their disorderly and predatory inclinations with impunity, infesting the neutral territory between the armies and making life well-nigh unbearable for those who dwelt there. The dangers and hardships of war were bad enough, but the Cow-boys and Skinners were worse.

After Joshua Hett Smith left Major André to pursue the road alone to White Plains, he stopped to see General Arnold at Beverly House, on his way to Fishkill to rejoin his family. What followed is best told in Smith's own words:—

"I mentioned to General Arnold the distance I accompanied Mr. Anderson [Major André], which gave him apparently much satisfaction. His dinner being ready, I partook of it, refreshed my horses, and in the evening proceeded to Fishkill to my family. Here I found General Washington had arrived in the course of the afternoon, on his return from visiting Count Rochambeau, and I supped in his company, with a large retinue at General Scott's. The next day I went on business to Poughkeepsie, and returned to Fishkill the ensuing evening.

It was on the 25th. of September, about midnight, that the door of my room where I lay in bed with Mrs. Smith, was forced open with great violence, and instantly the chamber was filled with soldiers who approached my bed with fixed bayonets. I was then without ceremony drawn out of bed by a French officer named Grovion, whom I recollected to have entertained at my house not long before, in the suite of the Marquis de La Fayette.

He commanded me instantly to dress myself and to accompany him to General Washington, having an order from the General, he said, to arrest me. I then desired of him the privilege of having my servant, and one of my horses, to go with him to General Washington, which he refused, and I was immediately marched off on foot the distance of eighteen miles."

Mr. Smith, seemingly, was not accustomed to such strenuous pedestrianism and one may well imagine his discomfiture at this enforced journey on foot in the middle of the night, with the prospect of a very unpleasant reception at the end of it. How unpleasant that reception was we have already seen in the account of Beverly House.

After Smith's escape from detention and removal to England, his house near Haverstraw did not figure in public affairs until August of the following year. At that time, the 20th. instant, to be exact, during the time when the allied armies were crossing the Hudson at King's Ferry, General Washington made his headquarters here. From the Diary of Claude Blanchard comes the following note:—

"On the 21st. the [French] army left Northcastle. In the evening I received orders from the general [Rochambeau] to carry a letter to General Washington, who was already on the other side of the North River, where we also were beginning to form some establishments. The Americans were already much farther off than I had supposed; I joined them nevertheless: General Washington was occupying Smith's house, famous owing to the fact that there André and Arnold had held their meeting. General Washington was taking tea; I took it with him."

Washington remained there till the 25th. of August, for on that date Blanchard records being with the Commander-in-Chief.

"On the 25th.," he says, "I went myself to the spot [King's Ferry] and saw many of the troops and much baggage cross. General Washington was there; they provided a pavilion for him, from which he examined everything very attentively. He seemed, in this crossing, in the march of our troops towards the Chesapeake bay and in our reunion with M. de Grasse, to see a better destiny arise, when at this period of the war, exhausted, destitute of resources, he needs a great success which might revive courage and hope.

He pressed my hand with much affection when he left us and crossed the river himself. It was about two o'clock. He then rejoined his army."

Thus the spot that had so nearly proved a place of ill omen to Washington's dearest hopes, not quite a year before this crossing of the French Army, now seemed to be a place of happy augury for the future, and of this augury Washington seemed in some way sensible. At any rate, so he appeared to the French military diarist, to whom we are indebted for the intimate details of the occasion, and the event of Yorktown justified his fond expectations.

XLV.

WASHINGTON'S HEADQUARTERS AND ANDRÉ PRISON AT TAPPAN

T HE village of Tappan, lying in the fertile valley which terminates on the Hudson at Piermont, is on one of the main lines of communication from the east: its position on the hills, and yet contiguous to the river being valuable and lending it considerable importance, as a camping ground. Although so small a settlement and one of so seemingly small importance, it was, however, the scene of one of the most historic trials of the Revolution, that of Major John André, the Adjutant-General of the British Army.

DE WINDT HOUSE, WASHINGTON'S HEADQUARTERS, TAPPAN

Library of Congress, Prints and Photographs Division

Tappan still may boast, as may so many of the historic towns of the Hudson Valley, of its famous dwellings, the Headquarters of General Washington and the house of Major André; the old Dutch church, alas, has gone, and only these two remain as little shrines for students of Revolutionary history. One may say that these two remain, but scarcely more, for both have suffered material changes, the changes that a modern craze for improvement inevitably precipitates. Washington's Headquarters has been so altered and added to that there is left only the back wing which in any way retains its original character. Although the house may never have been a building of distinctive beauty, it unquestionably had a rugged charm characteristic of the period and probably of the life of the original owner, John de Windt, a native of Saint Thomas, in the West Indies. Major André's house has taken on the aspect of a tavern and now contains an "enlarged and improved ball-room." while its exterior bears those detestable placards peculiar to all village general sweet shops.

The event most intimately associated with Tappan concern the circumstances of the trial and execution of Major André.

Immediately after Washington's return to Tappan from West Point on the 28th. of September, 1780, he summoned a board of general officers and directed them to examine the case of Major André and report the results. The board consisted of fourteen officers. It convened on the 29th. of September, and on that day arraigned Major André. After a long and careful deliberation, the board reported that:—

"Major André, Adjutant General of the British Army, ought to be considered as a spy from the enemy, and that agreeable to the law and usage of nations, it is their opinion that he ought to suffer death."

On the following day, the 30th. Washington endorsed that decision, with this statement "The Commander-in-Chief approves of the opinion of the board of general officers respecting Major André and orders that the execution of Major André take place to-morrow, at five o'clock, P. M."

Major André must have been a man of dauntless courage, for he at no time exhibited the slightest fear of death, but merely repulsion at the intended manner of his execution; he wished to

HOUSE WHERE MAJ. ANDRÉ
WAS CONFINED, TAPPAN

Library of Congress, Prints and Photographs Division

die as a soldier rather than as a spy. His only concern was for the feelings of his commander, Sir Henry Clinton, of whom he said, "Sir Henry Clinton has been too good to me: he has been lavish of his kindness: I am bound to him by too many obligations and love him too well to bear the thought that he should reproach himself, or others should reproach him, on the supposition of my having conceived myself obliged by his instructions to run the risk I did."

Major André had by his candour, youth, and extreme gentleman-liness endeared himself to the hearts of the Americans, and conse-quently, at the time when this letter was delivered to Clinton, he, Clinton, was led to believe through inferences that an exchange of prisoners might be effected, but Clinton, as a man of honour, could not countenance the exchange of André for Benedict Arnold.

At noon of the next day, the day of execution, a deputation appointed by Clinton arrived at Dobbs Ferry on the schooner *Greyhound* bearing a flag of truce. The deputation was unfortu-nately able to produce no new evidence which would lead General Greene, acting on the behalf of Washington, to alter his decision. At this point a letter to Washington from Arnold was produced, but had all their other arguments been successful, this letter would undeniably have left the General's decision unaltered, so bitter and full of invective as it was.

The first of October, at five o'clock, had been fixed for André's execution, but in consequence of the prolonged conference, the time was advanced to noon of the following day. André retained his composure to the end, and even on the morning of his execution, indulging in his favourite pastime, he made a small pen and ink sketch of himself, which is still preserved in a collection of letters at Yale University. He was executed at twelve o'clock, noon, on the 2nd. of October, 1780.

INDEX